STORMS OF
CONTROVERSY

STORMS OF CONTROVERSY

THE SECRET AVRO ARROW FILES REVEALED

THIRD PAPERBACK EDITION

PALMIRO CAMPAGNA

Third paperback edition published in 1998 by
Stoddart Publishing Co. Limited
34 Lesmill Road
Toronto, Canada
M3B 2T6
Tel. (416) 445-3333
Fax (416) 445-5967

Second paperback edition published by
Stoddart Publishing in 1997

First paperback edition published by
Stoddart Publishing in 1993

Hardcover edition published by
Stoddart Publishing in 1992

Canadian Cataloguing in Publication Data

Campagna, Palmiro
Storms of controversy: the secret Avro Arrow files revealed

3rd pbk. ed.
Includes index.
ISBN 0-7737-5990-5

1. Avro Arrow (Turbojet fighter plane). 2. Aircraft industry –
Canada – History. 3. Canada – Politics and government – 1957–1963.
4. Canada – Foreign relations – United States.
5. United States – Foreign relations – Canada. I. Title.

TL685.3.C34 1998 338.4'76237464'0971 C98-931322-0

Printed and bound in Canada

Every reasonable effort has been made to obtain reprint permissions.
The publisher will gladly receive information that will help rectify
any inadvertent errors or omissions in subsequent editions.

The information in this book in no way represents
the views, opinions, or thoughts of the
Department of National Defence.

*Stoddart Publishing gratefully acknowledges the
support of the Canada Council and the Ontario Arts Council
in the development of writing and publishing in Canada.*

For James Gilbert and all the children in the world. May their dreams become reality and not suffer at the hands of those unable to dream.

CONTENTS

FOREWORD

T HE ARROW CONTROVERSY CAUSED by the abrupt 1959 cancellation of the development of that years-ahead-of-its-time jet aircraft by the Diefenbaker government (followed immediately by the brutal destruction of all existing Arrows) has left a searing scar on the national psyche of Canada. The intimidating puzzle has been — why? Why the cancellation, why the destruction? In his work Palmiro Campagna lays out hitherto unavailable evidence from Cabinet records. His precise, unemotional documentation gives a new and brilliantly clear picture of the American political influence that used the United States' Bomarc system threat to cause the naive Canadian government to elect to invest in that worthless system and to cancel the Arrow.

The Canadian Cabinet argument was that Canada could not afford both programmes. The United States, as Campagna tells us, forced the Diefenbaker decision in favour of the Americans' nuclear-warheaded Bomarc system.

The explanation of the whys of the demise of the Arrow, as skillfully developed by Campagna, will not bury the Arrow controversy. But it will serve to illuminate the dim-bulb rationale that pervaded the tempestuous, reactionary Diefenbaker years.

The administration of John George Diefenbaker left its indelible, depressing footprint on the ego of a Canadian people anxious and capable then to become one of the world's leading high-tech nations. What a powerhouse of technology employment and high prosperity Canada would be enjoying today if the Arrow had survived and flown into our future.

Major General Richard Rohmer
Toronto

PREFACE
TO THE THIRD
PAPERBACK EDITION

In this latest edition of *Storms*, I add to a new appendix information about the Arrow that came to light in 1997, and I have included more previously unseen declassified documents.

The Arrow controversy remains alive and well. Proof of this was provided in an interview by the Canadian Press with former Conservative Cabinet Minister Pierre Sevigny in February 1998, which was published in every major newspaper across Canada. In the interview, Scvigny claimed that the destruction of the Avro Arrow was ordered by Avro president Crawford Gordon. Sevigny and the Canadian Press ignored the entire paper trail of government documents I provided in the first edition of *Storms* in 1992. In the ensuing firestorm of public opinion, Sevigny admitted that he had not seen these documents. Too often the word of such individuals is taken as truth simply because of their claims of involvement, but mostly these people talk out of their hats as they are not privy to inside information. As a result, rumours and accusations are easily spread and the debate quickly degenerates into an emotional, factless argument.

The Arrow controversy also lives on in cyber-space — numerous web sites are devoted to the issue. As well, there are many projects afoot to build small- and full-scale replicas of the Arrow. There is even talk that the U.S. might return the Avrocar to Canada. One model has languished in a hangar at the Smithsonian Institute in Washington since it was delivered to the U.S. in the early 1960s, and the other rests atop a pedestal at Fort Eustis, Virginia. I have discussed the Avrocar project in detail in my other book, *The UFO Files: The Canadian Connection Exposed*, which was pub-lished in a new edition in the spring of 1998. The CBC has aired a television movie called *The Arrow* that, though primarily a work of fiction, features many original flying sequences of the Arrow, beau-tifully restored.

In 1997, the Avro mole, code-named Gideon, long thought to have died in the Soviet Union, reappeared in Canada. Gideon has been implicated in the Soviet attempt to steal Arrow manufacturing secrets. His exact role in the Arrow affair and that of the KGB have yet to be determined. I urge any-one with new, legitimate information about Gideon and this covert episode to come forward.

There are also questions about the Arrow story that no one seems to ask. Why did several gov-ernment officials remain silent about their involve-ment in the destruction of the Arrow even though their names appear on the orders to blowtorch the aircraft into scrap? Why did all these people lie low, allowing John Diefenbaker to twist in the wind?

These questions may never be answered completely because many of the people involved are dead and denial of involvement runs deep.

James Dow, in his 1979 book *The Arrow*, wrote of the alleged meeting between Arrow president Crawford Gordon and John Diefenbaker in September 1958. Dow states that this encounter with a drunken, rude Gordon pushed Diefenbaker to cancel. The only eyewitness to this event, according to Dow, was reporter Grattan O'Leary of the *Ottawa Journal*. He was in an adjoining room when he overheard this discussion. O'Leary saw Gordon exit the room and Diefenbaker come out immediately afterwards. In his memoirs, Diefenbaker does not place much significance on this meeting.

Greig Stewart, in his 1998 book *Arrow Through the Heart*, describes a less volatile encounter between Diefenbaker and Gordon, but also maintains that the argument sealed the Arrow's fate. But Stewart states that it was member of parliament John Pallett and not Grattan O'Leary who was in the next room. Unless the prime minister had more than one adjoining room at the time, one or both of these two stories is incorrect. The truth and significance of this meeting may lie only in Diefenbaker's personal memoirs.

In the new appendices, supported by documentation, I finally establish the true costs of the Arrow program, and I have added intriguing information from former Minister of National Defence George Pearkes in interviews he gave to

Dr. Reginald Roy of the University of Victoria in 1967 that are only now resurfacing.

The new information and documents I provide on the Arrow and all of the recent developments about the story are testimony to the strength of the ongoing controversy. I wish to thank the legion of readers who have made *Storms* an overwhelming success. I would like to thank the staff of the Special Collections Branch of the University of Victoria, Chris Petter in particular, for allowing me to quote from the interview between George Pearkes and Dr. Roy; my editor, Jim Gifford; the staff at Stoddart; and for inspiration, my newborn daughter, Katia Marie.

Palmiro Campagna
Orleans, May 1998

PREFACE
TO THE SECOND
PAPERBACK EDITION

I WOULD LIKE TO THANK ALL those who have provided comments, both positive and negative, since publication of *Storms of Controversy* in 1992. The response has given me the impetus to continue my efforts in search of what was happening behind the scenes in the Arrow story. It has also led me into unravelling the mystery of and writing about the Avrocar, Avro's flying saucer for the United States Air Force.

In 1993, I had a chance to experience firsthand the "joys" of cancellation. I had been sent to Italy in September, for what was intended to be a four-year engineering assignment on the EH 101 helicopter programme. The family was moved and the house sold. In November, of course, the programme was cancelled courtesy of a political decision, and we were on our way back to Canada by December, some of our boxes not yet unpacked from the original move over there. It was not a pleasant experience.

After the dust had settled, I was able to renew my work on the Arrow. I was surprised to learn that many of the myths I had destroyed were still being flaunted, but such is life. Perhaps the new material will put them to bed. And what is this new material?

I have uncovered various memoranda and briefing notes which shed new light on both the Jetliner and Arrow developments. Included is what I have come to call the "smoking gun." This document should have been available in the mountain of material I had originally poured over, but either I had missed it or it simply was not there. The copy I did find was in a different area altogether and actually came to me via the good graces of serendipity. It finally puts many pieces of the puzzle together and names names.

In some of the correspondence that I received, I was asked if I had ever found anything more on "the one that got away." In fact, I have reviewed this matter and present some intriguing possibilities. Most people point to the photos of the destruction on the tarmac and note that they show five aircraft being destroyed. While pictures are worth a thousand words, not all is what it seems.

Is the story finally over? No, there are more documents out there, but the problem, like before, is finding them and getting them declassified.

Ottawa, October 1996

PREFACE
TO THE FIRST EDITION

THE STORY OF THE AVRO ARROW is one of emotion, intrigue, excitement, happiness, sorrow, and anger, but most of all it is the story of tragedy. What began as an entire nation working together to achieve the impossible ended with the destruction of that achievement. Several books and articles have since appeared, each trying to explain what went wrong. In these pages, for the first time in over thirty years, many of the remaining classified documents on the subject are finally allowed to tell their story. Admittedly, gaps in information yet exist, but what unfolds in these pages already tells a dramatically different story. I have quoted extensively from these documents so as not to distort or take their information out of context. Where matters become very technical, I have preferred to leave the explanations in the very words of the individuals who wrote them so long ago. I have included some of my own speculation in very specific areas, but I have left the reader to formulate personal conclusions on what happened to the Arrow. In the end, I address many of the myths and misconceptions that have developed over the years, trusting I have not created any of my own. I have attempted to document as much as possible in this regard.

Although it has been said that the Canadian aerospace industry suffered a major setback with the cancellation of the Arrow, I believe the country as a whole was affected psychologically. After cancellation, an ex-Avro employee commented that it seemed as if the spirit of the nation had died. Compare this to the U.S. experience: when the space shuttle exploded, American prestige was affected; however, Americans regrouped and forged ahead in the face of this adversity. With the Arrow cancellation, Canada decided it simply could not handle these types of projects, seemingly preferring to become a branch plant of the United States. From that point in time, we seem to have developed the attitude "If it's Canadian, there must be something wrong with it." Witness the recent television commercial concerning high-tech developments and Canada's 125th anniversary asking, "Can Canadians compete?" Would other countries even consider asking themselves such a question? It is time for our attitudes to change.

I am indebted to so many people, too numerous to mention, whose encouragement, advice, and insight are deeply appreciated. A few special individuals, though, must be highlighted. First and foremost, my wife, Jane Maxwell, for putting up with my long hours at the archives and the keyboard. Second, an absolute gentleman and brilliant engineer, Jim Floyd. Special thanks to Air Commodore Ray Foottit, the late Air Vice Marshall John Easton, and Dr. Oman Solandt for putting up with my questions; to Roberto Brun del Re, Vern La Rue, and Nancy McCallan for their early assessment of the manuscript; to Ken Lepper for providing some of the photos; and to Russ Carstensen.

Finally, I offer my thanks to those at the National Archives in Ottawa and Washington; the National Research Council in Ottawa; the Department of National Defence, which provided photos and information; the Dwight D. Eisenhower Library in Kansas; and the United States Air Force, which provided some photos. The documentation used is all declassified and available to the general public.

1 DREAMS

*Mr. Speaker, with the leave of the House I should like
to make a somewhat lengthy statement on the subject
of one facet of the national defence of Canada. . . . The
government has carefully examined and reexamined
the probable need for the Arrow aircraft and Iroquois
engine known as the CF-105. . . . The conclusion
arrived at is that the development of the Arrow
aircraft and Iroquois engine should be terminated now.*
Prime Minister John G. Diefenbaker,[1]
Black Friday, February 20, 1959

WITH THE ABOVE WORDS, over 14,000 employees at Avro Aircraft and Orenda Engines were released in a single afternoon. In all, over 25,000 people, including those working for various subcontractors, would be directly affected. There were rumours of suicide and the reality of a mass exodus of talented personnel from the country. Not only was a military project terminated, but the heart and soul of a nation were destroyed. Canada's aircraft industry would never embark on such an ambitious project again. Then, incredibly, one final blow was delivered. Five magnificent aircraft — and a sixth ready for taxi trials — were hacked and chopped and blowtorched to scrap metal, along with thirty-one others in various

1

stages of assembly. Engines, drawings, production line tooling, and the like were all ordered destroyed. Government records on the issue would remain classified for more than thirty years. The question is *why*.

Since the cancellation, several books and articles have appeared, each trying to explain some facet of the story. Kay Shaw, a former Avro employee, wrote *There Never Was an Arrow*, James Dow gave us *The Arrow*, and the Arrowheads provided the best picture and technical book, entitled, simply, *Arrow*. At least one stage play was produced, *The Legend of the Avro Arrow*, by Clinton Bomphray, and two books of fiction with the Arrow as the central theme have appeared. Not to be left out, several historians have included references to the Arrow story in various books on military history or on Canada's aviation heritage.

What exactly was the Arrow? Amazingly, many Canadians have never heard of it, despite the books and recently renewed interest by the news media. Was it truly a world-beater as some have maintained, or was it a mass of technical junk? Officially, Prime Minister John Diefenbaker and his colleagues had said that with production behind schedule, the aircraft would be ready at a time when the principal enemy threat would come from the intercontinental ballistic missile, not the manned bomber; therefore, the aircraft would be obsolete. It was also said the range of the aircraft was limited, and its cost was alluded to as high, although this was never put forward as the official reason for termination.

Were the costs of the programme beyond reach? If the aircraft was so good, why were other countries, namely the United States and Great Britain, not interested? Why did the government try to obliterate all traces of the aircraft after the project was cancelled? Why were any remaining government records locked away if the project was a disaster? Have the history books misrepresented the facts? Why have so many denied the truth? Or have they?

The 1950s were years of cold war uncertainty and post–World War II prosperity. In the United States, Richard M. Nixon had become President Eisenhower's Vice President. Nixon had already made a name for himself prosecuting suspected Communists, while fellow senator Joseph McCarthy was stirring anti-Communist sentiments throughout the country. In charge of foreign policy was John Foster Dulles, Secretary of State and hard-line anti-Communist, a sharp contrast to the more conciliatory President Dwight D. Eisenhower. In charge of the spy network was the Central Intelligence Agency (CIA), headed by Allen Dulles, brother to John.[2]

It was a period of espionage and intrigue. For example, revelations in the 1980s showed that, in the 1950s, the CIA was conducting covert hallucinogenic experiments on Canadians in Quebec, seemingly unbeknownst to the Canadian government. Meanwhile, both the CIA and Royal Canadian Mounted Police (RCMP) were involved in the hunt for Soviet agents, at least one of whom was actively involved in trying to obtain information on the classified supersonic jet interceptor being built by Avro Canada. Would these people and events play a role in the termination?[3]

During the Second World War, Britain saw the need to have its Lancaster bomber production augmented by companies in Canada. The National Steel Car plant in Malton, Ontario, was chosen since it was already building aircraft parts for the war effort. In November 1942, this company became a Crown corporation and was renamed Victory Aircraft Limited.

News of superior Lancasters being built by Victory reached Britain. In 1943, Sir Roy Dobson, managing director of A. V. Roe, Manchester, decided to pay a visit, along with Sir Frank Spriggs, managing director of Hawker-Siddeley. They were met by a young Canadian, Fred T. Smye, director of aircraft production at Victory, and his superior, Ralph P. Bell, director general, and were escorted on a tour of the existing aircraft companies in Ontario. Scott Young, in his ten-year history of the Canadian A. V. Roe company, recorded the following: "A few days later as the tour of Canadian plants progressed, Fred Smye heard the first hint in conversation that Sir Roy thought Canadians should have their own self-sufficient aircraft industry. From that moment on, Fred Smye never let go of the idea that it could be done."[4]

Two years later, Sir Roy reached an agreement with the Honourable Clarence Decatur Howe, an American engineer who had become Minister of

Munitions and Supply under the Liberal government of Prime Minister Louis St. Laurent. It was decided that Victory Aircraft would be taken over by Hawker-Siddelcy on a rental purchase plan, providing the management at Hawker-Siddeley agreed. Fred Smye, who had moved on to become assistant general manager of Federal Aircraft, resigned in order to become the first employee of the new company. Unfortunately, before Hawker-Siddeley could sign the agreement, the war in Europe ended and all contracts for more aircraft were cancelled. Weeks passed, and Fred Smye finally travelled to England to learn of any developments. On his return, Sir Roy followed. After a series of meetings with Minister C. D. Howe and Victory officials, A. V. Roe Canada was formed. The date was December 1, 1945. Fred Smye was appointed assistant general manager and would become the administrative force behind many of A. V. Roe's projects.[5]

In 1946, Turbo-Research Limited, a Crown company engaged in research work in the jet engine field, was acquired by A. V. Roe Canada. On December 2, 1954, it was decided to split A. V. Roe into separate airframe and engine companies. Fred Smye became vice president and general manager of the aircraft division, renamed Avro Aircraft, and Walter McLachlan was appointed head of Orenda Engines. However, A. V. Roe Canada remained as the overall parent company. Another major company, Canadian Steel Improvements, was soon added to the group, and in September 1955, Canadian Car and Foundry was purchased. In the midst of these acquisitions, the company designed and produced the Orenda, a first-class jet engine; the C-102 Jetliner, which introduced North America to jet transport; and the CF-100, a world-class fighter. Frank Spriggs of Hawker-Siddeley would eventually say to the A. V. Roe company, "You have demonstrated beyond question that you can talk with any aircraft or engine design teams in the world," words that would be echoed by Fred Smye himself over A. V. Roe's most ambitious project, the CF-105 Avro Arrow.[6]

Edgar Atkin was transferred from A. V. Roe in the United Kingdom to become Avro Canada's chief engineer. He and Canadian engineer Jim Chamberlin, Avro's chief aerodynamicist, began thinking about a replacement to the highly successful CF-100 subsonic fighter. In January 1952, with the departure of Atkin, James C. Floyd, also from the A. V. Roe Company in the United Kingdom, was appointed chief engineer. It was now his task to work with Chamberlin on the concept for the new aircraft, the Arrow. Floyd would eventually describe Chamberlin as "without a doubt the best technical man I have ever had the privilege to be associated with."[7]

Floyd had originally come to Canada in February 1946 to work on the C-102 Jetliner. This was a medium-range intercity jet transport, the first of its kind in North America. The story of the Jetliner is well documented in Jim Floyd's own book on the subject, but a few points are worthy of note here.

Commercial jet transport had not yet made its mark on the world scene and was considered a new technology. Then, on July 27, 1949, the British-designed DH Comet rose a few feet off a runway in England to become the first commercial jet to fly. Only two weeks later, on August 10, 1949, Canada's Jetliner flew for the first time. Unlike the Comet, the Jetliner flew for over an hour on its maiden flight, and up to altitudes of 13,000 feet. Floyd would later be awarded the Wright Brothers Medal for this effort, the first time this medal was awarded to an individual from outside the United States.

The Jetliner design was based on simplicity, safety, high speed, comfort, and economy and was able to operate from conventional airports with no special facilities. On April 18, 1950, the Jetliner delivered the first jet airmail in the world on a run from Toronto to New York in half the time it normally took. In *The Avro Story*, Jim Floyd wrote:

On arrival in New York we were whisked downtown, flanked by a siren-blasting escort of New York City police, straight through the city to meet the mayor.

The next day the New York press had pictures of the Jetliner flying over the city, with the following caption: "This should give our nation a good healthful kick in its placidity. The fact that our massive but underpopulated good neighbour to the north has a mechanical product that licks anything of ours is just what the doctor ordered for our overdeveloped ego. The Canadian plane's feat accelerates a process already begun in this nation — a realization that Uncle Sam has no monopoly on genius."[8]

The Jetliner broke records with every flight and garnered the interest and admiration of the U.S. military, several airline companies, and Howard Hughes. It became his personal jet for several months as he evaluated its characteristics and flight-handling qualities. In *Howard Hughes and TWA*, Robert Rummel, TWA's chief engineer, states:

The Jetliner, the first jet transport produced in North America, was an advanced, medium-range, 450-mph plane that first flew an amazing eight years before Boeing's 707. This extraordinary achievement is all the more remarkable considering that it was the first product of a new company in a country not dominant in the development or construction of aircraft. The design, developed by A. V. Roe Canada (AVRO), was conspicuously ahead of any competitive transport. The programme represented a giant bite for any company to chew in 1946, when the project was undertaken, no matter how extensive its resources or how well qualified the individual participants.[9]

The president of National Airlines, George T. Baker, was also interested. According to Rummel, Baker was ready to purchase four aircraft at one million dollars each with options for six more. The United States Air Force was prepared to order twenty for military training, and preparations were under way to have an American engine sent to Avro for testing. Howard Hughes also entered into serious negotiations for the manufacture of the Jetliner. However, because of the war in Korea, Minister of Munitions and Supply C. D. Howe had ordered all work to cease in favour of accelerated production of the CF-100 fighter. The Jetliner would not be put into production. Ironically, the CF-100 would go into squadron service in 1953, as the Korean conflict was nearing its end. Was the Korean War the true reason behind the Jetliner termination, especially with orders pending for its purchase and manufacture? In 1956, the revolutionary Jetliner would be ordered reduced to scrap. It would later be reported that no one wanted to buy the Jetliner and that it was of a poor design. It is unfortunate that this misinformation surfaced in Canada only. It is even more unfortunate that such a diatribe has been believed. The facts speak for themselves.[10]

In January 1952, the Royal Canadian Air Force (RCAF) realized that the CF-100 would eventually have to be replaced. After 1951, an All-Weather Interceptor Requirements Team was assembled to study Canada's air defence needs and to recommend performance specifications for a new all-weather interceptor aircraft to counter the perceived enemy bomber threat. The team consisted of representatives from the RCAF, the Defence Research Board

(DRB), the National Research Council (NRC), and the National Aeronautical Establishment (NAE). (The NAE had been established in December 1950 by the Canadian government as an aeronautical research and development centre administered originally by the NRC.[11])

The final report from this team was published on March 20, 1952, with a summary forwarded to A. V. Roe. Avro responded in June with two brochures entitled "C-104 Supersonic All-Weather Fighters." They described a single-engine and a twin-engine aircraft, neither of which fully satisfied the required combat performance. Still, on August 25, 1952, the RCAF requested that the NAE analyze these proposals. The NAE reply stated that the twin-engine design came closest to meeting the specifications, and that although weight was excessive aircraft performance estimates were realistic. It was recommended that further studies be undertaken.[12]

In March 1953, the RCAF issued Operational Requirement ORI/1-63, "Supersonic All-Weather Interceptor Aircraft," followed by RCAF Specification Air-7-3, "Design Studies of Prototype Supersonic All-Weather Interceptor Aircraft." Both were given to Avro with a requirement for design studies for the most efficient aircraft (in terms of size, weight, and cost) that could be developed for the engines that would be available at the time of some future production.[13]

Avro responded with report No. P/C-105/1, "Design Study of Supersonic All-Weather Interceptor

Aircraft," dated May 1953. It described a series of delta-wing aircraft of varying weights and sizes. It identified the pros and cons, risks and benefits for each. The report was studied by the RCAF and the DRB, who together concluded that the C-105/1200 — at a weight of 48,400 pounds and having a 1,200-square-foot wing area — would meet the requirement of Air-7-3. The requirements specification would eventually be issued as RCAF specification Air-7-4.

More information was requested on the aerodynamic claims, and it soon became clear that aerodynamic data had to be confirmed by wind-tunnel testing. Avro conducted the tests between August 27 and September 2, 1953, at the Cornell Transonic Wind Tunnel in Buffalo, New York. The resulting reports were sent to the NAE on September 18 for comment. In his September 28 reply to then Air Vice Marshall Douglas M. Smith (Air Member Technical Services), John H. Parkin, director of the NAE, stated, "[T]he Cornell wind-tunnel tests indicate that, aerodynamically, the C105/1200 configuration is capable of meeting its performance requirements, although it is important that wind-tunnel measurements be extended to higher Mach numbers as soon as possible." Parkin was stating that while results were good, they were somewhat limited in terms of the speeds tested and needed to be extended in order to evaluate the aircraft's performance at the higher velocities it was expected to achieve.[14]

The position of Air Member Technical Services

was directly responsible for the aircraft programme. He reported directly to the Chief of the
Air Staff, who in turn reported directly or through
the Chairman of the Chiefs of Staff to the Cabinet
Ministers. Hence, Air Vice Marshall Smith reported to Air Marshall C. Roy Slemon, Chief of
the Air Staff. Air Vice Marshall Max M. Hendrick
would replace Smith as Air Member Technical Services in 1955, and Slemon would be replaced by
Air Marshall Hugh Campbell in 1957. It would not
be until 1957 that a separate project office dealing
exclusively with the Arrow project would be created under the Chief of Aeronautical Engineering,
Air Commodore Gordon G. Truscott, who would
report directly to the Air Member Technical Services. Truscott had been a prewar officer, graduate
engineer, and pilot who supported the Arrow project.

As work at the Avro plant continued, the RCAF
conducted an investigation to determine if any foreign aircraft could satisfy the requirements. In his
submission to the Cabinet Defence Committee on
November 30, 1953, Liberal Minister of National
Defence the Honourable Brooke Claxton stated the
following:

With the object of economy and to avoid unnecessary duplication, every effort has been made to
determine whether future U.K. or U.S. aircraft
could meet our requirements. In the U.K. the
only aircraft for consideration is the Javelin
whose performance falls far short of the require-

ment. In the United States there is the Convair F-102 which is a single-engine, single-seat aircraft designed to carry a fully automatic armament which is now under development. This aircraft does not meet the range requirement set out and its manoeuvrability and ceiling are below our studied requirements. In addition, this aircraft is so highly specialized that if the planned development of any major element breaks down there is little flexibility in the design to permit substitution of alternate equipment. Further, this aircraft because of its design and layout does not have much development potential and is, therefore, liable to become obsolescent in a relatively short time. Adoption by Canada of this aircraft involves calculated risks greater than we are justified in taking. The RCAF, therefore have had A. V. Roe Canada work out an engineering proposal for an aircraft to meet our specification.[15]

The Minister went on to outline that the Treasury Board had authorized an expenditure of $200,000 on May 8, 1953, and an additional $300,000 on July 21. These monies had been spent on design studies and wind-tunnel testing. He stressed that if the programme were begun in earnest, a prototype could be completed by October 1956, with production by 1959. He then sought approval for the development to commence. Expenditures would be $26,925,000 spread over a period extending into 1958 and would include some

$4,000,000 in government-supplied equipment. Engines would be the most suitable ones found in either the United States or Britain. Two prototype aircraft would be built. Claxton was successful, and Avro was awarded a design and development contract in March 1954; the CF-105 design began in May of that year.

The RCAF specifications, which no foreign aircraft could meet, included a supersonic combat radius of 200 nautical miles, a combat ceiling of not less than 60,000 feet, a maximum speed at altitude of Mach 2, a rate of climb not more than 6 minutes to 50,000 feet, twin engines, a crew capacity of two, an all-weather capability, and a manoeuvrability of 2 g at Mach 1.5 at 50,000 feet without loss of speed or altitude. Also, the aircraft had to provide as much flexibility as possible for engines and armament capacity due to the uncertain availability of those under consideration. In the words of Claxton, the requirements had been developed by the RCAF "in conjunction with the DRB, the NAE, the United States Air Force, Department of Defence Production and various aircraft manufacturers both in the United States and The United Kingdom."[16] He had every confidence that Avro would be equal to the task.

Although the NAE had initially agreed that the C-105 configuration would meet its required performance, Air Vice Marshall Smith received another letter from Parkin dated January 15, 1954. This time, the NAE director noted that his comments of September had been premature. The full assessment of Avro's work was now complete and available in NAE Report No. LR-87, "Assessment of the Performance Characteristics of the Proposed A. V. Roe C105/1200 All-Weather Supersonic Fighter Aircraft." Essentially, the report concluded that the aircraft would not meet the required 200-nautical-mile radius nor the 2-g manoeuvrability because the supersonic drag (air resistance) was far greater than Avro's estimate. Smith, however, countered that even if drag were increased, the aircraft would meet the combat radius due to the increased fuel capacity Avro had included. He stated as much in a memo to the Chief of the Air Staff, Air Marshall Slemon, on February 16, 1954. On the question of whether the amount of drag calculated by Avro was correct, Smith noted that wind-tunnel testing to verify the numbers was ongoing. This would prove to be the beginning of a long series of disagreements between the NAE and Avro that would carry through over the length of the project.[17]

Despite assurances, the uncertainties about the aircraft's performance persisted, and the disagreements between the NAE and Avro increased. In an internal NAE memo dated September 29, 1954, the following is noted: "[O]ur opinions differ in various ways from those of the Company or the RCAF, and this has given rise to argument and possibly to some ill feeling, even to the opinion that the NAE is anxious to hinder the straightforward development of the aircraft. Nothing could be further from the truth."[18]

While the NAE saw itself as a legitimate scientific watchdog over a very complex project, its tone may have suggested otherwise; more than one official at Avro and the RCAF recalls that the NAE may have taken the role of honest broker just one step too far. The RCAF finally requested a meeting between the NAE, the DRB, and the U.S. National Advisory Committee for Aeronautics (NACA, later NASA) to discuss the differences between the NAE estimates of performance and those of Avro. At the time, it was believed that the best aeronautical minds were at NACA. The group published the "Joint Report on an RCAF–DRB–NAE Visit to NACA Langley Laboratories to Discuss Aerodynamic Problems of Avro CF-105 Aircraft," dated November 19, 1954.

The NAE had made its points, for on December 20 and 21, 1954, Avro was called to the carpet. A second meeting was held at NACA headquarters in Washington, with Avro engineers taking centre stage to explain the reasoning behind their more favourable performance figures. Jim Floyd and Jim Chamberlin were among those present from Avro. Items discussed included the NAE criticisms of drag calculations, use of wing negative camber rather than positive camber, and perceived problems with pitch-up, engine intakes, and overall stability.

On the crucial issue of drag, NACA backed Avro, stating, "It was basically agreed . . . provided that (a) the intake and ramp bleed area is investigated and cleaned up where necessary, and (b) the afterbody is well faired in after the nozzles, the zero lift drag at Mach 1.5 may be as low as .020. . . . The Avro estimate from area distribution and skin friction considerations was .0184. The configuration is considered to be generally reasonable with respect to drag."

Avro had proposed the use of negative wing camber rather than the traditional positive camber, which caused the NAE some consternation. Again, NACA concluded in favour of Avro: "It was agreed that there is little to be gained by conical positive camber for the particular mission of this aircraft. . . . Avro's reasons for going to negative camber were also understood and appeared reasonable."

The NAE thought the aircraft would be susceptible to pitch-up in supersonic flight. NACA stated, "It was agreed that the notch or leading edge extension proposed by Avro should alleviate pitch-up." Similarly, with respect to engine intakes, "It was generally agreed that the amount and the diffusion angle involved at the intake were not excessive."

Finally, on stability, Avro was proposing the use of artificial electronic stabilization, a radical departure from conventional design. According to the NAE, it was necessary to afford stability by making the aircraft inherently stable without the use of artificial electronic means. NACA stated:

It was generally agreed that while artificial lateral stabilization is undesirable in itself, the obvious aerodynamic [nonelectronic] cures such as a large increase in fin area could be unacceptable so far as performance of the aircraft is concerned. A concentrated test programme was recommended. . . . It was noted that problems of this type are not peculiar to the CF-105 configuration but appear to be associated with the mass distributions of modern high performance fighters.[19]

Avro had been vindicated on all counts by the NACA specialists. Floyd would later write, "If the NAE had been right, the Arrow would never have flown supersonically." Furthermore, NACA was affirming that the problems Avro was encountering were to be expected in supersonic aircraft design.[20]

Although many may not fully appreciate the technical significance of the arguments presented, they have been included because they have remained secret for so long, fuelling the speculation in some circles that the aircraft was technically flawed. Also, they demonstrate the technical expertise of the Avro team.

With the NACA experience behind them, the Avro team went back to work. Wind-tunnel testing continued. In all, seventeen scale models ranging in size from 1/80th to 1/6th scale were tested in the NAE facilities in Ottawa, the Cornell Laboratories in Buffalo, the NACA facilities in Langley Field, Virginia, and the NACA Lewis Laboratory in Cleveland.

Due to limitations in wind-tunnel testing, a complementary programme of free-flight model testing was carried out from 1954 to 1957. Eleven 1/8th scale models of the aircraft were mounted atop Nike rocket boosters of 45,000 pounds thrust and launched into the sky. At altitude the boosters would separate, allowing the model to continue flying. (The separation technique known as drag separation had been developed by NACA. Essentially, after expending its fuel, the heavier booster would decelerate faster than the model, thereby separating from it.[21])

The models themselves were a mix of crude and highly accurate representations of the aircraft designed to provide dynamic stability and control data. Each was fitted with a series of transducers and an FM telemetering system using standard radio broadcast frequencies. The models were tracked using radar and theodolites as well as film cameras. Nine models were launched from the Canadian Armament Research and Development Establishment (CARDE) at the range in Point Petre near Picton, Ontario. Two more were fired from the Wallops Island Range of the NACA Pilotless Aircraft Research Division in Virginia. Presumably, all of these models, constructed primarily of stainless steel, remain to this day under the waters where they splashed down over thirty years ago. They were considered expendable, so no attempts were made to retrieve them.[22]

Augmenting the scale model effort, Avro also built a series of mock-ups and test rigs. For example, an engineering wooden mock-up was built to check tolerances and sizing for the engine and armament packs as well as to examine cable and wire runs. To demonstrate pilot visibility during taxiing and ground handling, a mock-up of the front cockpit was mounted to a truck, simulating the height and attitude the pilot would experience. A test rig simulating the aircraft's electronics was added, as were others to simulate the landing gear and hydraulics. Finally, the most powerful digital computer then available, the IBM 704, was rented from IBM to handle the theoretical computations fed to it by a staff of thirty mathematicians, technicians, and operators.[23]

In four short years, outstanding even by today's standards, the most modern aircraft in the world was ready for roll-out. Along the way, Floyd had become vice president, engineering, and Chamberlin, chief of technical design. Chief engineer was now Robert N. Lindley with Guest Hake as project designer. But, despite the technical design and production achievement, the aircraft had yet to fly. Would it meet the stringent performance specifications? Would flight testing prove otherwise? Would other countries purchase it?

In a memo dated February 22, 1957, the RCAF officially named the CF-105 aircraft the Arrow.[24]

2 U.S. AND U.K. INTEREST

*If they were in our position, what would be their view
in continuing or abandoning the project?*
Question from the RCAF to the USAF during
a meeting from October 31 to
November 1, 1955.[1]

WITH ALL OF THE ACTIVITY being carried out
with NACA and Avro Canada's liaison with
Hawker-Siddeley in the United Kingdom, it is logical to assume that both the United States Air
Force (USAF) and the Royal Air Force (RAF) in Britain would have observed what was going on in
Canada with great interest. In the case of the
United States, General Nathan F. Twining, Chief
of Staff, USAF, had advised the Canadian Chief of
the Air Staff, Air Marshall Roy Slemon, that the
USAF was interested in a long-range interceptor and
had initiated a design competition among American manufacturers.

It was June 1954, and General Twining was ex-
pressing a specific interest in the CF-105, so much
so that he had requested the Air Research & Development Command (ARDC) in the United States
to evaluate the specifications of the Canadian
plane along with those in the design competition.

On July 15, 1954, Air Marshall Slemon replied and forwarded a copy of A. V. Roe's design study. He also stated he was pleased to open this exchange of information with the Americans. It was in keeping with the doctrine of requiring "the enemy to compete in the technological field with the combined brains and resources of the English-speaking Allies rather than the three components thereof . . . [because] such collaboration would be superior to the individual and in some cases overlapping efforts."[2] Slemon pointed out that approval to proceed with the CF-105 was based on the knowledge that neither the United States nor the United Kingdom had or were planning to develop a similar aircraft.

The exchange of letters resulted in a team of RCAF and Avro officials providing a briefing to the ARDC on August 26, 1954. The briefing was well received, and later in 1955, when USAF assistance was requested in arranging for special wind-tunnel testing at facilities not available in Canada, help was provided without hesitation.

Despite the progress Avro was making and their vindication at NACA headquarters the previous year, Air Marshall Slemon, together with Dr. Omond Solandt, Chairman of the DRB, decided an independent evaluation of the project was needed. A high-level technical delegation of USAF personnel was invited to visit Avro and study the programme between October 31 and November 1, 1955. The USAF team was headed by Major General G.E. Price, Director of Requirements and Deputy Chief of Staff (Development). It included members from

ARDC and the propulsion and fighter branches of USAF headquarters.[3]

The American team was told by the RCAF that increasing cost had led to a reappraisal of the project, that the defence budget was limited, and that, therefore, continuation could lead to the elimination of other desirable programmes. The USAF was requested to provide an opinion as to the "essentiality of the 105 Project to the defence of North America" and was asked flat out if it would abandon the programme under similar circumstances! The defence of Canada had expanded to include the defence of North America, and it is probable that the Canadians were hoping to interest the USAF in eventual acquisitions. Still, it is inconceivable that the question of continuing or abandoning the project would be put so bluntly, especially when one factors in the "Buy American" mentality that might shape any answer from the USAF. Also, one might ask how well the defence of Canada had been studied by the experts before embarking on the Arrow, and if Canadian confidence was so low that the RCAF had to keep running to the United States for answers and advice. Would this become a factor in the cancellation later on?[4]

The USAF team was also told that the development of a new engine, the PS-13, or Iroquois, was linked to the airframe development, and that cancellation of the airframe would remove justification to proceed with the PS-13. Finally, USAF views were sought regarding choice of missiles, fire control, development costs with respect to similar U.S. projects, and comparisons to other U.S. aircraft under development. To help in its deliberations, the USAF team was handed the latest facts and figures on the project, with the parting comment that Canadian requirements in terms of numbers of aircraft would be small and therefore unit costs would be high. Even at such an early stage, it seems every vulnerability was being exposed and the very future of the project was being placed squarely in the hands of the United States.[5]

During the ensuing discussions, the differences in performance between Avro's calculations and those of the NAE and the DRB were again tabled and discussed. The U.S. team also inspected the mockups and tooling bays in the plant and was told of the versatility that could be incorporated into the aircraft. A full briefing was provided on the Iroquois engine being developed by Orenda.

On technical soundness, the delegation thought the risks were reasonable for such an advanced design: "In their opinion to attempt to achieve Mach 1.5 and a 2-g turn at 50,000 feet was quite a technical advance, but they saw no reason why the design should get into any particular trouble. . . . The delegation did not seem unduly perturbed by the fact that there was a difference of opinion about what the performance might actually be."[6]

The USAF requirement for manoeuvrability was only 1.2 g at combat ceiling. Most aircraft will pull far more than 2 g, but to do it at altitude without losing power or height is quite remarkable even by today's standards. (G measures the force of gravity on an accelerating body. To appreciate g force, think of the feeling of being pulled sideways when you make a sharp turn in a car. Or think of a roller coaster; as you go screaming down to the trough, g builds up, so that when you abruptly curve and go upward again, you feel g force pinning you to the back of your seat.)

A list of U.S. aircraft under development or consideration was tabled. It included the short-range F-102B, the medium-range F-103 to be available by 1962 or 1963, the long-range F-101B, and the long-range LR-1x1 and LR-1x2. The conclusion drawn by the Americans was that the CF-105 would be the only aircraft available to supplement the limited altitude capabilities of the F-101B prior to service of the LR-1x1 interceptor.

In fact, the U.S. team admitted that if the LR-1x1 was given the go-ahead, it would probably not be ready for service until some five to six years after the Arrow, well into the 1960s. It was also noted that for the LR-1x1 to obtain the hoped for 100-mile acquisition range for targets, a technical breakthrough in radar development would be required, and this could further delay its in-service timing. There were also stated problems with the navigation, communication, and fire control subsystems of the aircraft.[7] The long-range project would eventually be cancelled, and some people would use this as justification for the Arrow cancellation, stating that the manned interceptor was considered obsolete. But given all the problems cited by the Americans, was the LR-1x1 not cancelled for technical reasons?

With respect to the F-102B, the Canadians asked if it could operate outside the Semiautomated Ground Environment (SAGE). SAGE was a ground-based surveillance and weapons control system which could transmit data to the aircraft and automatically guide it to the target. The answer was that the F-102 was not the best aircraft to operate outside of SAGE. Hence, the utility of the F-102 for target interception would be limited to the range of the SAGE system, even though the aircraft might physically fly beyond the SAGE perimeter. This range problem would later prove to be one of the limitations of the Bomarc missile, as well. The Arrow, however, was designed to operate well beyond SAGE and did not require the assistance of SAGE during the target interception process. In his memoirs, Prime Minister John Diefenbaker would intimate that it was the Arrow that could not operate outside of this sophisticated ground environment.

The medium-range F-103 was also discussed, but the USAF pointed out that no funds had yet been committed to this project and that technical advances in electronics would likely be needed to achieve its required performance. The Arrow appeared to remain the best aircraft that would be available in the time required, reinforcing the opinion that no American aircraft were suitable to meet the RCAF requirements.[8]

Considerable opinion was expressed on the PS-13,

which Orenda was designing as a titanium engine. U.S. engine manufacturers had experienced numerous problems with titanium; however, as pointed out by the Americans, their companies were trying to integrate titanium parts into existing engines, while Orenda was designing with titanium from the start. Therefore, they expected that Orenda would not encounter the same difficulties. Given the expected high performance of the engine, the American team also wondered how the performance of its LR-1x1 could be improved.[9]

The American team believed that the greatest technical risk area would be that of the integrated electronic and fire control system. The RCAF wanted the aircraft to operate within SAGE for a fully automatic interception of enemy aircraft as well as allowing manual control by the pilot outside the SAGE boundaries. The Americans argued this was counter to the flexibility provided by the two-man crew and two engines, and therefore the complexity of incorporating electronic "smarts" for operation within SAGE were not required. They also stated that since the proposed designer for the electronic and fire control system would be the Hughes Aircraft Corporation, a complicated design would overburden this company, which was already committed to American programmes. It was suggested that a less sophisticated system be chosen with only essential components provided by Hughes. RCA and North American Downey were suggested as potential suppliers.

In July of 1956, Fred Smye would be told by the

Chief of the Air Staff that the RCAF had selected RCA to provide the complete sophisticated system and that cooperation from Avro was expected. Avro had argued, unaware of the American advice, that such a system was too complex, too costly, not necessary, and could threaten the entire project. In short, after soliciting American advice, which in turn was echoed by Avro, the RCAF ignored it, only to have this part of the project terminated due to cost, as Smye had predicted.[10]

Finally, the American team was asked which missile suite it would prefer, the Hughes-designed Falcon or the Sparrow 2, currently under development by the U.S. Navy. Avro had argued with the RCAF that the best choice would be the Hughes Falcon because the Sparrow 2 had been designed for lower performance aircraft. The U.S. delegation essentially stated the same. The Falcon had been designed for greater height, could carry infrared or radar homing, and had the same "kill" probability as the Sparrow. Also, because it was half the size, eight Falcons could be carried by the Arrow instead of four Sparrows. The Falcon was also less expensive. In a conversation with this author in June of 1991, Dr. Solandt stated that the DRB had provided similar advice to the RCAF. However, Canadian Air Commodore Jack A. Easton thought that the American team did not know enough about the Sparrow to make an accurate comparison. He believed the Sparrow was better and this would eventually become the weapon of choice. Later, in late 1956, the U.S. Navy would abandon development of the Sparrow, only to have it taken over by Canada, adding yet another major development burden to the programme and one that was certainly not required.[11]

The U.S. team was then asked for its opinion of the Bomarc missile and its impact on the role of the manned interceptor. General Price indicated that this missile was being developed by Boeing aircraft as an addition to the manned interceptor. It was ground launched, with the Bomarc A having a range of 125 miles and the Bomarc B a range of 250 miles. Bomarc might replace the F-102 but Price "did not foresee the day of the phasing out of the manned interceptors as he felt there would always be a need for judgement and mobility in a weapon system."[12] In other words, once aimed and launched, the missile would destroy its target regardless of whether the target was truly a hostile aircraft or a civilian plane that had strayed off course and been mistaken for an enemy warplane. A man in an aircraft, on the other hand, could exercise judgement and caution by first identifying the target. Like the F-102, the Bomarc, an unproven missile under development, would be restricted to target acquisition within the SAGE network. The SAGE network itself would be subject to electronic jamming, a technology the Russians were known to possess. Eventually, the Bomarc would, in fact, prove to be a disaster, while the F-102 cum F-106 would remain in service until the early 1980s.

Throughout the two-day meeting, Avro was

asked to provide facts and information. The following is recorded by the RCAF within the conclusions of the meeting and speaks to the professionalism of the company:

It should be pointed out that the Company provided the meeting with complete facilities and information exactly as required in terms of quality and content. They made every effort to carry out the spirit of the requests made upon them by the CAS [Chief of the Air Staff] and did this to perfection. There was absolutely no indication whatever of salesmanship or extravagant claims and only the engineering staff made contact with the visiting party. They provided only the information that they were requested to do and stuck strictly to their terms of reference. Mr. Floyd provided a short discussion on the future potential of the aircraft, showed a film of the test models that had been made and fired and explained design characteristics of the mock-up. Mr. Grinyer described the design philosophy of his engine and its present status and timing. . . . Both engineers were most objective about the problems that they were facing, were not at all reticent to describe their difficulties, and the ways in which they had hoped to overcome them.[13]

A letter dated November 9, 1955, was sent to the Honourable Ralph Campney, Minister of National Defence, from Donald A. Quarles, Secretary of the Air Force. In it, Quarles stated that as a result of the evaluation it was recommended that "development and production of the CF-105 proceed as now planned."[14] He also included a summary of the meeting that showed a preference for the Arrow in northern areas or offshore by "a fair margin over the F-102B . . . due to the CF-105 having twin-engine reliability; having with its additional crewman, a better navigation and search radar capability; [and] being better adapted to operations from marginal airfields."[15]

The USAF liked the aircraft, had faith in the design team, believed that Orenda would succeed in developing the Iroquois, and wondered about the utility of this engine in American aircraft. It even gave Canada the go-ahead to proceed with the programme. One must wonder, "Which government was controlling the project?" Moreover, although increasing cost had been mentioned as a potential problem by the RCAF, money to continue was made available now that the Americans had spoken. The Americans had issued their decree and this was all that mattered. Still, why was the RCAF persisting on the complex fire control and Sparrow missile? What source of advice was more important than the Americans' on these issues? In conversation with this author, Dr. Solandt would only proffer that the RCAF wanted the absolute best and placed this above the actual requirements. And what of the NAE and the DRB?

From the same information available to the U.S. team, the DRB and the NAE had somehow concluded that the Arrow would probably be no better than the F-102. This assessment in a letter dated November 3, 1955, perhaps in anticipation of the American reply, prompted the following response from Air Vice Marshall Hendrick, Air Member Technical Services, on December 9, 1955. Commenting on the fact that numerous subsequent discussions had been held with the company and the DRB as well as the CF-105 Aerodynamic Subcommittee, he added:

[T]here is a wide difference of opinion between NAE and A. V. Roe on the possible performance of this aircraft. . . . We note your statement that you can find no serious grounds for differing with the NAE figures. I think it only fair to say however that we as a Service, can find no serious grounds for differing materially with the Company who are our contractors and the designers of this aircraft. . . . [U]nder the worst conditions the 105 is likely to be as good as or better than the 102 in aerodynamic performance. This is a statement which you have agreed on more than one occasion. . . . [T]he tactical and fighting advantages of the CF-105 by virtue of its two men, two engines, large radar, etc., give it such superiority as a weapons system as to justify continuation of the project. . . . We do not accept the contention that the 102B and the 105 are geometrically similar and that simple arithmetic comparisons of their performance can be made. . . . [T]he difference between the high wing and the low wing aircraft are sufficiently great to make such forms of comparison oversimplified and dangerous.[16]

In January 1956, Orenda received official notification that the USAF was interested in the Arrow only if it were to be fitted with the PS-13 Iroquois engine and not with the lower powered American J-75 engine, which was also being considered. In addition, it was disclosed that the USAF was interested in the Iroquois for other aircraft including their B-52 bomber.[17] Clearly, the USAF wanted the engine programme to continue. It must be realized that quite apart from the engine itself, the manufacturing and research knowledge gained from both the engine and airframe programmes would be of immense value to similar programmes in the U.S. and other countries, especially if they would eventually prove successful. A. V. Roe would be solving technical problems not only for itself but for the rest of the world, including potential enemies.

By January of 1957, John Orr, Director of Engineering Research at the DRB, was reporting that Avro and NAE performance figures were finally coming into agreement. Avro had reduced its 2-g manoeuvrability figure to 1.63 and the NAE had raised its to 1.62. As noted by Orr in a letter to the Chief of the Air Staff, this was still far superior to any other aircraft. Still, the cautions were evident, and by January 21, 1957, the NAE was claiming that its estimates were more accurate than Avro's. The bottom line, however, was that the Arrow was being shown to be a better aircraft by orders of magnitude above the rest, and later flight testing would show that the 2-g requirement could indeed be achieved.[18]

In February 1957, another meeting was held in Toronto. This time it was by the Advanced Interceptor Committee, chaired by General Boyd of the USAF. The committee agreed with Canadian thinking on the design and operational requirements for an aircraft like the Arrow, and in April 1957 the RCAF was informed that the USAF wanted to be kept up to date on all developments. It seemed that American aircraft programmes were indeed falling behind considerably in their schedules and the Arrow might fill the gap.[19]

As before, though, the NAE sent another letter to the DRB, this one dated June 20, 1957, and signed by the new director, D. C. MacPhail. Now the NAE was claiming the aircraft would break up in flight:

We understand that the CF-105 is to be equipped with an artificial stability augmentation system which goes considerably beyond what is being attempted in the design of other high speed aircraft. The essential difference is that the CF-105 system is required to provide augmentation of static directional stability, as well as the now generally required damping. The result of this development is that failure of the servo system can be expected to cause nearly instantaneous breakup of the aircraft in several regions within its normal flight envelope. . . . The reason for this work is, of course, that we believe it should be possible to design the airframe so that even if artificial damping is needed to provide acceptable handling characteristics, the safety of the aircraft is not dependent on its functioning satisfactorily. We know that the attainment of this standard of safety is being demanded and achieved by the British, French, and Americans and we are continually astonished that it is neither being demanded or achieved in Canada in the case of the CF-105 aircraft.[20]

The letter is most curious. By this time, the subjects of safety, lateral stability, and so on had been well addressed by the Avro team in its presentations to NACA and, as will be shown later, as discussed with experts from the United Kingdom. The tone in the letter is also somewhat strong and could lead one to believe that the NAE was again being more obstructionist than helpful.

In fact, the question of safety was paramount in Jim Floyd's mind and led him into several heated discussions with Harvey Smith, vice president of manufacturing. It was Floyd's opinion that if engineering realized during production — perhaps as a result of additional testing — that a given component might have a higher risk associated with it, then the component should be corrected if possible. This, of course, could lead to delays in production; with the tight schedules involved, delays would be unacceptable to Smith. The matter was resolved by Fred Smye, the president and general manager, who stated, "[I]n regard to safety of the first airplane, it is Floyd's unqualified decision as to whether or not the change is to be incorporated. . . . [I]f engineering feels that they must make the change for safety sake, it will be made immediately and it is not a matter to be discussed."[21.]

The NAE must have been aware of these policies through the DRB: in 1955, Crawford Gordon, then Avro's president and general manager, had personally supported a proposal to have a DRB individual attached to the project in the plant in Toronto; also, records show that the NAE fully supported the formation of aerodynamic and structural subcommittees of which they enjoyed participation. Under these circumstances, such a letter seems quite ludicrous.[22]

July 18, 1957, saw the visit of Dr. Courtland Perkins, Chief Scientist, USAF, to Avro. Dr. Perkins told Floyd the USAF had let a contract for a design study on a long-range interceptor complete with engine, missiles, and fire control system. The project was losing support in view of the aircraft weight and the situation in dollars for defence. He stated that should the aircraft be cancelled, there was a good chance that the USAF would consider the Arrow and that it should be kept abreast of all developments. He then outlined the requirements, which included the abilities to fly out to 250 nautical miles, loiter for one hour, proceed at Mach 3 for another 325 nautical miles, and to engage targets up to 70,000 feet at 1.2 g and Mach 3. It was a tall order, but Avro thought it might be achievable with some modifications and if refuelling were allowed during the loiter. Dr. Perkins asked to be kept abreast of all ideas.[23] One must indeed begin to wonder if, in a very subtle way, the USAF wanted Avro to do much of the work, perhaps thinking that U.S. manufacturers were unable to handle the project. On the other hand, maybe the USAF's strategy was a surreptitious attempt to find out just how capable Avro was. This author contacted Dr. Perkins several times during the preparation of this book in 1991. Dr. Perkins admitted to having visited Avro, but said he was not connected with the project in any way and did not recall what had been discussed at the meeting other than the circular wing flying saucer (Avrocar) being developed by John Frost of Avro. His parting comments on the Arrow were that he was not involved then and still is not today.

The whole subject of the Arrow was again reviewed, this time in Washington, between the Canadian Vice Chief of the Air Staff, Air Vice Marshall Larry Dunlap; the Air Member Technical Services, Air Vice Marshall Hendrick; and high-ranking officers of the USAF. Results of this meeting were reported at the 273rd Air Council meeting held October 19, 1957, in Ottawa. The Vice Chief of the Air Staff stated that the Americans thought North America must be defended against manned bombers and the intercontinental ballistic missile for the period 1960 to 1970. The United States also believed Russia could have a supersonic intercontinental bomber by 1965, possibly even a nuclear-powered one. Therefore, the American concept of defence was to counter with an in-depth array of complementary weapons: long-range interceptors that would attack oncoming bombers at a great distance with nuclear weapons, followed by surface-to-air missiles within the heartland should some enemy bombers get through the initial long-range encounter.[24]

The Americans had stated that surface-to-air missiles would necessarily be limited in range to 250 miles. (Presumably, this was due to the distance limitations of radar acquisition that would guide the missile to the target; that is, SAGE). Therefore, they would likely replace short-range interceptors as mentioned earlier, and perhaps some medium-range interceptors, as well, in the 1963 to 1965 period. There still remained the requirement, though, for a long-range interceptor that had the inherent advantages of flexibility, range, and human discrimination.

The Avro Arrow was regarded by the Americans as a long-range interceptor because of its radius of action and because of the geographical location of the bases from which it could be operated. Indeed, Dr. John J. Green, the DRB scientific adviser to the RCAF, had written the following in a memorandum dated June 10, 1954:

In computing combat radius different conditions are stipulated by the RCAF and the USAF. For instance, the USAF permits the use of external tanks, whereas the RCAF specification does not. If the combat radius of the CF-105 is calculated in accordance with the conditions permitted by the USAF specification, a figure of 782 nautical miles is obtained, which is not far short of the 1,000 nautical miles specified by the USAF. Incidentally, the combat radius based on the RCAF specification but with full internal tanks is 635 nautical miles for JP4 fuel and 665 nautical miles for JP1 fuel.[25]

Calculation of combat radius must also consider the type of mission to be carried out, but the memorandum from Dr. Green does point out some of the numerous other factors to be considered. This issue of combat radius would later become a source of confusion; the Prime Minister and others would state the figures incorrectly, giving rise to the mistaken belief that the Arrow's range would be so limited as to render it useless.

In addition to being regarded as a long-range interceptor, the Air Member Technical Services who was responsible for the Arrow development programme added that the aircraft would not only fill the gap from 1962 to 1965 but that its true potential could be exploited after 1965 to deal with the supersonic bomber threat through increased range and speed. Limitations to speed were thought to be due to thermal heating of the aircraft skin in supersonic flight, but the Air Member emphasized this might not prove to be the problem once thought. In supersonic flight, airborne particles and molecules strike the aircraft with such force that the skin heats up due to friction. This can cause the wings and other parts to distort because of uneven heating, possibly resulting in the loss of the aircraft.[26]

Meanwhile, at the Ottawa 273rd Air Council meeting, members were told that the Americans were pushing ahead with the Bomarc missile and were planning to improve the SAGE system. But the Bomarc and SAGE combination would only be useful against manned bombers and would be used primarily against the bombers that got through the initial encounter from the defending long-range interceptors. What about the intercontinental ballistic missile (ICBM), against which interceptors and the Bomarc would be useless? No decisions had yet been reached on how to counter the ICBM threat, but several weapons were under development. In an interview with this author on July 31, 1991, Air Vice Marshall John Easton confirmed that an anti-ICBM capability was being considered for the Arrow. The Americans had provided charts and estimates of proposed defensive weapons, performance capabilities of Russian bombers to 1965, costs of the Bomarc in relation to aircraft such as the F-106, hypothetical attack scenarios, and defence strategies against the supersonic bomber threat. It seemed the old subsonic Soviet bombers were slowly being replaced with supersonic bombers.[27]

The Air Member Technical Services stated that his own view, like the Americans', was for an all-encompassing programme of Arrow, Bomarc, and improved radar defences. The Vice Chief of the Air Staff agreed, but did not believe the economy could afford a variety of expensive weapons. At this same meeting, the Air Member Personnel, Air Vice Marshall J. Gordon Kerr, questioned the value of continuing with the Arrow given that it would be in use for only two or three years before the American long-range interceptors were ready and that less expensive Bomarcs would also soon be available. His position was to improve the ground environment and build missile bases. He, too, expressed the opinion that together "the cost of both Bomarc and the Arrow was prohibitive." This combined cost would eventually erroneously translate into only the cost of the Arrow as being prohibitive.[28]

Unfortunately, it appears that Air Vice Marshall Kerr did not fully understand the technical discussion that had preceded his comments on the need for long-range interception and the differences between aircraft and missiles for varying roles. This lack of understanding is not surprising, as he was a nontechnical participant. The question, though, is whether his comments deflected the course of the conversation or influenced the outcome. Did he expect the Americans to handle Canadian long-range requirements, or were they expected just to provide their aircraft without charge? The Bomarc was short range, yet why did he think it could replace the long-range Arrow? Was the Canadian air defence strategy truly thought out? And what of the future potential of the Arrow discussed at this same meeting? Was this group truly capable of discussing the question of defence and the role of the Arrow in an intelligent fashion, or were the concepts beyond their comprehension?

Like the United States, the Royal Air Force (RAF) in the United Kingdom was well aware of the CF-105 developments. In December 1955, the Minister of Supply for the United Kingdom requested permission from the Canadian government for a team of experts to visit Avro. The Director of the Royal Aeronautical Establishment, the Deputy Chief of Staff of the RAF, and others descended upon Avro in January 1956. It was acknowledged at the outset that the Arrow had been designed with Canadian geography in mind. However, this geography would not be unlike Britain if one considered the North Sea to be akin to the vast stretches of the Canadian northwest.

Conclusions from the British report agreed generally with the Americans. The U.K. team thought that Avro's claims were reasonable. They pointed to the differences of opinion between Avro and Canada's NAE and said that further wind-tunnel testing would be needed to augment the numerical calculations. Still, they addressed the contentious point of drag due to trim at supersonic speed. Explaining that this drag results when the elevators are deflected upwards to help control and stabilize the aircraft, the report goes on to state:

For the control derivatives (a), an analysis of NACA data on delta wings, suitably corrected for minor variations in geometry along the lines suggested by theory, would seem to support the values being quoted by the firm. We are therefore in disagreement with NAE on this point since they are suggesting lower control effectiveness. . . . Broadly speaking, the firm's estimates for thrust and drag are not seriously in error, i.e., probably not more than 5-10% optimistic. If we have understood the NAE estimates for trim drag correctly, we would say that they are over estimating the value of this quantity. . . . The amount of work done by the firm at this stage on the intake is especially laudable.[29]

The British experts were essentially agreeing that Avro's numbers were probably correct and that those of the NAE might be in error by a greater amount. It is known that the NAE received a copy of the U.K. results, but Jim Floyd does not recall having seen them. Still, this type of assessment might have upset those in the NAE who were certain the NAE was correct.

Further on, the report discusses, in some detail, the electronic automatic stability augmentation system, failure of which the NAE thought would cause the aircraft to break apart while in certain regions of the flight envelope. NACA had already stated electronic stability was feasible. Noting that failure of such a system could create severe problems, the British experts concluded:

Any aircraft of the performance of the CF-105 will require artificial stability and damping of some kind. . . . [W]hile most firms are adopting the philosophy of designing the aircraft to have the best possible inherent stability characteristics, and then bringing the aircraft to the required standard by the minimum of artificial means, this firm has taken the view that since artificial stability is required it should be exploited to the full. . . . Their arguments include the saving of weight . . . and better handling characteristics generally. The clear indication is that a high degree of reliability will be required from the system which may cause delays in development, since it is in any case very advanced in concept. . . . We were however impressed with the thorough and realistic manner in which they are tackling the project. Their avowed objective is to obtain a system reliability equivalent to that demanded of the engines on a twin-engine aircraft. . . . The CF-105 has a higher performance than the F-153 (Javelin) and the RCAF intends to equip it to a more effective standard than we could achieve in the same time. When fitted with British equipment the CF-105 would still be better than the F-153 but our less versatile weapons would tend to reduce its margin of superiority.[30]

The artificial stability system being discussed in this and the NAE letter are today part of the fly-by-wire systems, which are used in the most advanced jets, including the F/A-18 Hornet, Canada's newest fighter. More will be explained later, as fly-by-wire was indeed built into and successfully flown in the Arrow. Unlike the Avro engineers who were thinking towards the future, it is clear that the NAE wanted to take the lower risk traditional approach, but as had been pointed out by NACA and now the British team, the traditional approach would give poorer performance. In fact, given that the British report was released to the NAE before its memo of June 20, 1957, one wonders if the NAE was not simply extracting from selected portions of the report, leaving out the comments regarding the high degree of confidence the British team had in Avro. The F/A-18 is also inherently unstable, but it is precisely this feature that gives it its agility and manoeuvrability. The British report goes on to say that these types of controls will be "essential in higher speed aircraft and experience of them in the CF-105 would be invaluable." Indeed, this has proven to be the case.[31]

The visiting U.K. team also undertook to examine closely the building and manufacture of the engines and airframe and to look at planning, scheduling, salary, and morale of employees and numerous other like factors. The report states:

There is no doubt that the firm is capable with its present labour force and space of meeting the likely demands for the RCAF and in fact exceeding them considerably. An output of over 10 CF-105s per month on a single shift basis is well within the capabilities of the firm. . . . Orenda

Engines Ltd. . . . is excellently equipped and there is no doubt whatever of its ability to match the aircraft programme in mind by Avro Aircraft Ltd.[32]

The report finds remarkable the friendly relationship between the design and manufacturing staffs and the care taken in measuring the progress at every stage. The report concludes that the best choice for the RAF would be the Arrow "as is." So, yet again, independent experts from another country informed the RCAF that the project was sound, that they had all the confidence in the Avro engineers, and that they disagreed with the NAE on the major technical issues.

With respect to purchases, though, it was believed that the aircraft might be too costly if manufactured in Canada. To keep costs in check, licensing arrangements were proposed. The report itself had included cost and scheduling estimates for various production scenarios involving 100 aircraft produced in Britain at costs ranging between $3.2 and $3.7 million per copy. Then in May 1956, Air Marshall Pike (RAF) stated that although the Arrow was a very attractive aircraft, its proposed delivery date would be too late to meet the RAF requirement. Therefore, the chances of obtaining the aircraft would be small since Britain would rather obtain an aircraft that would be available sooner. Interest from the United Kingdom seemed to dwindle at this point, only to reemerge after the cancellation for the purpose of obtaining reports and technical data that might assist the United Kingdom in developing the TSR-2 aircraft.[33]

Meanwhile, on January 29, 1958, the Canadian ambassador to Washington, Mr. Norman Robertson, was the luncheon guest of Mr. James H. Douglas, Secretary of the Air Force. It proved to be a fateful meeting! With him were Lieutenant General D. L. Putt, Deputy Chief of Staff, Research and Development; Major General H. M. Estes, Assistant Chief of Staff for Air Defence Systems; and Dudley C. Sharp, Assistant Secretary (Matériel), Department of the Air Force. The purpose of the meeting was to discuss the CF-105. Mr. Douglas displayed considerable knowledge of the Arrow, Canada's concerns about foreign sales to reduce cost, and continental defence. He stated categorically that there was no place in the USAF inventory for the CF-105. He stated that the USAF was going ahead with the F-108 long-range interceptor because they believed it would be more advanced and capable. Later, of course, it would be cancelled.[34]

Still, the door had not been completely closed. The Secretary stated his personal view that in the context of continental defence, the USAF could purchase the Arrow in squadron strength to operate from Canadian bases and to be manned and maintained by the RCAF. The Canadian ambassador interpreted this as some form of charity and suggested that Canada wished to be a contributor to defence and not a beneficiary. He further stated there would be political problems with this arrangement.

General Putt speculated whether a plan through NORAD (North American Air Defence) could not be established that would call for more CF-105 squadrons than currently envisaged by Canada, with the difference being funded by the USAF. As an alternative, he mentioned that eight Strategic Air Command refuelling bases were being planned for installation in Canada and that perhaps a swap could be arranged; the purchase of CF-105s in exchange for work done in Canada in readying the refuelling bases.[35] On the one hand, it seemed the USAF was saying no, while on the other it seemed they were saying the Arrow was wanted and needed, especially for protection in the North.

In a priority message back to Canada, air staff in Washington indicated that the meeting had been far from conclusive, but that the opportunity was at hand for an official approach to the USAF. The message stated that the climate was favourable, and that apart from the meeting with the Secretary, there had been many indications that the CF-105 was being recognized as a very fine weapon. It does not appear, though, that General Putt's ideas for a swap were ever followed up, and it is not known what Norman Robertson's personal report on the meeting showed.[36]

As an early strategy at trying to interest the Americans further, notwithstanding this meeting, it was proposed that the Arrow be compared with the F-106 and F-108 aircraft to demonstrate the Arrow's superior capabilities. Performance characteristics for the American aircraft would be needed, and it was expected the information would be made available since Canada had always shared data willingly. This would not prove to be the case. In 1958, repeated attempts at trying to obtain the data on the American aircraft failed. A request was even made through Air Marshall Slemon, now Deputy Commander in Chief of NORAD, but this, too, yielded nothing. An exasperated staff officer would note, "The purposes of the letter are a) to pt. out to Senior Officers the importance of exactly comparable missions . . . and b) a last ditch effort to obtain F-106 operating data. . . . It would almost appear that the USAF are withholding this data. . . . 16 June 1958."[37]

American interest in the Arrow was changing at a time when the aircraft was beginning to prove its capabilities. Was the USAF truly disinterested in a project it had supported since inception? Had the USAF obtained the solution to the technical problems its own manufacturers were facing and was it now pulling back, or was it being told that it no longer had an interest in the Arrow by some other authority that felt threatened? According to John Orr, then Director of Engineering Research at the DRB, it is claimed that the USAF submitted a confidential evaluation of the technical and operational capabilities of the aircraft to Canadian officials. This report had supposedly been written by a junior officer subject to influence by U.S. aircraft manufacturers who might see the Arrow as a threat to business. This author located one other individual who claims to have seen such a report, but the report itself, if it exists, has not yet come to light. Still, why would anyone go to such lengths?[38]

The facts clearly demonstrate that the USAF kept the project moving, with the RCAF seemingly following orders. American officials had not only been sought after for consultation on the project but were asked directly for the go-ahead to continue. The situation evolving was not unlike that in the late 1980s with the design and development of the Israeli fighter, the Lavi. Just as the prototypes were commencing flight tests, the United States removed support and effectively killed the programme. The primary difference was that the United States was actually subsidizing the development of the Lavi and was likely well within its rights to pull out of the development if it so desired. Still, why did it not stop the project sooner? It is as if the Arrow and Lavi developments were simply a means of conducting research and development by exploiting foreign talent. In the case of Canada, this talent was being made available free of charge and always with the hope of a sale. But also in the case of Canada, why not purchase the aircraft? Was it really a problem with U.S. industry or were other factors involved? It is as if the more Avro and the Arrow proved themselves, the more important it became to stop the programme.

What is perhaps most distressing is the seeming lack of Canadian confidence in the programme, most notably from certain quarters of the NAE. Independent experts in both the United States and the United Kingdom were most impressed by A. V. Roe's technical talent and its grasp of the problems being faced. Both were also in disagreement with the NAE, and still the NAE persisted in raising problems that seemingly were not there, giving every impression, perhaps inadvertently, of trying to thwart the programme just to prove it was right.

What was it about this aircraft, which on the one hand was hailed by the international technical community, but on the other sparked a delayed lack of interest from foreign governments? Was it superior or not, and in which ways? What about that first flight? Would it prove to be Avro's undoing?

3 THE ARROW

Until recently, high-performance aircraft were not committed to production until after flight testing of one or more prototypes. . . . The Arrow programme is unusual in Canada in that even the first flying model has been built on production tooling.
Avro News, October 4, 1957[1]

THE CF-105, OR AVRO ARROW, had begun as a project under the Liberal government of Prime Minister Louis St. Laurent. However, after assuming power in June 1957, the Conservative government of Prime Minister John George Diefenbaker would mark the official unveiling of the Arrow programme on October 4, 1957. Remarkably, the aircraft had been built and made ready to fly in just four years, an incredible achievement. As a time-saving measure, Avro did not hand-build the first aircraft, but moved from drawing board to production line tooling and manufacture. This technique would be repeated thirty years later on the Stealth bomber using advanced, computer-aided design techniques unavailable to Avro at the time. As well, the man-hours expended in actual construction of the Arrow were twenty percent less than in projects of similar size and complexity.[2]

Aviation Week, one of the most prestigious journals of its day, reported, "Avro CF-105 Arrow has given Canada a serious contender for the top military aircraft of the next several years. The large, decidedly advanced delta-wing fighter was rolled out of the Malton plant a few days ago. . . . The Arrow's power, weight and general design leave little doubt of its performance potential."[3] Likewise, *Flight*, a respected international publication, would call the Arrow "the biggest, most powerful, most expensive and potentially the fastest fighter that the world has yet seen."[4]

As has been intimated, the Arrow embodied many technically advanced features. One of the most striking was the high delta-wing, tailless configuration. Early in the design, Avro had decided the delta was the most aerodynamically efficient platform for the high-speed and high-altitude performance demanded of an interceptor. It also provided for a large internal fuel capacity and, with some clever engineering, enough thickness in the wing root for stowage of the landing gear. To permit higher angles of attack and greater stability, and to alleviate pitch-up, Avro had extended and drooped the leading edge while adding a sawtooth cut, or notch. As the company had successfully argued with the NAE and NACA, this would create more favourable airflow across the wing and make the aircraft aerodynamically superior to others in its class.

Finally, Avro had added negative camber, a slight concavity in the upper surface of the wing that would help reduce the amount of elevator deflection required for stability and control (trim) during supersonic flight. Jim Floyd explains, "Camber has the effect of building in some elevator angle without the excessive control surface drag. The amount of camber chosen, which was 3/4 percent negative, was that which would give a good compromise between the positive angles to trim at low altitude, and the negative angles required at high altitude."[5]

A high wing (extending from the top of the fuselage rather than the underside) was chosen because it permitted flexibility in the changing of engine and armament packages without affecting the wing structure itself. It also allowed for easier attachment of the tailfin since the latter would not have to be carried through the engine structure. As for the tailless configuration, it "can be attributed almost entirely to our desire not to have to face the problem of putting a tail on top of an extremely thin fin out of the effects of wing downwash, or, otherwise, having to put it so low, again out of the downwash region, that our landing angles would be impossible. We felt that the problems associated with a tailless delta were more predictable and manageable."[6]

In selecting the tailless delta, Avro made use of experimental data that had been gathered by Avro Manchester when designing the tailless although subsonic Vulcan delta bomber and the Avro 707B and 707C research aircraft.

The Arrow was extensively "area-ruled." This concept involves aerodynamic shaping of the cross-sectional area of the fuselage along its length to reduce drag to a minimum. The concept is also known as the "Coke bottle" design, because the fuselage looks like a Coke bottle, pinched at the waist where the wing joins. The characteristic pinched waist of the fuselage was not immediately noticeable on the Arrow.[7]

Up front was the radar nose, which had been sharpened and extended as a result of applying the area-ruling principle for aerodynamic shaping. The nose was followed by the cockpit, which had been designed as an extension of the fuselage rather than as a separate bubble for good aerodynamic performance. This design is not unlike the Stealth bomber, which has a blended cockpit as opposed to the bubble cockpit of an F/A-18 Hornet. The cockpit canopy of the Arrow was of unusual design, opening and closing in clamshell fashion due to its size and weight as well as for ease of entry and exit. It was made of a magnesium alloy with partly glazed glass. In back, drag was reduced by trailing the canopy off into a spine running the length of the aircraft to the tail. This spine doubled as a conduit for controls and wire cabling. Inside the cockpit, positioned in tandem, were Martin-Baker C-5 ejection seats (some documents say Martin-Baker Mark 4). As for the cockpit layout, it was described by General Joseph Caldara, the USAF Director of Flight Safety, "unequivocally as the best layout he had seen."[8]

Breaking into the underside of the fuselage behind the cockpit and larger than the bomb bay of a

B-29 was the massive armament bay. To maintain a clean design and maximize supersonic efficiency, it had been decided to carry missiles internally. The concept of internal weapons carriage has spawned several misguided criticisms about an aircraft that would self-destruct if the weapons pack were lowered in flight. The idea behind the criticism is easily demonstrated if you extend your hand out the car window while driving down the highway; when you place the palm of your hand perpendicular to the direction of motion, the force of the wind tries to push it backward. In a high-speed aircraft, lowering a massive weapon pack in flight would have the same effect, except that instead of the pack moving backward, the whole aircraft would shudder and perhaps disintegrate. The criticism is purely academic, however, because on the Arrow the pack was not designed to be lowered in flight; only on the ground could it be lowered, removed, and replaced with a fresh pack, facilitating rearming and considerably reducing turnaround time. This concept also allowed easy reconfiguration of the aircraft for other roles including reconnaissance, bombing (nuclear), and scientific data gathering when fitted with the appropriate instruments.[9] But what weapon would be suitable for this aircraft?

In 1950, Cabinet had approved the establishment of a guided missile programme under the DRB. Work began on April 1, 1951, at the Canadian Armament Research Development Establishment (CARDE) in Point Petre, Ontario. Specifications for what was to be known as the Velvet Glove air-to-air missile were developed, and special laboratories were established at CARDE. By 1952, twenty test missiles had been fired, and by 1953 guided missile research made up over fifty percent of the work at CARDE. The first air-launched firing took place August 27, 1953, from an F-86E Sabre aircraft and was completely successful. Test firings continued with fixed-wing missiles, then controlled missiles, and finally missiles with seeker heads. By 1955, some of the development had been transferred to industry, over 300 missiles had been test-fired, and the development team had grown from a group of four to over four hundred engineers and scientists working in the DRB and industry.

Developed originally with the CF-100 in mind, the Velvet Glove programme was in itself a real success, contributing a wealth of information for further guided missile research in Canada. However, it would be inadequate for use with the supersonic Arrow and against an enemy supersonic bomber threat. Rather than upgrade the weapon for use on the Arrow, the project was terminated in favour of foreign missiles. The development had cost some $24 million.[10] (It is worth noting that one of the bright young scientists behind Velvet Glove was one Gerald Bull, of Iraqi supergun infamy.)

After the Velvet Glove, the Arrow was to have carried eight Hughes Falcon guided missiles controlled by the Hughes MX-1179 electronic fire control system. But the RCAF had ideas and an agenda of its own. Against the advice of the USAF, the DRB, and Avro, the RCAF requested design proposals for a more advanced fire control system that would be compatible with the Sparrow 2D missile being designed for the U.S. Navy. It was argued that the Sparrow would be less susceptible to electronic jamming than the Falcon since it operated at a much higher radio frequency band, and the RCAF disputed the Falcon's kill probability figures. (These figures predict how successful a weapon system is in destroying its intended target.) If this assessment was true, it is surprising it was not noticed by the DRB, Avro, or the USAF delegation that had advised the use of Falcon.[11]

The USAF had also warned that such an advanced fire control system was not required and that the design would stress the abilities of Hughes Aircraft, already burdened with USAF contracts. Instead, RCA, a less experienced player in the field of fire control systems design, submitted proposals and won the contract, which was negotiated on June 29, 1956, and made retroactive to June 20, 1956. The new fire control system was known as Astra.[12]

In 1956, the U.S. Navy abandoned the Sparrow 2 development, which was taken over by Canadair and Westinghouse in Canada, adding yet another expensive and unwarranted dimension to the project. In June 1957, Avro again suggested that Sparrow 2 development be abandoned, noting that a recent report by the DRB suggested that neither the Sparrow 2 nor the Sparrow 3 would be compatible with the Arrow.[13] Even the RCAF began to realize that development costs would be enormous and that Sparrow 2 might not be ready until 1965. Group Captain Ray Foottit, Assistant for the Arrow Weapon System, confessed he was not clear himself why the Chief of the Air Staff pressed for the Sparrow 2, except that the U.S. Navy was strongly recommending its continuance.

On August 30, 1957, Jim Floyd wrote directly to Air Vice Marshall Hendrick explaining the problems with the Sparrow 2. He added that Sparrow 3, also under development for the U.S. Navy, could be made compatible at a reduced cost, albeit with degraded capability. He believed this might suffice until the Sparrow X, capable of carrying a nuclear warhead, became available. Nonetheless, the RCAF pressed ahead with the Sparrow 2. Both the fire control system and the missile development would prove to be too large a financial burden and were eventually cancelled in September 1958. Still, the removable weapons pack, revolutionary in concept, allowed for flexibility in choice of weapons. With cancellation of the Sparrow, plans were made to equip the Arrow with Falcons and the originally proposed Hughes system.

With the weapons internal to the fuselage, how would the system work? Each missile was to be mounted on its own hydraulically activated, re-tractable launching mechanism. Because of their large fins, the four Sparrows would have sat partially within and partially outside the belly of the aircraft. The smaller eight Falcons would have been fully internal. Mounted on rail launchers, the missiles would have extended from their own individual weapons bay doors. The requirement for Sparrows was that all four be extended at the same time, with rear missiles extended further than the forward pair. Any missile or all four at once could then be launched. A sliding bay door arrangement was under study, with door opening or closing to be effected in 0.35 seconds and missile extension in no more than 1.25 seconds. Doors would open for extension and be partially closed during firing, reopening again to admit the rail launcher. Unfortunately, the development would not be completed, for termination of the entire programme would intervene.[14]

In terms of aerodynamics, Avro engineers had estimated that mounting missiles externally as in conventional aircraft would have increased drag by twenty percent. Yet critics have argued that if this was such a good concept, why had other aircraft designers not followed the same principles? In fact, the F-106 used an internal weapons carriage, and the concept was successfully tested on the F-111 in the 1960s.

A January 1990 article in *Interavia Aerospace Review* reported the following:

Why make sleek-shaped combat aircraft with low drag and low radar cross-section able to cruise supersonically and then hang on high-drag bombs or missiles with radar reflecting fins? It is illogical and would impose an unacceptable performance limitation on the next-generation combat aircraft.

Increased speeds and agility in fighters and the need to launch missiles in any attitude and under any G loading dictate semiburied or buried missiles, as well as ejector or rail-launcher systems able to match performance with aircraft attitude.[15]

The concept of internal weapons carriage has since been adopted in the Stealth fighter design and the proposals for the new advanced tactical fighter currently under development. It would seem that in the 1990s Avro would still have an aircraft of the future!

The requirement for such a large weapons bay necessitated stowage of the main landing gear in the delta wings. This caused a number of engineering difficulties, overcome by Dowty Equipment of Canada Limited. On retraction, the main gear with tandem wheels would be shortened, angled forward, and then twisted inboard for stowage. Given the 30-ton weight of the aircraft and resulting 200,000-pound compressive load on the main gear on landing, ultra-high-tensile steel with an ultimate tensile strength of 260,000 to 280,000 pounds per square inch was required. Use of aluminum was precluded, as was the use of butt joints and gas welding. Instead, large forgings were made using a die process. The main outer leg was the largest forging, weighing in at 1,000 pounds and reducing to 167 pounds after machining. Drop testing was used to check the performance of the liquid-spring shock absorbers, and over seven times as many calculations as performed on the CF-100 undercarriage were performed for stress analysis. Solutions to all the various problems put Dowty and Avro engineers at the forefront of metallurgical research. Likewise, engineers at Jarry Hydraulics were obtaining patents for the nosewheel steering mechanism they were developing.[16]

The Arrow employed two independent hydraulic systems. One pump on each engine supplied the "A" system, while another pump on each engine supplied the "B" system. In the event of the loss of one engine or system, adequate control could be maintained. The reason for highlighting the hydraulic system is because it, too, represented a technical advance. Special connections produced by Weatherhead of Canada were required: "the fluid connections produced by the company are leading the way in the field of high pressure, high temperature hydraulic systems. No standard fittings were available for the 4,000-pound-per-square-inch hydraulic system chosen for the Arrow."[17] This 4,000 pound-per-square-inch system was pushing the state of the art on hydraulic systems, which were traditionally of 3,000 pounds per square inch. The high pressure meant that the entire system could be made more compact and lighter than conventional ones; however, it also meant additional research to prove the concept. In fact, Avro engineers and their subcontractors made enormous strides in developing and using high-

temperature alloys such as magnesium and titanium, high-pressure hydraulics, fuel technology for
supersonic flight, and human engineering. Supporting these advances, Avro maintained a huge metal-
to-metal autoclave pressure chamber, a special
heat-treat furnace, a giant skin machining mill,
and a 15,000-ton rubber pad forming press (then
the largest in the world).[18] Added to this was an
overall quality control system so exacting that it
was said by one employee that inspectors used
magnifying glasses and special instruments when
judging the precision of tolerances on given components.

Discussion of the engine intakes, which also incorporated technical advances, is most complicated
and therefore best summarized by a direct quotation from the British engineering report discussed
in Chapter 2:

The intake has a 12 degree ramp and a boundary
layer diverter below the ramp to improve pressure recovery. The diverted air (1% of engine air)
is used in the air conditioning unit. . . . There is
a porous strip on the ramp through which the
ramp boundary layer is sucked. This was found
in the tunnel to prevent a serious loss of efficiency when the intake was spilling. At the end
of the intake diffuser there is a two-position by-
pass annulus which serves the double purpose of
avoiding excessive spillage and of removing the
duct boundary layer. The maximum bleed is 8%.
This air is ejected round the engine nozzle. In

this way the firm claim that they avoid appreciable sink drag. . . . The wedge shock is on the intake lip at Mach 2.3. Tests have shown that to avoid unsteady flow at the compressor face at reduced mass flow, it is necessary that the shock should be well ahead of the lip, and the firm have accepted some preentry drag to achieve this. Measured values of pressure recovery at Mach 1.5 and Mach 2 are 96% and 86% respectively, both at the engine match points. These values must be regarded as being very good. Flow distribution is claimed to be very good. The intake is insensitive to incidences up to 9.5 degrees and angles of yaw up to 6 degrees which were the greatest angles tested. It is our opinion that there is every hope that the intake will work satisfactorily and efficiently, due to the careful thought which has gone into its design. The firm have wisely avoided variability, since there is hardly a case for it at Mach 1.5.[19]

The last sentence is a reference to the fixed ramp angle of 12 degrees. Other designers were using variable intake geometries, but these required servomotors and sensors in order to alter the geometry in relation to the speed of the aircraft. This incurred a weight penalty and added complexity; Avro had wisely decided it was not required.

Early in the design it was decided that some form of power assist would be required to help control and fly such a large aircraft in supersonic flight. The extra power would assist the Arrow to respond immediately to the pilot's commands from the control stick and thus provide a high degree of manoeuvrability. It would also help control an otherwise unstable aircraft at certain speeds and altitudes. This was the electronic stability augmentation system so feared by the NAE. Today, it is called fly-by-wire.

In conventional systems, the pilot's stick and rudder controls are mechanically linked (via steel cables or rods) to valves that control high-pressure fluid flow to actuators. These, in turn, operate the aircraft's control surfaces, such as ailerons, elevators, and rudder. External position sensors, gyroscopes, and automatic flight control systems are also mechanically linked via the rods and cables. Unfortunately, response time in these conventional systems is not immediate, and the pilot must exert some force to move the control stick. It was not until the 1970s that fighter aircraft, namely the Panavia Tornado and F/A-18 Hornet, began employing a system known as fly-by-wire. In this arrangement, the rods and cables are replaced with electrical wires. An electrical signal command is sent via the pilot's control column to electro-hydraulic actuators, which move the control surfaces. Reaction time is almost instantaneous, and weight is considerably reduced since a system of wires and rods, pulleys and bell cranks weighs far more than electrical wiring. Variations of this system had been employed in experimental aircraft, including the high-flying SR-71 Blackbird, whose design began in

September 1959, seven months after the Arrow's termination.[20]

And then, there was the Arrow! As discussed in the British report, Avro engineers broke convention by deciding on a design that was essentially unstable at certain speeds; the engineers instead provided stability through electronic means. Just as the British report predicted, this became the way of the future in the 1970s with the Panavia Tornado and F/A-18 Hornet aircraft. Today, fly-by-wire has been incorporated into civilian aircraft; the next step will likely be "fly-by-light," whereby the electrical wires will be replaced by fibre optical cables.

The Arrow embodied three modes of flight control: normal, automatic, and emergency. Emergency mode still used some mechanical linkages (rods and cables) and was a backup to the fly-by-wire system, a fact seemingly missed in the NAE memo that had claimed that safety was not being considered on this project. Both normal and automatic modes were fly-by-wire. Normal mode was described in the pilot's operating manual as follows:

[W]hen the pilot exerts a force on the control column grip to move the elevators (ailerons), a force transducer on the control column transmits an electrical signal . . . fed to servos, which convert the electrical signals into a mechanical movement by means of hydraulic pressure. The servos are known as parallel (or command) servo and differential (or damping) servo, depending on outside forces acting on the aircraft, to maintain stability. . . . [T]he electrical output at the transducer is directly proportional to the force exerted at the grip. The control column will move as the force is exerted, as with a conventional flying control system, but it is not moved directly by the pilot. Movement of the control column follows the positioning of the elevators (ailerons) by the command circuits, but as the response of the system is instantaneous, the control column will appear to be moved by the pilot.[21]

To give the pilot some sense of "feel" on the control stick, an electrical, artificial feel system was introduced. The control stick force required to move the control surfaces was made to feel proportional to the amount of g force the aircraft was pulling. This system would be similar to making the power steering in a car artificially feel as though it was not there, requiring the driver to exert more force than expected. In an aircraft, the lack of "power steering," so to speak, would let the pilot "feel," or sense, the motion of the ailerons and other control surfaces.

In automatic mode, the aircraft was to be fitted with an automatic flight control subsystem. Fly-by-wire control would be as before except that the aircraft could be controlled from the ground, such as from the computerized SAGE system. Automatic control would limit the range of the aircraft to that of SAGE, but only while in the automatic mode. The electronic control system also provided an auto-navigation function by allowing the aircraft to be flown via information from a computer.

Completing the flight control system was the damping system. This system provided artificial stabilization in flight by picking up instabilities from sensors and adjusting control surfaces automatically, requiring no action from the pilot. All three axes of flight — pitch (elevators for up and down motion), roll (ailerons), and yaw (rudder) — were embodied with numerous redundancies to ensure flight safety in the event of system failure or malfunction.[22]

Overall, the electrical systems in the Arrow needed eleven miles of wiring, and the analogue computers included both vacuum tube and transistor technology. The effectiveness of the flight control and damping system would later be proven in flight testing: Jan Zurakowski, the Avro test pilot, would shut down one engine during a 60-degree climb with full afterburner, and experience absolutely no sideslip or roll. Clearly, the Arrow was in a class of its own and at least twenty, if not thirty, years ahead of its time in terms of design philosophy, materials, and manufacturing techniques![23]

Powering a 30-ton aircraft to supersonic speeds and allowing for a 2-g turn at 50,000 feet without loss of speed or altitude requires tremendous power. Add to this the safety requirements needed in case of engine trouble somewhere over the vast expanse of Canada, and the choice of a twin-engine configuration is explained. It is noteworthy that twenty years later, Canada would again choose a twin-engine fighter, the F/A-18.

Initially, Avro had decided on the RB-106 engine under development by Rolls-Royce. By 1954, Rolls-Royce had abandoned the project, so in August of that year an analysis of alternative engine types was completed. Included in the study were the Curtiss-Wright J-67, Pratt & Whitney J-57 and J-75, De Havilland Gyron, and Bristol Olympus. The J-67 was deemed the most suitable, and considerable design work to accommodate this engine had been done when, in 1955, it became clear that this, too, would be abandoned, this time by the USAF. It was decided that an untried aircraft and unproven engine would make for a high-risk situation, so the P&W J-75 was selected to power the first five aircraft, designated Mark 1s. A new, more powerful engine, the Iroquois, would power subsequent aircraft, designated Mark 2s.[24]

In September 1953, Avro's Gas Turbine Division, later to become Orenda Engines, decided to build a supersonic engine. In twenty days, a proposal was put before the Hawker-Siddeley Group Design Council, which had been visiting in Malton. Project Study 13 was endorsed by the Council in October. On December 17, 1954, the first test engine was run.[25]

In a memorandum to the Cabinet Defence Committee dated February 25, 1955, wherein he requested approval for the PS-13 development and tooling, the Minister of National Defence, Ralph Campney, pointed out that Orenda Engines had already invested $9 million of its own money in the development. The first prototype had run successfully, and two more prototypes were due to run before June 1, 1955. Campney further stated that the RCAF had completed a study on the suitability of available engines:

> This study indicates that the engine is more advanced in design and concept than any engine being developed in the U.K. or U.S.A. The engine was supersonic in concept from the beginning. The design incorporates a transonic first-stage compressor producing an exceptionally high mass flow. . . . [E]mphasis on mechanical simplicity coupled with the extensive use of titanium, has produced prototype engines which are about 1,000 pounds lighter than other engines in the same power class. An accepted way of comparing engine performance is the thrust produced per pound of engine weight. The PS-13 at its 20,000-pound rating exceeds the Gyron by 22% and the J-67, J-75, and RB-106 by over 50%. These comparative figures are of great importance, particularly with respect to increased performance at high altitudes. . . . In fact, the PS-13 is the only engine likely to be available on time to give the CF-105 its required performance.[26]

It has been argued that such an engine design was too costly, and that less expensive if not technically comparable engines could be acquired elsewhere. The Minister refuted this argument, saying:

Studies carried out indicated that there is little
or no advantage either in time or money in
building an engine under licence as opposed to
Canadian design. This stems from the fact that a
licensing agreement can only be undertaken
safely when the engine has been type-tested and
modified to a point where its detail configuration is comparatively static. The comparative
costs are a matter of statistics but general information and experience indicates that there is no
significant difference in costs where the design
staff, development facilities, and production capacity are available at home. Furthermore, the
advantages of expending this money and effort in
Canada rather than in another country places the
PS-13 engine in a very favourable light.[27]

Campney then praised the technical competence of
the design team. He believed that by developing
this engine Canada would remain in the forefront
of jet engine technology. Unfortunately, this thinking would be lost in the years to come.

The PS-13, or Iroquois, was approximately 19
feet long and 4 feet wide. It was rated at 19,500
pounds dry thrust and at up to 26,000 pounds with
afterburner for a total of 52,000 pounds from both
engines. Plans for a 60,000-pound limit, more than
adequate to power today's fighters, were in the
works. On November 1, 1957, dry thrust runs of
over 20,000 pounds were demonstrated. At a combined 60,000-pound thrust with afterburner for a
60,000-pound aircraft, the Iroquois would have pro-

vided a thrust to weight ratio of 1:1, propelling the Arrow at better than Mach 2 and later Mach 3, assuming that limitations due to structural heating could be overcome. Orenda had pioneered the development and use of titanium as well as methods for machining and welding this material. Advances were also made in lubrication design, with the engine consuming only ten times more oil than a 200-horsepower automobile engine of the day.[28]

On January 30, 1957, the Minister of National Defence requested an increase in funding to the overall project of $46,390,000 over the previously approved $216,790,000. The following reasons were given: the airframe required some redesign due to additional requirements imposed by the Astra control system; some costs were initially being carried by the USAF but were now being passed on to the RCAF, which had assumed the full development; redesign was required due to the decision to fly with the Pratt & Whitney J-75 engines on the Mark 1 aircraft; the costs of materials and wages were rising; and surprisingly, or perhaps not, the PS-13 Iroquois engine development was so successful, it was entering a phase of higher expenditure earlier than anticipated.[29]

The Minister indicated that the engine had completed 1,500 hours of development running, achieving a thrust of 16,100 pounds — 20,000 with afterburner. By November of that year, it had completed 3,200 hours of development running, including a 100-hour endurance test and the aforementioned 20,000-pound static run. On November 13, the Iroquois was flight-tested on a B-47 aircraft on loan from the USAF.[30]

Initially, eleven aircraft had been scheduled for procurement, but this was reduced to eight pending the next Cabinet Defence Committee review. This review would take place in October 1957 under the newly elected minority Conservative government. In a memo dated October 22, the new Minister of National Defence, the Honourable George R. Pearkes, would report that the Chiefs of Staff were recommending that twenty-nine aircraft be ordered for immediate procurement. The cost would be $157 million to be spent in 1958–59 and another $273 million over the next three fiscal years. The first eight aircraft would be used as test aircraft to develop the airframe and engine, although they could be modified for service later. The remaining twenty-one would prove out proper weapon and operational functioning and performance.[31]

With such technical advances being achieved, it is easy to understand why the USAF was continually after news of developments. Fortunately, the "We can't do it here" mentality had not yet hardened in Canada thereby unencumbering the engineering creativity of those involved. Also, as a result of these accomplishments, Canada was developing and attracting some of the best talent in the business from around the world. Simply put, Canada and A. V. Roe were where it was at!

4 UP, UP, OR AWAY?

*Mr. Quarles's answer was cautious in realizing the
Canadian dilemma but stated that in general terms
they [USAF] would like to have interceptors in Canada
in place of those cancelled. . . . General Twining
reiterated that the manned bomber would remain in
the threat for a number of years.*

Top-secret message from Air Vice Marshall
Hendrick to General Foulkes, April 7, 1959[1]

ON OCTOBER 4, 1957, official roll-out of the first
Arrow, numbered RL25201, took place. John
G. Diefenbaker and his Conservative government
had been elected earlier in the year. His Minister
of National Defence, the Honourable George
Pearkes, was on hand for the unveiling of what
had begun as a Liberal government project. In his
address, Pearkes discussed the relative merits of
missiles versus interceptors, concluding that the
two were complementary and that both would
eventually be required.[2] He appeared to be echoing
the American philosophy.

On this same day, the Soviets launched Sputnik
into orbit. The artificial satellite captured the
headlines and sent shivers across North America:
attack from space by missile was now achicvable.
It has been said that Sputnik was a factor in the

demise of the Arrow, but it does not appear to have been a major factor in events to come.

On December 4, 1957, the first engine runs with J-75 engines installed took place. Taxi trials commenced December 21.

Among the many innovations developed for the Arrow was telemetry, used in the scale-model free-flight program. After the taxi trials, the Flight Test Instrument Section at Avro placed transmitters throughout the aircraft to provide real time in-flight information to ground-based personnel. This system, which was not unlike the one used later in the manned space program, would add significantly to the overall safety of the flight test program. The pilot could be warned in-flight if he were reaching critical limitations of which he might otherwise be unaware. The data would also help the engineers to optimize the design and provide clues in the event of an accident. A flight simulator was also developed, but neither Avro test pilot was able to control the simulator; both men "crashed." Did this mean the simulator had inherent problems, or did it really mean the Arrow itself was not flyable?[3]

The big day arrived on March 25, 1958 — first flight. An Avro employee would write:

There she stands, off the end of the runway, with Zura at the controls making a final check. . . . As she stands with her power plants throbbing, she looks one beautiful, compact form but the 9,500 people anxiously watching know that final form was shaped out of some 40,000 parts which they had created and drawn on paper, cut and formed into highly specialized metal, assembled into small and large units in order to produce that final, complete aerodynamic shape.[4]

Janusz "Zura" Zurakowski, Avro's chief development pilot, world-renowned for his superb aerobatic skills, was ready for takeoff. The flight lasted 35 minutes, achieving a speed of 250 knots and a maximum altitude of 11,000 feet. The purposes were to assess the handling qualities of the aircraft, check the responses of various controls and aircraft subsystems, and familiarize the pilot. Zurakowski writes:

The aircraft flying characteristics were similar to that of other delta wing aircraft like the Javelin or Convair F-102, but the Arrow had a more positive response to control movement. The unpleasant part of my first flight was the feeling of responsibility, combined with the realisation that the success of this aircraft depended on thousands of components, especially electronic and hydraulic, with only a small percentage under my direct control. But total responsibility for the flight was mine.[5]

The flight was essentially flawless; only minor snags were noted by the pilot. On landing, Zura was mobbed by a throng of jubilant employees and hoisted into the air. It was a proud moment for the company and the country, not unlike the landing of the first space shuttle in the United States.

April 2, 1958, saw flight number two. Speed was again limited to 250 knots, or Mach .45, due to the failure of the nose landing gear door to retract. The maximum altitude achieved was 30,000 feet, and a flight time of 50 minutes was recorded.[6]

Minor adjustments were made to the nose door micro-switches, and the next day, April 3, the Arrow was flown supersonically — a truly spectacular achievement for such a new, complex, and unproven machine. Flight duration was 1 hour 5 minutes. A speed of Mach 1.1 was recorded at an altitude of 40,000 feet. Almost insignificant snags were again noted. For the seventh flight on April 18, Zura would report an altitude of 49,000 feet at Mach 1.52, still accelerating and climbing. An RCAF pilot, Flight Lieutenant Jack Woodman, would take flight number eight for familiarization, and flight nine would belong to Wladyslaw "Spud" Potocki, Avro's second development pilot. Meanwhile, Zura began flight testing Arrow number RL25202 in August and then flew supersonically on the first flight of RL25203 in September.[7]

General conclusions from RL25201 testing were that the aircraft had achieved a high degree of reliability in a total flight time of 8 hours 10 minutes. Handling characteristics and performance agreed well with estimates. Handling at supersonic speeds and higher altitudes was good, and the yaw damping system was a considerable help for accurate flying. In one instance, one of the aircraft experienced a rippling of the engine nacelle skins, and the affected panels were changed to a heavier gauge on all aircraft. The change was considered minor and was effected in a matter of days, with minimal impact to the flight schedule or overall performance.[8]

At age forty-four, Zura gave up test flying and joined the Engineering Division as a staff engineer. This left Spud Potocki, Peter Cope, and Jack Woodman as the Arrow test pilots. Spud completed the first flights on two more Arrows, numbers RL25204 and RL25205. These five aircraft would be the only Arrows to fly. None of the Mark 2s, fitted with the Iroquois engines, would ever leave the ground. The first Mark 2, Arrow RL25206, was ready for taxi trials when the project was terminated.[9]

As good as the Arrow was, two significant incidents did occur during the flight tests. On flight number eleven, on June 11, 1958, with Zura at the controls, the main landing gear failed to extend properly, causing the aircraft to veer off the runway. Unfortunately, there was no warning light to signal the pilot whether the gear was in proper position or not, leaving Zura unable to try to correct for the problem before touchdown. The investigation pointed to a failure in the chain that controlled the mechanism for extending the leg. Modifications were put in place for subsequent aircraft.[10]

On November 11, 1958, Arrow RL25202 with

Spud would experience tire burst and would also veer off the runway. The resulting investigation, using data from the telemetry system discussed earlier, showed that on touchdown the elevator had moved fully down. The resulting backlift meant that only a portion of the aircraft's weight was actually on the wheels. When Spud applied the brakes, the wheels locked and the aircraft skidded. Both problems would later give rise to the mistaken belief that the undercarriage was unreliable.

Other problems included failure of the indicator lights, some buffeting at lower altitudes, and a strong oscillation during one of Spud's flights, which, according to telemetry, was generated by the aircraft, not the pilot. The telemetry system itself was a source of minor problems and delays. Still, Spud would achieve Mach 1.96–1.98, or approximately 1,300 miles per hour, and the aircraft would fly to over 58,000 feet. Even with the lower powered J-75 engine, no Arrow had been pushed to its performance limit.[11]

Jack Woodman was the only RCAF pilot to fly the Arrow. As the government's representative, it was his duty to assess the aircraft's performance. He noted that approximately 95 percent of the flight envelope had been explored. At some speeds and altitudes, the aircraft was somewhat difficult to fly, while at others the handling qualities were very good. The aircraft accelerated from subsonic to supersonic speed smoothly, with the controls becoming less sensitive. Several years later, Jack would recall:

The aircraft, at supersonic speeds, was pleasant and easy to fly. During approach and landing, the handling characteristics were considered good. . . . On my second flight . . . the general handling characteristics of the Arrow Mark 1 were much improved. The yaw damper is now performing quite reliably, although turn coordination is questionable in some areas. The roll damper is not optimised as yet, and longitudinal control is sensitive at high IAS. . . . On my 6th and last flight I reported longitudinal control to be positive with good response, and breakout force and stick gradients to be very good. Lateral control was good, forces and gradients very good and the erratic control in the rolling plane, encountered on the last flight, no longer there. . . . [E]xcellent progress was being made in the development . . . [and] from where I sat the Arrow was performing as predicted and was meeting all guarantees.[12]

Along with engineering progress on the Arrow, a number of other developments were occurring. By July 1956, Jim Floyd and his research team had already begun thinking of the future development of the Arrow. They could see an increase in level speed up to Mach 2.5, with a later stage increasing to Mach 3. To use long-range missiles, performance of the aircraft could purposely be degraded, allowing the missile to do its own manoeuvring after launch. Avro had also noted that — due to some increase in profile drag, induced drag, and weight — only 1.65 g would be pulled at Mach 1.5 rather than the required 2 g. This was closer to the NAE estimate reported in Chapter 2, which had been revised upwards from 1.38, but it was still far above any other aircraft. However, the Mark 2 with Iroquois engines was being optimized to Mach 2, and due to certain changes to the engine, better performance would be achieved than the specification called for, with 2 g at Mach 2 and 50,000 feet.[13]

In a three-day meeting in Ottawa beginning March 6, 1957, Floyd and others from Avro met with DRB and RCAF representatives. The DRB had just completed a study that showed a definite requirement for interceptors, in addition to guided missiles, for the period 1960 to 1970. The DRB agreed that a Mach 3 capability would be most desirable, as well as a ceiling of 60,000 feet and a range up to 1,000 miles. Dr. Watson of the DRB also agreed with the concept of degrading the airframe performance to allow for weapons with greater range and inherent manoeuvrability, and he was supported by the RCAF. It was also believed that weapons with atomic warheads should be able to be carried.[14]

Meanwhile, quite apart from the development of the aircraft, a memo dated June 6, 1957, pointed out that a dedicated project office should be established within the RCAF. Until October 1957, no government project office dealt exclusively with the Arrow. The Air Member Technical Services, Air Vice Marshall Hendrick, was ostensibly the project manager, but his staff's responsibilities were spread over a number of other programmes. As a result, the coordination of the various government laboratories such as those of the NAE and CARDE was very loose. In October, Hendrick established the Assistant for the Arrow Weapon System project office headed by Group Captain Ray H. Foottit, who would report through the RCAF's Chief Aeronautical Engineer to the Air Member Technical Services.[15]

In a letter to Fred Smye dated December 4, 1957, Foottit exercised his new authority and accused Avro of mismanaging the project. The accusation centred around a reduction in performance of the Arrow with Iroquois engines predicted in Periodic Performance Report Number 12. Foottit thought the RCAF should have been apprised of this as early as the spring of 1957. However, Avro *had* kept the RCAF fully informed, through a letter to Wing Commander Ed Bridgland dated September 23, 1957. Perhaps due to the lack of a project office and to technical wording in the correspondence, confusion was inevitable. In fact, Ray Foottit explained to this author that he never saw the letter; quite possibly it was lost or misplaced because it would have been received just before the setting up of the Arrow project office. There was similar confusion regarding the aircraft scheduling, which did not sit well with Foottit.[16]

The matter persisted into 1958, prompting J. L. Plant, former Air Vice Marshall and now Avro general manager, to write to the RCAF. In his letter dated February 18, he expressed the need for a central clearing point for all communications between the company and the RCAF. He believed the misunderstandings that had developed were the result of "backing and filling" with respect to conversations between RCAF personnel and various members of Avro.[17] In a letter dated March 8, 1991, Ray Foottit explained to this author that at the time of his memo to Fred Smye, he and the RCAF thought Avro was witholding information about potential problems. It seems that this had been an earlier characteristic of Avro during the CF-100 programme, back when Edgar Atkin was chief engineer before Jim Floyd. The RCAF was worried that the company might be returning to old ways. Having been personally stung, Foottit wanted to nip any withholding in the bud. All was eventually straightened out, and Foottit continued to have the highest regard for the engineering team at Avro. In the same letter to this author, he stated, "They were the most professional team I had ever worked with."

March 31, 1958, saw the reelection of John Diefenbaker, this time into a landslide majority Conservative government. Despite the earlier approval his minority government had given the Arrow project, Avro now worried that the situation might change for the worse. As if in anticipation of things to come, the Air Industries and Transport Association of Canada had presented the Prime Minister with a comprehensive brief dated December 2, 1957. The brief included a listing of the achievements and capabilities of the entire aircraft industry, with a series of appendices covering each company. Its aim was to brief the Prime Minister for an approaching NATO meeting. It stated:

> It has been our experience in the past that the potentialities of the Canadian aircraft industry and its allied companies have not always been clearly appreciated. The picture of the industrial side of Canada as it has recently developed is not as well known as its natural resources. The traditional notion of Canada as basically a storehouse of raw materials seems to remain firmly fixed. . . . This brief has attempted to indicate the industry's proven ability in scientific efforts of research and development as well as production. Such achievements as all-weather fighters, supersonic aircraft, [and] light and heavy transports . . . are ample proof. . . . The conservation of our existing resources cannot be taken for granted. . . . Lack of an immediate and long-range programme will result in a deterioration of the industry's effective operating capacity. . . . We believe the industry at the moment to be in serious jeopardy.[18]

Likewise, and perhaps also in anticipation, the RCAF was preparing its own case to keep the Arrow project going. In a memo dated March 28, 1958, the Chief Aeronautical Engineer for the RCAF compared the costs of the Arrow to those of the USAF's F-106, F-102, and F-101 in order to determine if these American aircraft were less expensive and whether there was justification in purchasing these instead of the Arrow. Conclusions from the memo indicated that

> Arrow costs compare favourably with the somewhat less sophisticated aircraft in the U.S.A. . . . It has been interesting to learn that RCAF flyaway costs for the CF-100 from production were less than for the comparable F-89 Scorpion. Similarly, quantity production of the F-86 and T-33 was undertaken in Canada at a lower per aircraft cost than from U.S.A. production. . . . [Q]uantity production of an aircraft as complex as the Arrow can be undertaken in Canada at a cost comparable to that for production of a like aircraft in the U.S.A.[19]

The memo was in line with the Air Industries brief, which independently stated "that for both fighter aircraft and light utility planes, there were up to 15% fewer man-hours per pound (of airframe) required to produce Canadian aircraft, compared to the U.S. industrial average for comparable aircraft." Unfortunately, these briefs would be to no avail.[20]

On May 12, 1958, another variable entered the equation. Canada and the United States officially signed the NORAD agreement, although it had been August 1, 1957, when this integrated Canada–United States Air Defence Command was established. In the subsequent debate on NORAD in the House of Commons that June, there was some question whether the agreement committed Canada to purchasing SAGE and Bomarc, since these were already on the American agenda.[21] Recently released records seem to imply this indeed was the case, and that the RCAF interest went back several years before.

The threat of Soviet attack from the North had given rise to three electronic defence networks: the Pinetree line, the Mid-Canada line, and the Distant Early Warning (DEW) line:

> [A]ir defence planning in the U.S. and Canada had recognized the need for introducing some degree of automation into the Pinetree line which was both an aircraft control and warning line. Development of different concepts and pieces of equipment had been occurring on both sides of the border. The U.S. pressed ahead vigorously with their SAGE concept and by April 1958 it was accepted in Canada that, in the interests both of technical interworking and economy, the only sensible thing to do was to extend the U.S. automation across the border. This meant the introduction of data processors at the radar sites and additional communications to route this data to computing centres. In addition the USAF were introducing Bomarc missiles into their automatic network which meant new ground-to-air data communications in addition to voice.[22]

The above quotation from the records of the Canadian Department of Defence Production suggests that the government was wholeheartedly following the American lead without giving necessary regard to Canada's real defence needs. The sensible thing to do was not to introduce SAGE, Bomarc, and the associated complex systems willy-nilly but rather to develop and follow a precise defence policy for Canada. As will be shown later, the SAGE and Bomarc system was being set up for the defence of the American Strategic Air Command. The defence of Canada would be a by-product. Could Canada afford both SAGE and the Arrow? Was the system even needed for defence? As it turned out, the answer to both questions was no. Moreover, the memo implies the decision to go with the SAGE and Bomarc system was made in April, four months before the now famous Defence Minister George Pearkes's trip to Washington, where he tried to sell the Arrow to the Americans only to return sold on the SAGE and Bomarc system instead. The Arrow does not appear even to have been a factor in the equation, although it should have been, especially in the interest of "technical interworking."

On July 8, U.S. President Eisenhower and his Secretary of State, John Foster Dulles, arrived in Ottawa for a three-day meeting to discuss, among other things, defence issues. It is surprising that neither the U.S. Secretary of Defence nor the Secretary of the Air Force was present. After all, the Arrow's first flight had taken place weeks before, and any discussion of defence would surely have involved the Arrow and USAF interests. The

Department of Defence Production memo quoted earlier states:

This decision [April decision to acquire SAGE/Bomarc] resulted in the realisation that, for the SAGE/Bomarc program, we should be faced with a situation very much like that of DEW line and be unable to contribute significantly to the production of major items in Canada. Therefore when the President and Mr. Dulles visited Ottawa on 9–10 July 1958 the general nature of the problem was explained to them and that experience on DEW Line indicated that something more specific would have to be done either to enable us to participate immediately in the SAGE/Bomarc programme or some other alternative planned.[23]

In other words, the Canadian government would not be content with simply allowing the Americans to install their systems in Canada, as had occurred with the DEW line effort. Canada wanted a share in the transfer of technology and the building of components, noting the potential for business from the United States as extensive. Neither Eisenhower nor Diefenbaker spoke openly on the SAGE and Bomarc question in their official announcements, and this three-day meeting appears to have been largely ignored in terms of its impact on the Arrow decisions to come. What is not clear is who made the decisions on SAGE and Bomarc in April 1958. In his memoirs, Prime Minister

Diefenbaker explains that Cabinet was briefed on April 28, 1958, on the need for both missiles and interceptors for air defence.

What *is* clear is that in their addresses to the public that July, the Prime Minister and the President jointly announced the formation of the Canada–United States Committee on Joint Defence. What was the purpose of this committee if not to determine the alternative discussed in the Department of Defence Production document — namely, to bring in SAGE and Bomarc in such a way that Canada could share in the production of components? It certainly does not appear that the Committee was established to determine ways and means of getting the Arrow into the U.S. industrial base and the hands of the USAF. (The announcement of the establishment of this joint committee had been planned as early as May 1958, according to American records.[24]) The Defence Production document adds: "Conversations on production sharing therefore commenced in August 1958."[25] The fate of the Arrow was sealed, knowingly or not, with the Americans, because the truth was that Canada could not afford both the Arrow and the SAGE and Bomarc system.

Archival records have, after thirty years, revealed the top-secret briefing document prepared for Defence Minister Pearkes for his discussions with the U.S. Secretary of State. It is dated July 8, 1958. Pearkes explained that if Canada had not been a "northern outpost" of the United States but rather an island, air defence requirements would be significantly reduced. However, by virtue of our geographic location, Canada was compelled to spend nearly half the defence budget on air requirements. He complained that despite close cooperation between the two countries, the United States had never accepted a Canadian aircraft, nor had there been any success at a joint development. He then addressed the problem of defence against the manned bomber and the Arrow:

[W]e have had under development in Canada a supersonic aircraft known as the CF-105. . . . We have had the greatest possible cooperation with the United States Air Force in the development of a type of aircraft which was considered by both countries to be a requirement for the air defence of North America during the 1960s. . . . [T]he total United States content in the CF-105 will be approximately 20% in the development and preproduction aircraft and 10 to 15% if this aircraft goes into production.

The development of this aircraft to date has cost $250 million, and its development will be continued for the next two or three years, to cost about $530 million, making a total of $780 million. Our requirements for this aircraft will be relatively small, somewhere around 100, and therefore the individual cost of the aircraft will be about $5 million, plus the cost of development. If this were the only requirement for our air defence, we could perhaps make provision for it in our succeeding defence budgets; but in order that aircraft of this type and the type to be used by the United States can operate in Canadian airspace we will be required to introduce SAGE into Canada.

The introduction of SAGE in Canada will cost in the neighbourhood of $107 million.[26]

Pearkes went on to describe that the radar and communications nets would now require improvement and that NORAD was recommending Bomarc missile base installations in the Ottawa–North Bay area. He explained how all these new commitments would increase the defence budget by twenty-five to thirty percent. He then asked for some form of cost-sharing and wondered if the United States would consider equipping squadrons at Harmon Field, Newfoundland, and Goose Bay, Labrador, with the Arrow.

The briefing highlights several important points. First, SAGE was not required for the Arrow as suggested above, but rather was a requirement for the Bomarc missile and some U.S. aircraft. This fact had been pointed out by the visiting U.S. teams, who had also seen no need for SAGE with the Arrow due to its two-man crew. Second, use of Bomarc was required because of NORAD recommendations to round out the American chain of defence, and not for Canadian defence considerations. Third, Canadian requirements for aircraft would be small, in the order of 100, thereby driving the per unit cost higher. Finally and perhaps most importantly, the government could shoulder the

Arrow costs, but not with SAGE and Bomarc included. Nowhere in the brief is the technical superiority of the Arrow discussed. Instead, it reads like a pathetic plea for aid, something the Canadian ambassador had told USAF Secretary James Douglas would never be accepted. It seems that at no time was the need for SAGE and Bomarc — an untried, unproven missile — ever questioned. The response to Pearkes from Secretary Dulles is not known, but it would seem that Minister Pearkes went on to his meeting in Washington in August with the SAGE–Bomarc issue almost as a fait accompli. Then, when the United States, through Secretary of State for Defence Neil McElroy, told Minister Pearkes in Washington that there was no requirement for the Arrow in the U.S. inventory, the CF-105 programme was effectively dead. Was McElroy speaking the truth, or was he also fully aware that without the Arrow, the SAGE–Bomarc issue would be resolved in favour of the American requirement?

On August 28, 1958, Minister Pearkes told the Conservative Cabinet that the Cabinet Defence Committee (CDC) had reviewed the air defence requirement and had agreed

to recommend that two Bomarc bases be created in the Ottawa area and North Bay area, and two additional heavy radars installed in Northern Ontario and Quebec with associated gap-filler radars. It was also proposed that negotiations be started with the United States for the cost-sharing

and production-sharing of the Bomarc bases. . . .
The committee had referred to the Cabinet for
consideration proposals to cancel the CF-105
programme and to investigate additional missile
installations and a possible alternative interceptor to the CF-105. . . . He himself had recommended cancelling the CF-105 programme in its
entirety. . . . [T]he change in the nature of the
threat and the very great cost of development
and production had brought him to make the
recommendation he had . . . after very careful
study of all the factors involved. . . . He went on
to describe the SAGE system and the steps that
had to be taken to introduce it, whether or not
the government decided to proceed with the CF-
105. He also described the U.S. intentions on
Bomarc and how they related to Canada. . . . It
was cheaper than the CF-105 in terms of men
and money, and just as effective. . . . Their own
F-106C was comparable in performance to the
CF-105, it would be available for squadron service several months earlier, and it cost less than
half as much.[27]

Why did SAGE have to be introduced? How could
Pearkes state that the Bomarc would be just as effective, and why was the F-106 suddenly comparable in performance to the CF-105? What were his
advisers telling him?

In conjunction with his verbal statements,
Pearkes circulated a secret brief prepared by the
CDC. It stated, in part: "The first phase is now well

advanced and a decision as to whether or not to go into production is urgently required. . . . This aircraft is now in the test flying stage and flights to date indicate it will meet its design requirements. The engine for the aircraft, which is part of the Arrow programme, is also undergoing air tests. These tests indicate that it also will meet its design requirements."[28] This appears to be the only instance in which the technical performance of the Arrow was mentioned, although it was promptly ignored in the rest of the brief. Had the programme been in trouble technically, it would have seemed natural to consider cancellation, but every indication was being given that the Arrow would be a success. Pearkes himself had said it could be accommodated financially, without the burden of the SAGE and Bomarc system. So why was it even being discussed? If anything, it should have been the SAGE and Bomarc question on the block. Incredibly, no one questioned the logic, and the Chiefs of Staff themselves thought the requirement for few aircraft without U.S. acquisitions would make the project too costly, especially since cheaper American aircraft were available. It is not clear who prepared the secret brief, but members of the CDC included the Chairman of the Chiefs of Staff, General Charles Foulkes, as well as the Chief of the Air Staff, Air Marshall Hugh Campbell.

The secret CDC brief elaborated on the Bomarc missile and its capabilities, followed by this noteworthy paragraph: "It will be recalled that the early requirement in 1953 was for nineteen squadrons, a total of between 500 and 600 aircraft. This has now been reduced to nine squadrons and consideration has been given in the last few months to reducing the requirement to five squadrons of about 100 aircraft now that the Bomarc missile is to be introduced into the Canadian Defence system."[29]

As far as the CDC was concerned, the introduction of the SAGE and Bomarc system was already an assertion, not a recommendation. Its introduction, and *not* the cost of the Arrow, was the reason for having reduced the number of Arrows down to 100. The original requirement appears to have been for a one-to-one replacement of the CF-100. With its greater capability and coverage, fewer Arrows would be required for the same task. Is this why the July brief stated that Canada's requirements would be small? In later testimony, General Foulkes, Chairman of the Chiefs of Staff, would state that the reduction was due to the fact that eleven auxiliary reserve squadrons that were to get the Arrow were taken out of the picture due to the length of time needed to train the auxiliary pilots on such complex aircraft. Whatever the reason, the Arrow cost alone was not it. Finally, the brief stated that the enemy threat was changing and would come from ballistic missiles instead of manned bombers, so the interceptor would lose its importance. Did Minister Pearkes truly believe in the Bomarc, or was he simply being given no choice in the matter?

As will be recalled, the RCAF memo of March 28

comparing the costs of American aircraft had shown the Arrow as very similar, and the July top-secret brief had indicated that the government would likely be able to support the Arrow if the SAGE and Bomarc system were not a factor. Why then was the CDC's brief now attempting to blame cost as the reason for recommending cancellation? The CDC's comparison to American aircraft was to the single-engine F-106D, which was not at all comparable.

Appendix A of the committee brief shows the average cost per Arrow for a quantity of 100 as $12.6 million, whereas the cost for each of 100 F-106Ds is shown as $5.59 million, a very large differential. Unfortunately, the tables compare apples with oranges. The F-106 is shown with Falcon missiles, the very ones originally recommended by the USAF and Avro but shunned by the RCAF. The Arrow cost, however, is shown with the more expensive Sparrow, the RCAF choice, plus its remaining development costs and the remaining development costs of the airframe and engines. To make the two aircraft somewhat comparable, the comparison should at least be done with the same weapon system for both. On September 3, the government did just that, and now, with the Falcon in the Arrow, the cost decreased to $8.91 million dollars each, a differential of $3.32 million from the F-106D. In addition, Canada would not only have had a superior aircraft but a viable aircraft industry, with the money spent on purchasing the aircraft remaining in Canada.[30] The costs quoted in the July top-secret brief to the Secretary of State included $530 million on development and $5 million on flyaway for a total of $1,030 million, or $10.3 million per copy, a number for which provision could be made in the defence budget.

There is also the matter of including the remaining development costs in the final numbers. The debate on this inclusion continues to this day. For example, the November/December 1989 issue of *Military Forum* carried the headline "What Do Weapons Really Cost?" In its discussion of the B-2 Stealth bomber, the article stated:

> Opponents of the B-2, who want to make the plane look more expensive, use a different measure of unit expense — "total cost." Mainly, this adds in the cost of R&D it took to set up the B-2 production line in the first place. "Stealth" is at the cutting edge of technology, so R&D costs are considerable: $22 billion so far. . . . The total cost unit price figure for the B-2 is the much quoted $500 million. This represents the amount of investment the taxpayer has shelled out to get a single B-2 on the runway. But if that plane crashed, it would not cost $500 million to replace it. Building a new one on the existing line would take $274 million, the flyaway price. That is the amount of money taxpayers have at risk when the plane goes up in the air.[31]

The Arrow, too, was on the cutting edge, so by adding in the remaining development costs, the unit cost of each Arrow was much inflated. If one were to crash, its replacement cost would actually be the lower flyaway cost of $5 million dollars, equal to the F-106 cost. The flyaway cost would be reduced even more, down to $3.5 million dollars per copy, as will be shown later.

One is left to wonder if the factors studied by the CDC were truly understood or if the committee was reacting to some external influence. The secret CDC brief stated that the Soviet threat was moving towards ballistic missiles, yet Bomarc was a defence against the manned bomber only, with all the limitations discussed in previous chapters. SAGE, on the other hand, was now being stated as a necessity with or without the Arrow. The inescapable conclusion is that the government had made up its mind, with the aid of the Americans. That is, the acquisition and use of the SAGE and Bomarc system would proceed in accordance with American wishes. Since it would be impossible to afford it as well as the Arrow, the Arrow would have to go, no matter how good it would eventually prove to be.

How strongly the Americans wanted the SAGE and Bomarc system is reflected by the following in Jon B. McLin's book, *Canada's Changing Defence Policy, 1957–1963*:

There was also some concern about the cost to Canada of the Bomarc–SAGE package (which also included expenditures for additional, "gap-filler" radar stations); this concern was manifest

at the August 1958, meeting between the delega-
tions headed by Pearkes and McElroy. It went so
far as consideration of the consequences of a refusal by Canada to accept the missiles; the consequence would be, Canadians were told, the
emplacement of at least one more Bomarc squadron in the U.S., south of the Great Lakes. But
the proposal received the approval of the Chiefs
of Staff Committee and, having been approved
by the U.S. administration, was a matter for the
Diefenbaker government to decide.[32]

In other words, with the Bomarc's limited 250-
mile range, any attempt at using those missiles
would create an air battle over Southern Ontario
and Quebec. Further, we now know, and undoubtedly it was known to the Canadian team then,
that the Bomarc was only effective with a nuclear
warhead. Use of such a weapon over Southern Ontario and Quebec would be catastrophic to major
Canadian cities and the populace. The threat of
such a consequence was tantamount to coercion
on the part of the United States: "Accept our missile bases or we will give you nuclear devastation
over your most populated regions." If this threat
were realized by Minister Pearkes, he would have
reasoned that the only way to reduce the risk and
save these regions would be to have the bases
moved northward. Acceptance of the bases,
though, would mean the death of the Arrow, a
death that would require a palatable excuse for the
cancellation.

In the Cabinet discussions following the Minister's recommendation to cancel the programme, one of the topics was the potential layoff of over 25,000 employees. The numbers were tabled by the politicians from the affected regions and not by Avro. The counter argument was that these people would surely find other employment in Canada's vigorous economy. There was discussion that neither the United Kingdom nor NATO (North Atlantic Treaty Organization) would be interested in purchasing the Arrow and that it was useless against the ballistic missile anyway, a perceived threat against which *no weapon* of the day could defend, especially not the Bomarc. It was noted that the United States was equipping itself with both missiles and aircraft; should Canada not do likewise? (This presumably was a reflection back to the American philosophy of long-range interceptors at the fore and missiles in back should any enemy aircraft get through.) The point went unanswered. It was asked if cancellation would forever make the RCAF completely dependent on the United States for equipment; this, too, seems to have gone unanswered. Instead, it was stated that on military and financial grounds, the Arrow should be cancelled and probably should never have been started. Aircraft manufacture under licence was the way ahead, but to cancel now and procure a U.S. aircraft for manufacture under licence would be a "serious political mistake."[33] The Cabinet deferred its decision.

Records show that on September 3, 1958, Avro

officials learned that the programme was in trouble. Fred Smye and John Tory, a director at Avro, met with the Prime Minister and, later the same day, the Minister of Finance and the Minister of National Defence. Unfortunately, the Avro officials had not been privy to the secret documents discussed earlier. Their recommendation, as before, was to dump the Astra and Sparrow systems and to go with the Hughes MA-1 and Falcon. Revised cost estimates as discussed earlier were later tabled to the Cabinet, showing the reductions and savings available. An air defence option of using Bomarcs only was also cited at $520.3 million, assuming no cost sharing with the United States.

What was not stated or was perhaps simply ignored was that the interceptor would provide a reusable platform, whereas the missile would be a one-shot deal. Furthermore, if that shot happened to be against a civilian target by mistake, results would be catastrophic. Fred Smye has written that Minister Donald Fleming was most interested in the cost reductions and set up the next meeting with Minister Pearkes. According to Smye, Air Marshall Campbell was also present. Minister Pearkes and Air Marshall Campbell were apparently quite negative to the idea of dumping the Astra and Sparrow system. Smye also met with the Minister of Defence Production, Raymond O'Hurley, and his deputy, D. A. Golden, and says these ministers had not been made aware of the cost savings possible by switching to the Falcon and the Hughes system. Minister O'Hurley asked his deputy to check on this and asked if savings would also arise from a switch in engines. Smye replied that the company had investigated this and found there would be no savings. Curiously, this entire exchange was either not brought up or not recorded in the Cabinet discussion that would follow.[34]

Back in Cabinet, Ministers Pearkes and Fleming reported on these discussions and introduced new factors. Now, it was being said the aircraft might well be obsolete before going into service because it would be supplanted by missiles. Also, for the first time, records show that the Chiefs of Staff were divided on the issue. The Chief of the Air Staff believed there was a useful role for the aircraft, in contrast with the ministers' statements, but the Navy and Army Chiefs thought the matter should remain under review for a year. Their reason was that the enemy threat appeared to be rapidly changing from one of bombers to one of missiles; presumably they wished to wait a year to see how it would evolve. They did think, though, that the programme was expensive and would perhaps not be the best way to spend so much money. The costs of the SAGE and Bomarc system and the F-106 seem to have gone unquestioned, although General Foulkes, the Chairman of the Chiefs of Staff, was of the opinion that the Bomarc would give the best defence for the available money.[35]

Fleming, the Minister of Finance, whose personal records still remain closed as of this writing, reported on the discussions with Smye and Tory. It was his contention that if the Hughes and Falcon system was good enough, as Avro had said, then engines and airframes from the United States should also be good enough. It seems the Minister was grandstanding, for in his meeting with Smye and Tory, Smye reports, the Minister was seriously interested in the idea of replacing the Astra and Sparrow combination if it meant cost savings. Minister Pearkes added that the RCAF had made a conscientious decision to go with the Astra and Sparrow system. Had he forgotten that even the USAF, let alone his own Defence Research Board, had recommended against this system? Or, having been given the American threat of placing Bomarcs just south of the Great Lakes, was Pearkes pressing for Astra and Sparrow knowing full well that to continue would kill the whole Arrow programme once and for all? And why did Minister O'Hurley not speak up on the potential cost savings? The issue of cancellation was deferred to the next meeting of the Cabinet on September 7.[36]

Cabinet documents for the September 7 meeting open with the following:

> *The Prime Minister* opened the further discussion of the proposal of the Minister of National Defence to cancel the CF-105 programme. . . . [T]he serious problem still requiring consideration was the effect on employment and the general economic situation.
>
> *The Minister of Finance* said that in considering matters of defence he naturally put the safety of

the country ahead of finance. . . . Now, however, the military view was that the programme should be cancelled. . . . The arguments for continuing were that Canadian military requirements should be found in Canada, that cancelling the programme would throw upwards of 25,000 men out of work with serious effects on the economy, and that national prestige should be taken into account. . . . [M]ore important, the military authorities had now decided that the aircraft was not necessary.[37]

When had the military finally asserted that the Arrow was not necessary, and who was responsible for this assertion? Both Minister Pearkes and General Foulkes had been recommending abandoning the programme in favour of the Bomarc, but as of the last Cabinet meeting the decision had remained inconclusive. Further, there was no mention of the economies to be gained, as had been discussed earlier.

The Finance Minister wondered if a middle ground might be pursued between cancelling and going into production, but thought that there was none. He worried about the 25,000 layoffs, but reiterated that these people would be absorbed into the economy. He repeated the erroneous figure that the Arrow cost would be twice as much as a U.S. aircraft and that the economy could not support this. He also stated that cancellation now could be used advantageously as a political ploy by claiming that the government was abandoning an ill-fated Liberal administration project. The savings could then be allocated elsewhere, such as for Northern development. It was thought this would be a blow to Canadian prestige, but at what cost could the latter be maintained?[38]

After the Finance Minister's address, the discussion continued with the following comment, which would ring true for years to come:

> In the forthcoming winter, unemployment would be higher than it was last year. Cancelling now, apart from the effect on the employees concerned, might well be the one psychological factor which would result in a break in the economy and lead to a drastic downturn from which recovery would be extremely difficult. The programme should be allowed to continue over the winter and a decision taken then as to its future.[39]

It was further argued that continuing the programme for even a short time would mean that orders would have to be placed for raw materials. This would result in the completion of only a few aircraft, whose individual cost would then be astronomical. Still, immediate cancellation could result in a recession.

As to defence requirements, there was still the option to purchase American F-106 aircraft. The Americans were now prepared to consider cost-sharing on the Bomarc, so on economic and military grounds the decision to cancel would be seen as "good housekeeping" by the Canadian public.

The new piece of information in the discussion was the American proposal. With these new American overtures, the fate of the Arrow was most definitely sealed. Still, the decision was again deferred, and no one questioned the need for or relevancy of the Bomarc. As stated earlier, the Bomarc was only effective with a nuclear warhead. By relocating the Bomarcs northward, the most populated region of Canada would be spared direct nuclear consequences. From the U.S. perspective, it is no wonder they were prepared to move their Bomarcs northward. Why have nuclear radiation and fallout rain on the United States when it could all be done over Canada?

On purely military grounds and protection from enemy attack, the records of the Department of Defence Production state:

[T]he Americans now are interested in terms of their own defence in the installation of Canadian soil of not only Warning Lines and communications, but also actual weapons, such as Bomarcs, to bring down enemy bombers. However, the concept of area defence in depth, combined with the fact that the whole complex of radars, computers, communications, aircraft and missiles are part of a single defence system indicates that no division can be made between air defence of Canada and air defence of the United States.[40]

The Americans were interested in protecting their own Strategic Air Command by positioning missile bases in Canada. As the record further shows, the Arrow "was designed to meet the specific requirement of the Canadian perimeter of the North American defence areas."[41] The Arrow's purpose was dropped in favour of the American requirement. The document reasons that to build the sophisticated radar and support centres required would unduly strain the Canadian defence budget, and that the only solution would be to enter into defence sharing "whereby Canada has allotted to it the production of certain components of weapons systems for the joint use of the two countries."[42] In other words, by following American defence policy and entering into production sharing, Canada would be relegated to building piece parts as dictated by the United States. Apparently, there was never a consideration that perhaps the United States could build piece parts as governed by Canada. Essentially, it appears that Canada was left in the awkward position of having to find a good reason for cancelling the Arrow, where none existed.

On September 17, 1958, Crawford Gordon, president of A. V. Roe, the parent company to Avro and Orenda, visited with the Prime Minister. Many have contended over the years that Gordon entered the Prime Minister's office under the influence of alcohol and proceeded to make demands. In his memoirs, the Prime Minister would write of the meeting, "[I]n no way could it be described as a nasty personal confrontation. I do recall that he began his presentation in a blustering fashion."

According to James Dow's book on the Arrow, outside the Prime Minister's office was Grattan O'Leary from the *Ottawa Journal*. Allegedly, the Prime Minister said that he had just informed Mr. Gordon that the Arrow would be cancelled because it was too expensive and could not be sold to the Americans. Dow writes:

> If Diefenbaker had finally settled on a decision to cancel the Arrow, a flat announcement to that effect could have destroyed his government. His instinct for political survival would have told him there was a need to prepare his ground. On the one hand, he would have to portray Avro in the worst possible light by vilifying the company and pulling every possible dollar into the costs of the programme he would show the public. He would also have to throw out some propaganda to show that Canadian defence would not be compromised by termination. This would mean downplaying the bomber threat and introducing Bomarc missiles in a way that would overplay their performance. He would not, for obvious reasons, agree to seek interceptors in the United States, at least not for the time being.[43]

Would Dow have come to the same conclusion had he known or had access to the records of the Cabinet discussions mentioned earlier, wherein Minister Pearkes and General Foulkes had given their proposals recommending cancellation? Also, if Diefenbaker was concerned about his political future, why would he confide his decision to someone from a newspaper? Why did Crawford Gordon not disclose the decision to the media? Finally, why did Grattan O'Leary not capitalize on his newfound information? There is also the inconsistency with the Prime Minister's memoirs. Knowing there had been a witness to the event who could claim otherwise, why did the Prime Minister not disclose all? These questions remain unanswered if one accepts the notion of John Diefenbaker as the sole mastermind behind the cancellation.

On September 21, 1958, the Prime Minister reported to the Cabinet that he had met with Crawford Gordon, president of Avro. Gordon had reiterated the need to cancel Sparrow and Astra and had also stated that Avro had been told the U.S. government would be willing to provide the weapons at reduced cost. The Cabinet remained divided on the question of complete cancellation, stating that the psychological impact would be enormous, not to mention the financial impact of cancellation. Still, to continue the programme could impose a high cost on the Canadian economy and contribute to inflation. On military grounds, there were questions regarding the views of the Chiefs of Staff, which appeared at odds from earlier recommendations to continue the programme for at least a year. It was known that the Chief of the Air Staff required interceptors: *"The Prime Minister* suggested that a compromise should be considered on which possibly the Cabinet could agree. He thought such a compromise might involve carrying on the development programme until March but not beginning the production programme on the Arrow or the Iroquois at this time."[44] It was believed that the economy, at least, could better handle cancellation in March rather than at the present time.

Cabinet then approved the installation of Bomarcs and two additional heavy radars and gap-filler radars for the Pinetree system. It was further decided that no production order for the Arrow or Iroquois would yet be made, and that a comprehensive review of the requirements for the programme would be completed before March 31, 1959, such that a final decision either way could be made. The Chiefs of Staff were instructed to report if any additional missile installations or any interceptor aircraft like the Arrow would be required.[45]

On September 23, Prime Minister Diefenbaker finally announced that Astra and Sparrow would be terminated. He also revealed that the cost per aircraft would be reduced from $12.5 million to $9 million by using the Hughes and Falcon weapon, but implied that this was still too costly. In fact, the top-secret brief of July 8 had stated that to acquire the Arrow, SAGE, Bomarc, and associated support would increase the defence budget twenty-five to thirty percent. In October, the *Financial Post* would report identical figures.[46] But rather than questioning the SAGE and Bomarc system, it became popular to tout the alleged obsolescence of the Arrow and to overinflate its cost. In a series of articles for *Maclean's,* Blair Fraser incorporated numerous other inaccuracies about the aircraft, well documented in E. K. Shaw's *There Never Was an Arrow.*[47] It seems the media was on the "dump the Arrow" bandwagon. Had Diefenbaker succeeded in his plan, as surmised by James Dow? Why was there no forceful outcry against the media from the RCAF? Perhaps attitudes would have been different if access to these secret and top-secret documents had been available then.

In November 1958, Air Marshall Slemon, now at NORAD headquarters in Colorado, was quoted as saying interceptors would be required for some time to come. This was interpreted negatively by the government, as it had just recommended Bomarc and was stating the Arrow might be obsolete. The following is recorded for the December 22 meeting of the Conservative Cabinet:

> The Prime Minister said he had been shocked by the statement Air Marshall Slemon had made about the Arrow. It was not a question of whether Slemon's remarks had been misinterpreted or not but whether he should have made a statement of that kind at all. Avro had put on a tremendous publicity campaign and this played right into their hands. If the government decided to continue development, it would be accused of giving in to a powerful lobby. Pressure was coming from other sources in Ontario, too. Even if he thought the decision reached last September

was wrong, he was determined, because of what had happened since, to adhere firmly to it. The future of the CF-105 would have to be discussed before Parliament opened.

The Minister of National Defence pointed out that it was still his understanding that development would be terminated by March 31.[48]

Clearly, Diefenbaker was upset that a senior officer appeared to be speaking against government policy. However, in his September announcement he had said the programme would be reviewed in March. Why then did Minister Pearkes believe termination would occur at that time?

The Minister went on to point out that in Paris, earlier in the month, the United States had made very clear it was not interested in the Arrow and that the U.S. decision not to proceed with interceptor development except for the long-range F-108 would strengthen the Canadian government's position to abandon the Arrow. Yet the Arrow was considered long-range by the Americans. In his memoirs, Finance Minister Fleming says that John Dulles, Secretary of State, added that the American aircraft industry was "slack" and that under these circumstances there was no way foreign aircraft could be ordered.[49] No other reasons were put forward, yet the Americans knew their refusal to purchase would mean the end of the programme.

Back at Avro, work was progressing, although not without some trepidation. Canadian Pratt & Whitney had submitted a proposal to the Department of

Defence Production offering less expensive and improved J-75 engines in place of the Iroquois. The RCAF had rejected a similar proposal in July, and now in September a similar rejection was forthcoming. Significant savings would not be realized through cancellation of the Iroquois, and performance of the aircraft would be significantly affected. Orenda had also been approached by France for possible use of the Iroquois in the Mirage IV fighter. The French Air Ministry had deemed the latter as more promising than the J-75 and were looking at totals upwards of 300. Then, on October 31, France concluded that the Iroquois programme had or would cease to exist and could therefore not risk obtaining it for their own programme.[50]

It is not known how the French learned of this; had they heard through official channels, or did the damaging press articles make their mark in Europe? Were the Americans involved? Needless to say, Charles Grinyer, vice president of engineering at Orenda, tendered his resignation. He was persuaded to return, but only after Fred Smye obtained assurance from Defence Production Minister Raymond O'Hurley that the project would not be cancelled. Meanwhile, Smye submitted a letter dated October 21, 1958, to Pearkes in which he stated:

[O]n the basis of installing the Hughes MA-1 fire control system, and the adoption of the Falcon and/or Genie missiles, and as the result of other substantial economies and savings proposed by the company, it is now estimated that we can produce and deliver 100 operational Arrow aircraft, complete in all respects including the Iroquois engine and the MA-1 fire control system, for approximately $3,500,000 each. . . . [T]he Company would be prepared to enter into a fixed price contract on the basis of $3,750,000 for a completed, operational aircraft.[51]

The new figures made the Arrow more than comparable in cost with U.S. aircraft, since all previous estimates had been assuming a flyaway cost of $5 million per aircraft, not $3.5 or $3.75. Pearkes sent the letter to General Foulkes, Chairman of the Chiefs of Staff, and to the Department of Defence Production and the Chief of the Air Staff. The new figures seemingly made cancellation on the basis of cost very difficult to justify.

On October 27, 1958, Crawford Gordon, president of A. V. Roe, sent reassuring words to his shareholders. He reiterated Slemon's words on the need for interceptors and also quoted James H. Douglas, Secretary of the USAF. In a statement on September 27, Douglas had said that Soviet statements about their new long-range bomber were being believed, and for this reason the United States was embarking on a similar long-range interceptor development.[52]

Jim Floyd had been in the United Kingdom on business but was well aware of the controversies back home. On November 7, 1958, he wrote the following to Avro president J. L. Plant:

> In reading some of the press reports, I believe that too much emphasis has been put on unemployment aspects of the decisions to come, and there is no doubt in my mind that if the Arrow was a "dud," or not required for the defence of Canada, we should not wish to proceed with it solely on the basis of "keeping people busy."[53]

Floyd felt that while the question of keeping the team together and fully occupied was of paramount importance, all arguments for continuation of the Arrow programme must be based on its military effectiveness. In the six-page letter to Plant he outlined his discussions with the senior RAF personnel at the Central Fighter Establishment and Bomber Command in the United Kingdom and also Sir Thomas Pike, and recommended closer co-operation between them and the principals in the RCAF and the Canadian Minister of Defence. He noted that the U.K. military establishment at least was convinced of the threat from manned bombers, since it was known that the Russians were developing the Bounder, and that in the face of electronic jamming (which the Russians were known to have) the two-man interceptor was recognized as perhaps the only means of defence. He spoke of intelligence estimates that pushed the threat from missiles into 1964–65 and discussed a study to determine if an anti-ICBM missile might be carried in the Arrow's weapons bay. He thought that perhaps the politicians did not have all the facts in the case or that they had too many, namely surrounding the whole question of the Bomarc problem and the American influence.

In December, in light of the September 21 statement by the Prime Minister, the RCAF reviewed the entire Arrow project. In justifying the need for interceptor aircraft, the following points emerged:

(a) Primarily in peacetime to expose violation of national airspace and to take whatever measures deemed necessary to prevent recurrence. In wartime, reconnaissance aircraft are targets the same as any other enemy aircraft and would no doubt be present for strike assessment, target planning, etc.

(b) The manned interceptor has the advantage of human judgement which can be brought to bear on unforeseen enemy countermeasures. The interceptor is equipped with a variety of counter ECM [Electronic Counter Measures] features which can be selected by the human operator(s) as the situation dictates.

(c) The manned interceptor has the flexibility to redeploy to any suitable base within the defence system as dictated by the tactical or strategical situation. The limiting factor would be the ground environment.

(d) An alternative supersonic two-place all-weather interceptor that generally meets the operational requirement is defined in OCH 1/1-63. This aircraft would have to be equal to or superior to the Arrow Weapons System.[54]

The memorandum, written by Group Captain E. H. Evans, Acting Chief of Operational Requirements, went on to discuss the mission profiles, reiterating speed and altitude requirements. It seems that at least some in the RCAF had the technical facts.

By December 27, five aircraft had been fitted with the P&W J-75 engine, with the first four aircraft having completed over 50 hours of flight time in total. Of the Mark 2 Arrows, that is, those to be fitted with the Iroquois, the sixth and seventh were in final assembly. Arrow RL25202, which was undergoing some repair of damage from a landing accident, was also being modified to accept the Hughes MA-1 fire control system in place of the cancelled Astra. Fourteen development Iroquois engines had been built, 6,700 hours of test running had been completed, and 22 of these hours had been logged on the B-47 flying test-bed aircraft. A further ninety-six engines were on order. Likewise, two MA-1 systems were on order from Hughes.[55] Employment at Avro and Orenda was now in the order of 15,000, and an RCAF memo noted: "As of September 23, 1958, the companies were instructed to keep commitments to the minimum necessary to continue the programme as authorized by Cabinet."[56] The statement is noteworthy in that it supports the company's later contention that it thought development would continue at least to March 31, 1959. (Diefenbaker would later charge that the company should have known cancellation could be imminent.)

In adopting the Hughes systems, the RCAF on December 29 also agreed to adopt the twenty-first Arrow as the production standard. Essentially, the design for producing Arrows was frozen with the Mark 2 Arrow 25206. However, flight testing of the Mark 1s and Iroquois had revealed some deficiencies that would be carried over into 25206; plans were made to correct them by Arrow 21.

Specifically, due to increasing weight and reduced thrust in the Iroquois engines as well as an increase in weight of the airframe, the RCAF expected that Arrow 25206 (unlike the first five aircraft) would reach an estimated speed of only Mach 1.9, whereas the twenty-first aircraft, number 25221, would easily reach Mach 2, with speed limited to structural heating as discussed earlier. Arrow 25206 might not perform the 2-g turn at altitude, but 25221 would easily achieve 1.62 g. Likewise, 25206 would reach an altitude of 55,000 feet, while 25221 would clear 59,800. Similarly, the engines for 25221 would achieve their full design specifications of thrust, weight, handling, and reliability.[57] It must be remembered that these wcrc calculated numbers which would be proven through flight testing. In fact, Arrow 25202 would

reach Mach 1.96–1.98, as recorded by pilot Spud
Potocki, and altitudes of 58,000 feet would be
achieved during the flight test program.

On December 30, 1958, Jim Floyd again wrote to
John Plant. He had met with John Pallett, the
Member for Peel County, who had told him that
Diefenbaker was only keeping the project alive to
prevent massive layoffs at Malton, where the
Arrow was being built. Pallet had said that according to Diefenbaker, the RCAF had given no indication of the need for the interceptor. This is
incredible in light of the Chief of the Air Staff's
comments: "Pallett . . . said quite definitely that if
the RCAF have, in fact, a requirement for the
Arrow, this has never filtered down to the politicians, and that he is sure Diefenbaker considers it
a 'dead duck.'"[58]

On January 1, 1959, the following was recorded
by the Assistant for Arrow Weapon System office
on the status of the Arrow 2 aircraft:

> Very few engineering problems are expected in
> the production or flight testing of the Arrow 2
> airframe. . . . System problems are expected to
> decrease in number by 40% compared with
> those encountered in Arrow 1 flying. The re-
> maining problems expected to arise will be di-
> rectly related to Arrow 1 to Arrow 2 system
> configuration changes. . . . The new problems of
> unknown magnitude in the electrical, air-condi-
> tioning, power plant, armament, and electrical
> systems should be of a minor significance be-

cause of considerable running and/or flight testing in other installations, leaving for solution primarily compatibility and reliability problems.[59]

On January 12, 1959, Air Marshall Hugh Campbell wrote a lengthy summation of the programme to Minister Pearkes. He discussed the achievements in the flight test programme and noted the economies being gained from the switch to the MA-1/Falcon/MB-1 weapon system. These included increased range in the supersonic mission from 238 to 358 nautical miles, and in the subsonic mission from 347 to 506 nautical miles. This was due in part to the smaller Falcon system, which meant additional fuel storage capacity was gained, but also from the flight testing, which showed estimates of drag from wind-tunnel testing to be greatly improved. Campbell also reiterated the successes being obtained with the engine programme. He summarized the situation with the following:

(c) The adoption of the MA-1/Falcon/MB-1 fire control and weapons to the CF-105 programme has reduced the development time and will permit operational aircraft to be delivered for squadron use by September 1960 in place of the spring of 1961.

(d) The result of substituting MA-1/Falcon/MB-1 for Astra/Sparrow together with a close analysis of the programme has resulted in an overall saving of $642.9 million for 37 pre-production and 169 production aircraft or a $452.5 million saving on the programme for 100 operational aircraft.

(e) The programme submitted on 13 August, 1958, for 100 operational aircraft listed a fly-away price of $5.0 million, exclusive of sales tax, for 80 production aircraft. This programme also showed an anticipated recovery of 20 aircraft from the 37 aircraft development programme.

(f) For the revised programme from which 100 operational aircraft will be obtained, the fly-away cost for 92 production aircraft is $3.75 million. This programme includes the recovery of 8 operational aircraft from the 20 aircraft development programme.

(g) The rate of annual expenditure for the revised programme reduces the yearly spending for the programme submitted to CDC 8 August, 1958, from a 1959/60 forecast of 385 million and peak of 447 million to a 1959/60 forecast of 162 million and a peak of 245 million.

(h) The revised programme from which 100 operational aircraft will be obtained would cost approximately $702 million from 1 April, 1959.[60]

By the end of January 1959, fifty-nine flights had been completed for a total of 62 hours 45 minutes. A total of 7 hours 16 minutes had been flown at supersonic speeds in excess of 1,300 miles per hour, without full throttle being applied to the J-75 engines. The aircraft had flown supersonically on only its third flight and had exceeded 1,000 miles per hour on its seventh flight. Aircraft 25202 was now being fitted with the MA-1-C fire control system. Aircraft 25205 had flown for the first time on January 11.[61]

For the Mark 2s, manufacture of 37,280 parts was ninety-eight percent complete for Arrows 25206 to 25208. Subassembly of 8,034 parts was seventy-nine percent complete. Arrow 25206 was expected to be complete with Iroquois engines by February, and acceptance was planned for March. Material was on hand for the completion of the remaining aircraft for a total of thirty-seven. All was progressing as it should; however, spares for the aircraft were inadequate and could cause a delay in the programme. In a memorandum from the Assistant for Arrow Weapon System, it was emphasized that "All the above delays are directly attributable to CDs [contract demands] awaiting DM's [Deputy Minister] signature."[62] In other words, the government was to blame for delays and lack of spares for the thirty-seven aircraft. Twenty days later, with all progressing well and costs extensively reduced, the programme would be prematurely terminated.

From the above, it is clear that Canada had a

first-rate interceptor. Although costs were high, they were nothing out of the ordinary for this type of development and compared well with American programmes, despite the fact that the Arrow was a superior aircraft. It is also clear that decisions to acquire the Bomarc had been made in April of 1958 or earlier, and that this issue was discussed between the President and the Prime Minister in their July meeting, along with the prospect of sharing in defence costs. At this same meeting, Defence Minister Pearkes told the Secretary of State that Canada could afford the Arrow but not with the Bomarcs included. Then, in August, Pearkes was told that Bomarcs would be installed just south of the Great Lakes if Canada would not accept them. This would mean nuclear war over the most densely populated regions of Canada. Pearkes returned from this meeting only to recommend termination of the Arrow in favour of Bomarcs. Canada's entire defence policy was still being manipulated entirely by the United States, which was now most decisive in stating it would never purchase the Arrow. But what did the Americans stand to gain if the Arrow were terminated?

In the Cabinet discussions, no one seemed to listen to the Chief of the Air Staff, who maintained that interceptors would be required. Among those not listening was Charles Foulkes, the Chairman of the Chiefs of Staff, who was in favour of the Bomarc. Further, no one seems to have questioned the utility of the Bomarc for the defence of Canada, although it had been clearly shown it was purely for the defence of the American Strategic Air Command. Finally, attempts were made to show that the Arrow was costing too much, when in reality the problem was one of the combined cost of the Bomarc and Arrow together. Even the Minister of Finance admitted he would not let financial concerns get in the way of defence, although he noted that the military themselves were recommending against the Arrow — so why should further moneys be spent on it? What about those arguments of potential mass layoffs, recession, national prestige, and the resulting psychological impact on the nation?

5 MUTILATION

People who ought to have been privy to, if not directly responsible for the decision to scrap the Arrow — Diefenbaker, O'Hurley, Pearkes, Golden, Miller — have all denied prior knowledge of the destruction.
The Arrow, James Dow[1]

JANUARY 13, 1959, saw the Arrow subject discussed again by the Conservative Cabinet. Minister Pearkes read from the memo he had been given the day before by the Chief of the Air Staff. He said that the Hughes plus Falcon system could be integrated into the aircraft. This would mean an increase in radius of action from 238 to 354 nautical miles for a supersonic mission and from 347 to 506 nautical miles for subsonic. The delivery schedule would also be advanced. In addition, he noted that the handling and performance of the five flying aircraft were "extremely reassuring."[2]

Despite these facts, Pearkes went on to state that the United States had over 800 interceptors in service and funds to procure another 650. The USAF had just cancelled the F-106C and F-106D in favour of the long-range F-108, which was not dependent on SAGE and which was now on the

NORAD inventory. He said that 100 interceptors from Canada would be a relatively small contribution and, besides, the Arrow's range was limited to 300 and 500 miles. In fact, range was dependent on the type of mission being flown, because figures in nautical miles are longer than statute miles. Pearkes further stated that the Bomarc would afford a less expensive means of defence and that Canada could rely on the United States to provide any required interceptor defence. But the United States had not yet committed itself to cost sharing, and the prospect of paying for these programmes, even with some reductions, was still great. Perhaps cancellation of the Arrow was even a condition of cost sharing. In any event, it seemed nothing was going to prevent the Minister from killing the Arrow, although a decision was not immediately taken, as March 31 was the stipulated deadline. Why did no one challenge the Minister's remarks, and how did the F-108 get on the NORAD inventory? Was Canada not a participant in the decision? The F-108 was not even on the drawing boards and would eventually be cancelled, yet the Arrow was flying and proving itself in every respect. Were the other Cabinet members aware of the U.S. decision to install Bomarcs just south of the border, and of the implications?[3]

Some documents obtained from the United States may add additional information. The first is a National Security Council secret document dated December 30, 1958, which says:

In its desire to assist Canada's defense production industry, the Canadian Government is confronted with a dilemma. On the one hand, the Government has emphasized the rights of Canada as a sovereign power and the relationship of defense production to Canadian industrial and scientific growth; on the other hand, it is faced with the economic reality that Canada does not have the resources to finance the more expensive weapons systems for modern defense. The Government's difficulty is exemplified by its recent decision to reduce drastically the production of the Canadian-developed CF-105 supersonic interceptor aircraft and to introduce into the Canadian air defense system the U.S.-produced Bomarc missile in its stead.[4]

The U.S. paper had it wrong. The Bomarc was introduced on U.S. insistence, and the Arrow programme had not been drastically reduced because of cost. The requirement for the Arrow for the auxiliary squadrons had been eliminated due to problems of training, if General Foulkes is to be believed, and the introduction of the Bomarc would cover part of the role slated for Arrows. Added to this was the increased capability afforded by the Arrow over other aircraft, and of course the numbers would then be reduced. Reducing the numbers would naturally drive up the unit cost of those ordered; however, it would be the added cost of the SAGE plus the Bomarc system that would strain the budget.

A second document obtained from the United States is more telling. A memorandum on production sharing between the United States and Canada dated June 1, 1960, was issued from the office of the Deputy Secretary of Defense, USAF. It refers to the National Security Council paper of December and contains the following:

> Prior to the NSC paper, and following a visit of the President to Canada in July 1958, Canada took the following actions with the understanding that her defense industry depended largely upon U.S. channelling defense business into Canada: Cancelled the CF-105 and related systems contracts; decided to make maximum use of U.S. developed weapons, integrated into NORAD; worked with the U.S. toward a fully integrated continental air defense.
>
> The U.S. in turn established a Production/Development Sharing Program with Canada with the first quarterly meeting in October 1958. Since then, policy obstacles impeding a free flow of business have been modified in a number of areas such as: Buy American Act; duty free entry of defense goods; security programs of mutual interest (for example Bomarc); cost sharing agreements have been worked out; and possible joint development programs are being explored.[5]

This memo fixes the cancellation in 1958 along the lines of Minister Pearkes's understanding. It also suggests a degree of bargaining, with the Arrow as a chip.

At the January 28 meeting of the Conservative Cabinet, the Minister of Finance indicated his budget for 1959–60 would show no provision for the Arrow save for cancellation charges. It would appear that the decision to cancel was indeed set and now just had to be made formal, with the review in March being nothing more than academic. The Prime Minister wondered if Avro might produce an aircraft under licence from the United Kingdom, the Blackburn, to soften the blow of resulting unemployment. Minister Pearkes indicated that this aircraft was not yet in existence, but that an aircraft from Grumman in the United States might be built as a replacement for the F-86 Sabre, which was becoming obsolescent. He was not prepared to replace the CF-100.[6]

At the February 3 meeting, the Prime Minister stated that his Chiefs of Staff had not raised any new factors about the manned bomber threat that might have any bearing on the decision to cancel, and that cancellation was now just a matter of time to decide what to do about maintaining employment at Avro. It was stated that the sooner the decision to cancel, the more would be saved on cancellation charges. The following day, Minister Pearkes indicated that the new price per aircraft with the Hughes and Falcon system was estimated at $7.81 million, excluding $28 million in cancellation charges for the Astra and Sparrow system. Although the cost had been reduced from $12.6

million per aircraft, he stated he still could not justify this expense for 100 aircraft. He also added that there was nothing now suitable in the U.S. inventory of interceptors and that if the manned bomber threat was decreasing, it would be preferable to concentrate on missiles for defence. In addition, his Chiefs of Staff were continuing their investigations into requirements for more missile installations and for alternative interceptors. The Prime Minister stated that a meeting of the Cabinet Defence Committee would be required before a final decision could be made.[7]

The CDC met February 5, 1959, at 3:30 p.m. General Foulkes, the Chairman of the Chiefs of Staff, had indicated that the Chiefs of Staff "were still of the opinion that the changing threat and the rapid advances in technology, particularly in the missile field, along with the decreasing requirements for manned interceptors in Canada, created grave doubts as to whether a limited number of aircraft of such extraordinarily high cost would provide a defence return commensurate with the expenditures."[8] The acting Minister of Defence Production, Howard Green, stated that by cancelling immediately rather than March 31, $15 million could be saved. The Secretary of State for External Affairs, Sidney Smith, agreed with the decision to discontinue development now. Both seemed to have missed the facts that the Arrow cost was decreasing and that the money spent would remain in Canada, not to mention the technology and talent.

Additional discussion points included an increase to the Bomarc bases under consideration. Also, it was reiterated that Canada could not be expected to provide every type of defence needed and that Canada was already providing airspace, expenditures on warning systems, communications, Bomarcs, and a share in the ballistic missile early warning system. In addition, the NORAD agreement would allow U.S. interceptors to be temporarily stationed in Canada if required. Still, the Chief of the Air Staff was asked if interceptors would be needed. He replied that 100 to 115 would be necessary, no matter where they came from.[9]

At this meeting, the CDC finally agreed to recommend cancellation, despite the comments from the Chief of the Air Staff, Air Marshall Campbell. The Cabinet record includes the following:

The difficulty in the situation was the changing nature of the threat and the fact that the services had to consider now what might be required for 1961–62–63 and up to 1965. If an attempt were made to obtain the best possible defence against the manned bomber, and assuming that the defence budget would be roughly the same order of magnitude as at present, no provision could be made for defence against missiles which most regarded as the principle threat three and four years hence. It seemed that a calculated risk had to be taken for the period 1961–63, to be in a better position to meet the missile threat which would follow that period. At present it was estimated that, to provide 100 CF-105s with the

MA-1/Falcon/MB-1 weapons system, would cost $781 million. It was still not possible to estimate precisely the cost of reequipping the Air Division (in Europe), but it could well be in the neighbourhood of $500 million and this could not provide for a replacement for the CF-100.[10]

The record of this meeting is interesting in that at no time does it state that the Army and Navy Chiefs of Staff might be worried about not getting their share of the defence pie should the Arrow go into production. Sharing the pie has been a favourite argument from those who have proposed that the Arrow was too costly. Surely, if there was any strength to this argument, such comments from the Army and Navy representatives would have been recorded. In fact, it seems it was mentioned only once (as reported in Chapter 4) and not to any substantial degree.

Second, if the concern was over missiles, why was the Chief of the Air Staff still requesting interceptors? Why was he being ignored? Third, the reequipment of the Air Division in Europe seems to have been included more as a red herring than anything else at this stage. It was being discussed, but no real plans were afoot to reequip this division. Again, the reasons being put forward for cancellation were not due to the cost of the Arrow itself but to the fear of not having funds at some point in the future for building defences against some imaginary threat. Was this fear a reaction to U.S. policy again? In fact, cost would not even be stated as the official reason for cancellation and would be repeatedly denied by the Prime Minister and the Minister of National Defence. Cost would become the historians' favourite reason for the cancellation.

The CDC's decision to terminate was tabled to the Conservative Cabinet members at the February 10 meeting. Minister Pearkes added that he did not believe Russia would launch an attack unless it had a large arsenal of ballistic missiles that could not be defended against by conventional means; however, he could not give assurance that interceptors would not be required in the future, nor that they would not have to be procured in the United States should the Arrow programme be discontinued. However, with the manned bomber threat diminishing, he believed it was cheaper to defend against any remaining bomber threat with the Bomarc, especially since the United States had just agreed to pay $91 million of the total $110.8 million forecast for two Bomarc squadrons in Northern Ontario and Quebec. Therefore, cancellation would be even better, since Canada could obtain its defences now almost free of charge. Did Minister Pearkes honestly believe this, or was he now relieved to know that the useless nuclear Bomarc could be safely placed in Northern Canada with only the Arrow as a sacrifice?[11]

The issue of reequipment of the European squadron was brought forward again. It would cost $400 to $500 million to replace the obsolete F-86 Sabre. This time, the point was made that such a plan would give the appearance that Canada was defending Europe with aircraft while the United States was defending Canada with aircraft. The reply to this irony was that the Air Division in Europe would be reassigned a strike attack role, which would therefore require different aircraft types suitable for this purpose. Furthermore, Canadians at home would be manning the Bomarc bases and associated warning lines, so it was not true to say the United States would be defending Canada. Besides, the F-108 operating from Greenland and Alaska would be complementing the RCAF squadrons of CF-100s. The comment about reassigning the role of the Air Division in Europe to one of strike attack almost suggests that it was being done for political reasons so that it could be argued that the Arrow was not suitable for number-one division.[12]

On February 14, 1959, the Conservative Cabinet agreed to the decision to cancel the Arrow programme. It was believed that when the announcement was made as much as possible about the production-sharing arrangements with the United States should also be given. No Member present was opposed to the decision, although the Minister of Labour expressed concern over the layoffs that might ensue. With respect to a decision not being made before March 31, it was noted that the September statement was considering the world climate, namely the possible invasion of Quemoy by China. Like Korea and the CF-100, this invasion might have accelerated the development of the interceptor should Canada have become involved in the conflict. Because this world situation had passed, the need for the aircraft was negated and so termination would be justified. Finally, it was agreed that other Ministers, in particular the Minister of Defence Production, Mr. O'Hurley, would have to be present for any official vote on cancellation. Also, it was thought the company should be notified at the same time as Parliament.[13]

On Tuesday, February 17, 1959, the Prime Minister told his Cabinet that a draft statement on termination had been prepared. It included a discussion of the production-sharing arrangements as well as the acquisition of the Bomarc and nuclear weapons. It was decided that Friday would be the most appropriate time for the announcement. The Cabinet record says that the Cabinet

(a) agreed that the development of the Arrow aircraft and Iroquois engine be discontinued, effective as of the time of announcement;

(b) that an announcement concerning this decision, the production sharing with the United States, and the acquisition of atomic weapons be made in the House of Commons, probably on Friday;

(c) that the contractors be notified of the termination of their contracts at the same time; and,

(d) that an agreement be made with the United States, in the form of an exchange of notes, for the implementation of the agreed arrangements on the sharing of the costs of Bomarc and SAGE installations in Canada and the associated extension of radar coverage.[14]

On Thursday the 19th, the Prime Minister told his Cabinet that the CBC was planning to broadcast a programme on the Arrow the following Sunday or Monday, and that his statement should be made before the programme aired. He asked Ministers Pearkes, Fleming, Smith, O'Hurley, and Fulton to redraft his statement one final time. Then, on February 20, 1959, "Black Friday," John Diefenbaker rose in the House of Commons to cancel the Arrow and Iroquois programmes.[15]

In his address, Diefenbaker stated that the reason for cancellation was the rapidly changing threat. Enemy bombers were being replaced by more effective ballistic missiles, against which the Arrow could not defend. In effect, the Arrow would be an obsolete weapon, and so continued expenditures for it were no longer justifiable. He then quoted the price per aircraft at $7.8 million dollars and stated that this did not include the $303 million spent in development up to September 1958. He stopped short of using cost as his reason, perhaps because he knew the costs were decreasing. He further discussed the Bomarc question, but failed to indicate that this weapon had been pushed onto Canada by the United States, although the Americans were now prepared to pay nearly two-thirds of the cost.[16]

Back at Avro, officials received a telegram from D. L. Thompson of the Department of Defence Production. In it, he apprised the company of the termination and ordered the company to cease work immediately. To comply with this request, Avro had no choice but to lay off its employees effective immediately, since they would no longer have anything to work on. A similar telegram had been sent to E. K. Brownridge at Orenda. In all, some 14,000 employees were left jobless that afternoon. What had been described by employees as a family would soon be scattered, and the psychological impact on the nation would become greater then expected.[17]

Details of the political storm that followed the cancellation are well covered in James Dow's book *The Arrow.* What is not covered, follows here. On March 4, 1959, the RCAF established a Termination Group under Group Captain A. H. Lieff. Before this, the RCAF had asked the DRB if the NAE could make use of the Arrow in research. The initial reply from the DRB, dated February 10, 1959, was quite optimistic and outlined some candidate projects for which the Arrow would be useful.

On March 11, following termination, another reply came from the DRB. It stated that the RCAF had indicated that five aircraft and fourteen engines could be made available for research. However, the DRB believed that the operation and maintenance would have to be contracted to Avro at a cost of $7 million over three years. Expenses for an engine programme would cost another $6 million, with another $1 million needed to run the engine test facility, reputed to be among the best in the world. The reply concluded:

> It is obvious from the foregoing that the expenditures involved are far in excess of the present level of expenditure in aeronautical research activities in this country. Further, even assuming that funds were available in the amount indicated, it seems doubtful whether the foregoing represents the best investment therefor. Accordingly, it would appear that expenditures of this magnitude could only be justified on the basis of other considerations, e.g., maintaining a nucleus of engineering talent in the firms; providing test facilities to other countries; or for Air Force purposes.[18]

On March 13, Air Marshall Campbell advised Minister Pearkes of the DRB reply, indicating the costs and the fact that the Arrows had only flown a total of 65 hours, but that 1,000 hours were required to ensure airworthiness and reliability. He also explained spare parts were in short supply and concluded: "Considering the development left to be done, the difficulties in supporting the aircraft and the cost of doing the research flying from Avro . . . it can be said that there is no use in the RCAF or NAE for these aircraft. . . . Since there is no practical use for the Arrow or its major components, the RCAF intends with your approval to . . . make the necessary arrangements to dispose of the Arrow airframes and Iroquois engines."[19]

The Air Member Technical Services, Air Vice Marshall J. Easton, had confirmed with Dr. Field of the NAE that there would be no use for the aircraft. In a handwritten reply dated March 19, George Pearkes concurred and said he wished to be informed "of the proposed method of disposal of the airframes and engines" before the action was taken.[20]

It is difficult to imagine that the DRB and the NAE were turning their backs on an acknowledged advanced aircraft and engine. Surely these would have been a bonus to aeronautical research and funds would have been found. The comment on a lack of spare parts was blatantly incorrect, since there were enough parts for the assembly of thirty-two more aircraft. At best, spare parts were in short supply for all thirty-seven, but then only because no contracts had been signed, as discussed earlier. In speaking to this author in June of 1991, Dr. Omond Solandt, who left the DRB in 1956, could only speculate that the NAE would not have been able to conduct any useful research with the aircraft because it simply did not have the required equipment for the work. In telling the RCAF it could not use the aircraft, the NAE did not necessarily mean the aircraft was useless. One is left to wonder, though, if the NAE was not interested because of their earlier criticisms of the Arrow.

On March 19, a telegram was sent from J. L. Bush

of the Department of Defence Production in Ottawa to C.A. Hore of the same Department in Malton. Hore was advised that the wooden mock-up was to be destroyed and the metal mock-up was to be sent to the Crown Assets Disposal Corporation, since the RCAF had advised of no further use for either.[21]

In a memorandum dated March 26, 1959, to Minister Pearkes through the Deputy Minister, Air Marshall Hugh Campbell wrote about the disposal of the aircraft and engines:

Two methods may be followed:

(a) Declaring as surplus matériel to Crown Assets Disposal agency. This course is not recommended for the reason that this agency has the prerogative of selling this matériel in its original state. This course could lead to subsequent embarrassment, that is, airframe and engine could conceivably be placed on public view or even, in fact, used as a roadside stand. This, I am sure, you will agree is most undesirable.

(b) Relinquishing any DND interest in the airframes and engines to DDP for ultimate disposal by that agency. In this case DDP can reduce it to scrap. This course is recommended.[22]

On April 7, 1959, Hugh Campbell sent the Minister an update in which he advised that arrangements had been completed for the return of the B-47 aircraft to the USAF as well as return of the MA-1 systems. He asked for the Minister's approval concerning the scrapping.[23]

That same day, Bush advised Hore that the RCAF had no further plans for flights of the completed aircraft and expected they would be turned over to the Department of Defence Production for mutilation. However, two aircraft were to be kept in a whole state as they might yet be required by the Department of National Defence.[24]

Bush went on to discuss the disposal of engines, jigs, and tooling. He stated flatly that "Recognizable components and aircraft are to be mutilated to the extent that they cannot be assembled in the form of an aircraft."[25] He further ordered that one complete cockpit be made available to the Institute of Aviation Medicine and that one complete set of drawings, technical reports, and related production material be retained. Bush also stated that the B-47 that had been used in the testing of the Iroquois was to be returned to the USAF, and seemed to indicate that the RCAF wished to have this aircraft scrapped, as well. It was indeed cut to scrap.

On April 8, the Minister replied to Air Marshall Campbell with approval for the scrapping. Whether he consulted first with the Prime Minister is not known. However, the previous week, on April 3, Minister Pearkes had attended a luncheon in Washington in the office of Neil McElroy, the U.S.

Secretary of Defense. General Charles Foulkes and Air Vice Marshall Hendrick, now Chairman, Chief of the Joint Staff in Washington, were present along with numerous other high-ranking officers and embassy officials. A top-secret message on the meeting notes the following:

> Mr. Pearkes asked Mr. Quarles opinion on the need for Canada to provide interceptors in place of the cancelled Arrow. Mr. Quarles answer was cautious in realizing the Canadian dilemma but stated that in general terms they would like to have interceptors in Canada in place of those cancelled. Mr. Pearkes mentioned the improvement of northern bases in Canada to allow American interceptors to operate therefrom and Mr. Quarles admitted this was one way in which this need could be met.[26]

The Minister and his staff had argued that the era of the manned interceptor was over, but with the five Arrows still intact, the Americans were saying that interceptors were a requirement. No-one — not Pearkes or Foulkes or Hendrick — prevented the axe from falling in light of this information. After the fact, Foulkes himself would write memoranda explaining that interceptors were now a definite requirement and should be procured.

On April 14, Group Captain Lieff advised Bush that the RCAF had no requirement for any airframes or engines and that all should now be scrapped. He specifically stated that the RCAF did not wish to have the aircraft disposed of in its whole state. On April 20, G. W. Hunter, Assistant Deputy Minister, advised Raymond O'Hurley of the Department of Defence Production that disposal action was being taken. However, he indicated that four aircraft were being retained pending decisions from foreign governments as to possible use. This was contrary to the directions given by Lieff.[27]

Hunter further advised that the fifth aircraft, which had been undergoing repair, was in fact now being dismantled. This aircraft could only have been Arrow RL25202, which explains why it does not appear in the photos of the destruction on the tarmac outside the plant. Was it truly destroyed, or was it dismantled and hidden for posterity? On April 22, Hunter updated his statements. He now contended all five aircraft were being held intact pending disposal. He stated, "No decision has been made to reduce these aircraft to scrap."[28]

This was an extraordinary statement in light of earlier correspondence. He went on to say there had been some interest from the United Kingdom. In fact, it was Avro's Jim Floyd who was attempting to tell the government that there was overseas interest, but there is no indication in the files of direct communication between Canada and the United Kingdom, the United States, or any other government, although Campbell informed the Minister that the five aircraft would be held pending news from the United Kingdom. The Minister agreed, but nothing was forthcoming.

Meanwhile, Assistant Deputy Minister Hunter provided a draft statement for O'Hurley explaining that the Mark 2 aircraft could not be allowed to attempt a speed record run because considerable preparation and months of flight testing would be required first, should the matter be raised. He stated that first flights with the Iroquois were scheduled for April or May, and that at least six months would be required in flight test before attempting the record. This estimate would have been impossible to predict until after the first flight. Hunter also noted some USAF interest, but nothing that had come in officially.[29]

Meanwhile, Frank Miller, the Deputy Minister of National Defence, and D. A. Golden, the Deputy Minister of Defence Production, were in communication. In a letter dated April 27, 1959, Miller states:

(a) there is no intention of allowing the completed aircraft to be flown, maintained in service, or left in the whole state. . . .

(c) the aircraft, as a whole aircraft, or airframe or engine will not be put up for disposal as such but will be reduced to scrap after all useful and creditable material has been removed.

I would appreciate confirmation of your understanding and agreement.[30]

Golden replied on May 12. He was in complete agreement, although he stated that the five completed Mark 1s were being retained pending news from the United Kingdom.

On May 15, Bush sent the following telegram to Hore: "It has been confirmed that there is no requirement for any Arrow aircraft or Iroquois engines. It is therefore in order to proceed with reduction of the Mark 1 airframes and Iroquois to scrap as previously discussed."[31]

Fred Smye's dream, and the dream of a nation, was over.

There was renewed talk of allowing Arrow 25206 to attempt a speed record. Hunter again wrote to O'Hurley in the negative, reiterating the costs involved and the problems of flying an untried engine. Still, the archival records are interesting in that they contain the draft of his memo, which says: "The establishment of a world's speed record would not enhance the military value of the aircraft but the publicity may have made the decision to discontinue production more difficult."[32] From the word *but* onwards, the sentence is crossed out. Breaking the record would definitely enhance the military value, and the publicity would have been devastating to those who wished to cancel! Indeed, the Americans were continually priding themselves on their ability to set world speed records.

There are at least two letters on file from concerned Canadians requesting that one airframe be preserved for posterity. One is dated May 8 and the other May 13. Minister Pearkes replied to the first that the Arrow could not be preserved for economic reasons and that several hundreds of thousands of dollars could be recouped from the sale of the scrap. This from a programme that had cost several hundred million! To the second letter, Minister Pearkes responded that the Arrow "would be inadequate for the defence of Canada" by the time it would come into service.[33]

By July 7, the Department of Defence Production had reported that three of the five aircraft were completely dismantled. The fourth and fifth would be finished by July 10 and 17. The remainder in the plant had been taken apart. The Iroquois engines were being retained pending possible interest from the United States by General Electric and from the United Kingdom by Bristol-Siddeley, but the Crown Assets Disposal Corporation requested and received confirmation of the disposal action on the same date. Finally, the records show that the United Kingdom did make contact with the government and Avro in July, and on July 22 a team of engineers arrived. These engineers, however, were interested only in the technical data that might assist them in the development of a new delta aircraft, the tactical strike and reconnaissance TSR-2. With its Mach 2 performance and 66,000-pound double engine thrust, the TSR-2 would surely be a world beater. In September 1959, the technical data were sent; two prototypes would fly by 1965. The project was eventually scrapped by the U.K. government in favour of the U.S. F-111. Like the Arrow, it was said that the TSR-2 would have cost twice that of comparable American aircraft, and it, too, was cancelled after considerable expenditure in development. Not surprisingly, the TSR-2 would be reduced to scrap, just after flight trials were beginning to prove its worth. Was American influence as prevalent in the TSR-2 as it had been with the Arrow?[34]

On January 21, 1960, Hore advised the Arrow Termination Coordinator in Avro that the records and publications that had been retained could also be destroyed, since the RCAF saw no further use for them. A confirmation that this order was carried out has not yet been found.[35]

In the sequence of events leading to the cancellation, every reason for continuing the programme had been ignored. Costs were decreasing and the aircraft was proving its capabilities, having achieved a speed of Mach 1.96–1.98 and a height of 58,000 feet, all with the lower-thrust J-75 engines. The schedule was also advancing forward. The aircraft would be fitted with a proven weapon system, and range was greater than had been previously calculated. Rather then press the Arrow into service in Europe, thereby increasing the numbers to be manufactured, which would in turn lead to further reductions in the flyaway cost, the government decided to redefine the European role to one of strike attack, a role for which the Arrow was not entirely suited.

The official reason for the cancellation was given as the decrease in threat from the manned bomber and increase in threat from the ballistic missile. Yet less than two months after the cancellation,

Canadians were being told that the bomber threat was real and that interceptors would definitely be required, a stand maintained by the Chief of the Air Staff all along. Anyone who believes that the nature of the threat could change so rapidly, seemingly month-to-month, is entirely unaware of the network of intelligence gathering that goes on in the world. The threat was not changing so rapidly, but it was a convenient excuse that the average individual could never question.

Finally, when the decision to cancel was handed down, it is incredible that Canada's NAE was not in a position to accept the aircraft for research purposes. The most advanced aircraft in the world would instead be blowtorched to scrap, on orders from the RCAF! After all the discussion on cost, only a few hundred thousand dollars would be recouped from this multimillion-dollar investment. Like the Jetliner and the Velvet Glove, the Arrow would be no more.

6 WHY?

The CF-100 was incapable of policing Canadian skies against intrusions from aircraft similar to the U-2.
Cabinet Conclusion, July 15, 1960[1]

IN MAY OF 1958, the NORAD agreement, which effectively made the United States and Canada joint partners in the defence of North America, was signed. The Arrow would have been a logical contribution from Canada's perspective. This view had been expressed by James Douglas, the U.S. Secretary of the Air Force, as well as by his military advisers, who in January of 1958 had been seeking ways of keeping the Arrow programme alive. However, even as NORAD was being signed, other quarters in the United States were ignoring the Arrow and pushing for the installation of Bomarcs, knowing Canada would be unable to afford both. The solution for supporting major defence programmes then lay in the defence-sharing arrangements that were established as a result of the Eisenhower-Diefenbaker summit of July 1958. Unfortunately, these arrangements and NORAD were bent on ensuring that American defence policy and weapons would prevail, for the defence of

151

the United States. This is not to imply that the concept of shared continental defence was incorrect, but certainly the implementation of this concept and its consequences needed further development in certain areas; otherwise, and as it turned out, Canadian companies would be relegated to the production of component parts rather than complete complex platforms, and Canada would be forced into installing useless weapons.

In the files of the Under-Secretary of State for External Affairs for Canada, Norman Robertson, there is a confidential article that expounds on this theme. It is not known if the article was written by Mr. Robertson himself, but the indication is that it was published by the The Economist on February 5, 1959. Robertson's article is titled "Canada's Defence Dilemma." A search of The Economist back issues reveals an article entitled "Dilemma for Canada's Defence Industry" in the April 11, 1959, issue. This article discusses the defence production-sharing arrangements and the apparent contradiction between Canada's vision of total independence and the need for industrial integration with the United States in the area of military technology. It appears to be a sanitized version of the confidential article found in the Robertson files.

The confidential version begins: "The logic of North American defence needs now faces Canada with a dilemma: how to 'integrate' its defences with those of the United States while retaining its full national sovereignty."[2] Indeed, the question of maintaining sovereignty had arisen during the discussions to cancel the Arrow.

The confidential article contends that the Conservative government fully accepted the doctrine of complete integration of air defence for North America just as the previous Liberal government had. (The signing of the NORAD agreement certainly demonstrated this acceptance.) Accordingly, the article argues, Canadian and American defence could not be integrated without American strategic concepts prevailing. For example, it says:

> The Distant Early Warning line was built entirely on American insistence. When some members of the Liberal ministry proposed that, if it had to be built, Canada should at least do the work and send the bill to the United States, the idea was vetoed by Mr. C. D. Howe, the former Minister of Commerce, on the ground that it was a crackpot idea, anyway. The Canadian decision was, in effect, equivalent to saying: "It's all nonsense. But if they think they need it, we cannot and should not stop them. Only don't lets take the responsibility ourselves."[3]

This view may be somewhat simplistic, but probably is not far from the truth. The article explains that at the service level, because of the smaller Canadian air force, RCAF recommendations invariably followed those of the USAF and that if Canadian geography had been different, that is, not situated between the United States and Russia, installation of the SAGE and Bomarc System would never have been recommended. One should recall that it was a Defence Production document that stated the Bomarcs were purely for defence of the American Strategic Air Command and not for Canada. Recall also that the Canadian delegation had been told that bases would be established just south of the Great Lakes if Canada did not accept the missile on Canadian soil — the implication being nuclear strikes over populated Southern Ontario and Quebec. The price for following U.S. doctrine would then, according to the article, mean abandoning hope of ever producing "end items" like the Arrow. Instead, Canadian industry would be reoriented for the production of component pieces subcontracted from American industry.[4]

This is exactly what transpired when, after cancellation of the high-tech Arrow, Canadian industry was afforded the opportunity of building low-tech pieces of the Bomarc missile, since Canadian industry simply was not geared for the missile and its associated production. Even this may have turned out differently had the Velvet Glove programme not been cancelled in favour of American weapons. However, the acquisition of the SAGE and Bomarc system did present tantalizing economic and technological prospects, which would have overshadowed pure defence issues. Unlike the case of the DEW line cited earlier, Canada was now intent on sharing in the production effort to a much higher degree. A Department of Defence Production document quoted earlier contains the following:

Conversations on production sharing commenced in August 1958. The cancellation of the Sparrow and Astra programs in September lent an impetus to this as what had previously started as a ground environment problem was now seen to involve the whole Air Defence Weapon System.

Meetings with senior U.S. officials took place in October 1958, and by November 1958, agreement was reached in defining our short- and long-term objectives. Under the short-term objectives an effort was to be made to see what participation could be achieved on SAGE/Bomarc programs. Under the long-term objectives a study was to be made of the principles and procedures necessary to enable future Canadian participation in North American defence supplies.[5]

The Arrow was not discussed in this Defence Production document. It is as if it never existed and was therefore never part of the equation, except in the American memorandum on the production-sharing programme, quoted in a previous chapter, which implied that cancellation was part of a deal. The fate of the Arrow had willingly been placed into the hands of the Americans from its inception, and would end there. In signing the NORAD agreement and the defence-sharing arrangements, Canada had essentially agreed never to develop high-tech aircraft again. What is sad is the ease with which all was accomplished. Allegedly, the Prime Minister had never officially discussed the matter of signing the NORAD agreement with his Cabinet. General Foulkes would later say the military had stampeded him into it, a fact denied by the Prime Minister. Meanwhile, the Department of Defence Production seemed more interested in the potential of the U.S. market opening its doors to Canada than with the decreasing capability to compete without sound research development, and manufacturing capabilities afforded by programmes like the Arrow. The RCAF, on the other hand, was torn between aircraft and missiles as defences, and threats may have coerced the Minister into accepting the Bomarc.

Returning to the Department of Defence Production, a good example of how eager the government was to get into the U.S. market and how caught up it was in the idea of production sharing is given by a teletype message received by a Mr. Thompson at Defence Production on March 6, 1959. In part, it reads:

Re Project Mercury [U.S. space programme]. Saw Silverstein 5:30 yesterday and advised him proposal for Canada to offer 30–45 senior engineers of Avro and Orenda was under active consideration in Ottawa. . . . In my judgement this proposed deal represents the most significant move we could make in production sharing. 1. NASA next to its counterpart in USSR is the ultimate scientific centre in the world. . . . 2. That the Canadian govt. could claim credit to itself in terms of PR is obvious. 3. It could become a

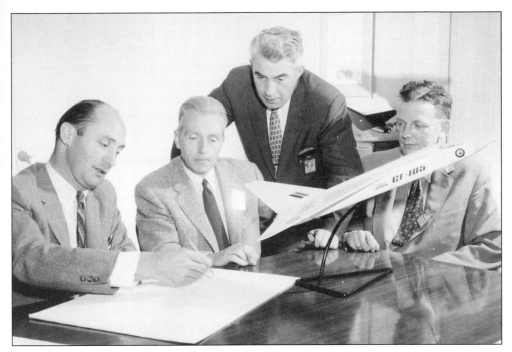

The Arrow Dream Team. *(Left to Right)* Bob Lindley, Jim Floyd, Guest Hake, and Jim Chamberlin. (JIM FLOYD)

October 4, 1957, the official roll-out of the Arrow. (DEPARTMENT OF NATIONAL DEFENCE)

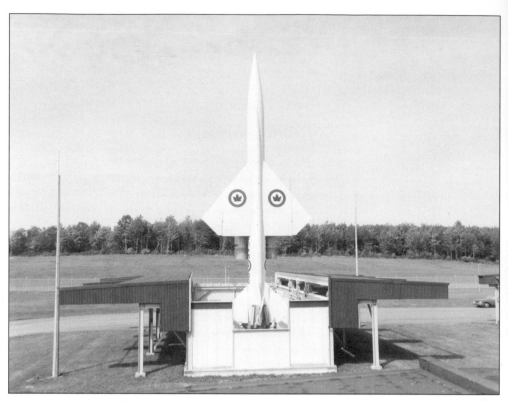

The Bomarc missile, untried, unproven, and on guard for the Strategic Air Command — in Canada. (Department of National Defence)

The CIA U-2 spy plane. Its only defence — altitude. In 1959 its only enemy — the Arrow! (U.S. Air Force)

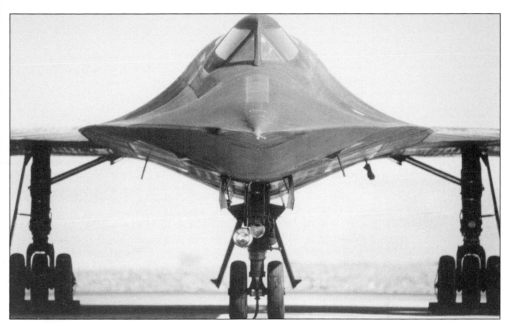

The Arrow wasn't yet in the grave when the SR-71 Blackbird, a titanium super spy plane, hit the drawing boards at the famous "skunkworks" of Lockheed in September 1959. (U.S. Air Force)

The Arrow. Note the cockpit configuration in comparison to that of the SR-71.
(Department of National Defence)

The old and the new: the Avro CF-100 and Avro CF-105 at the ready. (Department of National Defence)

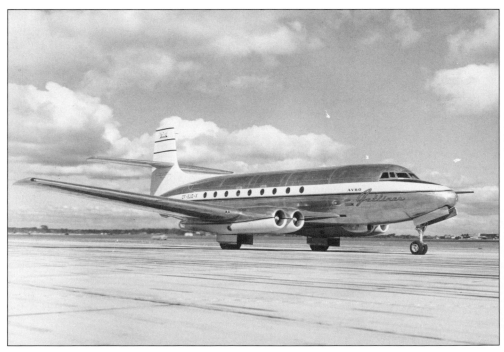

The Avro Jetliner, the first commercial jet to fly in North America. Terminated and then destroyed in 1956. (Jim Floyd)

The Avro CF-100 over the white cliffs of Dover. (Jim Floyd)

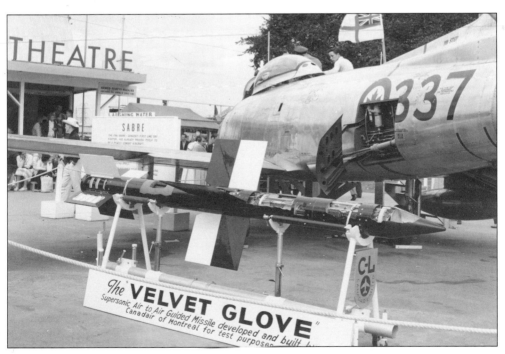

The Velvet Glove, the considered weapon package for the CF-100 and the Arrow. A promising effort terminated after $24 million spent in research and development. The alternative — American missiles. (Department of National Defence)

The Arrow with speed brakes extended. (Department of National Defence)

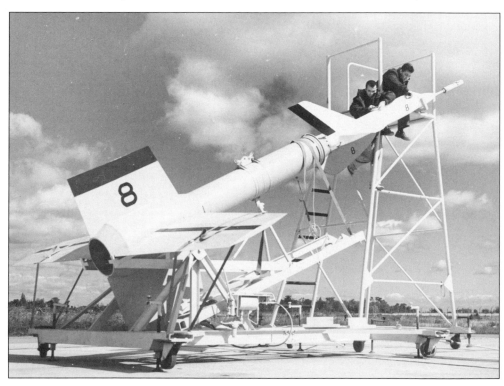

Free-flight rocket models of the Arrow were instrumented and then launched to obtain flight data for the Arrow design. (Jim Floyd)

The USAF F-117A Stealth fighter. Fly-by-wire controls and internal weapons carriage — currently the wave of the future. (U.S. Air Force)

The Arrow. It, too, had fly-by-wire controls and internal weapons carriage. In 1957 it was the wave of the future. (Jim Floyd)

All that remains of the Arrow for public viewing. Blowtorched remnants of a once-great aircraft and the scarred psyche of a nation. Could more pieces be out there somewhere? (KEN LEPPER)

great fulcrum to help pry production sharing deals loose. . . . 4. As the top ten percent of propulsion and aeronautics team in Canada (30–40 people) are intent on leaving Canada anyway to seek employment elsewhere and as what will be left will not meet the aims of Cabinet agreements with Avro-Orenda it seems in my personal judgement that Canadian govt. should support this proposal albeit I can only base my judgement on the Canadian govt. policy as it is known to me at this time.[6]

The author of this message was obviously well intentioned. It is ironic, though, that the same people who would be denigrated in Canada over the years to come, in a seeming campaign of discreditation for building an expensive obsolete aircraft, were being touted and sought after as among the best in the world by the ultimate scientific centres in the world. It is no wonder Avro engineers wanted to leave Canada: their industry had just been decimated; their dreams and lives shattered; and their brilliant achievements largely ignored! The deal went through, and Jim Chamberlin and twenty-five others from Avro wound up at NASA. As for the defence-sharing arrangements themselves, the same U.S. memo and the National Security Council paper quoted in earlier chapters both explain that the arrangements were not working as Canada had hoped.

The reasons for cancellation then seemed steeped in the Canadian government's willingness to be led or persuaded by the dictates of American defence policy. Coupled with this was a lack of confidence in our own capabilities, a confusion and lack of understanding of new technology (missiles), and a certain greed for potential (but not definite) economic prospects down south. In the absence of good reasons to terminate this highly successful programme, the diminishment of the manned bomber threat was put forward as the official reason for cancellation, perhaps because it was known that the average Canadian would be unable to dispute it in the absence of any secret intelligence information. But such information was available and was reported on. The article "Intelligence Schism" published in *Aviation Week* on March 2, 1959, pointed out the variance between the Canadian government interpretation of the same intelligence information the U.S. government had — namely that the Russian threat from new bombers under development was very real.[7]

That the United States was writing Canadian defence policy was further evidenced in early 1960. The Commander-in-Chief of NORAD, American USAF General Laurence Kuter, recommended that nine CF-100 squadrons in Canada be replaced with six squadrons equipped with supersonic aircraft such as the American F-101B. Speaking to his Cabinet on February 6, 1960, almost a year after the decision to cancel, Prime Minister Diefenbaker appointed a special committee to study the NORAD request. The Cabinet record indicates that Diefenbaker stated the following:

If the Committee reported that security demanded the acquisition of these aircraft, then that would have to be the decision. To purchase them, however, would cause great difficulties. It would place him and the Minister of National Defence in impossible positions. On the other hand, failure to reequip would be bad for the morale of the RCAF. He thought the public had been convinced of the wisdom of the government's decision to cancel the Arrow. To obtain other aircraft now in the face of statements that the threat of the manned bomber was diminishing and that the day of the interceptor would soon be over would be most embarrassing unless a reasonable explanation could be given. Additional Bomarcs in Canada might be an alternative. The committee should first examine carefully what had been said publicly by himself and other Ministers about cancelling the Arrow and, in the light of that, consider what was possible. In any event, the safety of the nation should be the paramount consideration no matter what the consequences. He had been against cancelling the Arrow but had been persuaded otherwise.[8]

These comments from Diefenbaker are astounding. When Air Marshall Slemon had reaffirmed the need for interceptors back in November 1958, the Prime Minister was very upset that Slemon, a Canadian, was undermining the government position, which was to study the situation until March

1959. But when the need for interceptors came from an American, the statement had to be treated with seriousness even though the situation could prove embarrassing. (The reader may remember that the Chief of the Air Staff had always maintained that interceptors would be required but, like Slemon, was ignored.) There was no discussion of cost impacts; rather, the security of the nation was "paramount" regardless of consequence. This echoed the Finance Minister's sentiment in the September 7, 1958, meeting when he said he would not jeopardize the safety of the country but, given that the military view was one of cancellation, he found it difficult to justify further expenditures.

Second, Diefenbaker was now saying he had been against cancellation. This may be partly true, given the number of meetings and discussions before the decision. But exactly what did he mean when he said he had been persuaded otherwise? Was the destruction of an industry based on persuasion? Who had persuaded him? Was he simply being polite in not naming his Minister of Defence and Chiefs of Staff? Could anyone else have had an input to the decision? In the Cabinet discussion following his comments, it was concluded that the acquisition of U.S. aircraft could not now be explained to the Canadian public in light of the Arrow decision without losing total credibility.[9]

At a meeting on May 14, 1959, the Cabinet assured itself that the recommendation from NORAD was only tentative and had not come directly from the United States. The Cabinet thought that the decision to introduce supersonic aircraft would therefore not have to be taken yet. The Cabinet was clearly stalling for time to avoid having to go before the Canadian public with an about-face. What would the Prime Minister have done if the request had come directly from the United States, and how more direct could it be than via NORAD? At this same meeting, Minister Pearkes added that the interceptors would only be used for the defence of the U.S. Strategic Air Command and would afford little security to Canadian cities, an unbelievable comment since this was precisely the raison d'être for the Bomarc. Pearkes reiterated the difficulty in defending a decision to buy American aircraft now. As a result, the decision to acquire the American planes would be successfully delayed. This was pure politics and had nothing to do with the safety and defence of Canada. The decision would finally become palatable when combined with a U.S. purchase of thirty-five Canadian CL-44 aircraft in exchange for sixty-six aging F-101B Voodoo aircraft in 1961.[10]

Weeks before the cancellation, the United States, secure in the knowledge that the Bomarc bases would be built, began offering to share the cost. Rather than change Canadian thinking into saving the Arrow, Minister Pearkes stood firm in his resolve that no money should be spent on a weapon that would soon become obsolete, especially now that the same protection would be afforded by the much cheaper Bomarc. The Americans, though, knew that aircraft would not be replaced by missiles, and said as much not two months after cancellation. Still, the nagging question remains as to why they were not ready to purchase the Arrow, especially since they were aware of how technically advanced it was.

The most obvious answer would relate to intense lobbying from American aircraft builders, who would fear competition from the Arrow and Avro. As discussed earlier, John Orr of the DRB has since claimed that American industry influenced a USAF technical report on the Arrow, which was purportedly sent to the Prime Minister in the hope of persuading him into cancellation. As well, Jon McLin has stated in his book, *Canada's Changing Defence Policy, 1957–1963*, that intense pressure was applied on the U.S. administration in the hope of thwarting the CL-44/Voodoo deal, because the CL-44 was a Canadian product and American policy on foreign acquisitions was entrenched in the Buy America Act. Further, Finance Minister Fleming claims in his memoirs that John Foster Dulles told him at the Paris meeting in December 1958 that the American aircraft industry was in a slump and that he could therefore not justify purchasing a foreign aircraft, the Arrow. Was this all a reaction from American industry, or did Secretary Dulles have another reason? Certainly, Boeing would have been lobbying hard for sales of Bomarc, their missile.

With the exception of Minister Pearkes possibly trying to prevent a nuclear disaster, as discussed earlier, the reasons for the cancellation of the Arrow are incongruous. First, the airframes and engines were recognized worldwide as being in advance of anything else, and flight testing was proving this. This point was made by the United States, the United Kingdom, and France, which was negotiating for the Iroquois. Only in Canada were unfounded doubts being expressed. However, this author has uncovered a previously secret report prepared by the Canadian Armament Research and Development Establishment (CARDE), which was asked to study the effectiveness of the Arrow with the Astra weapon system.[11] Completed in April 1958, the report was most favourable; however, *it was not released from* CARDE *until 1961*, two years after cancellation! Second, the Arrow programme was sustaining a brilliant aeronautical industry, which was attracting top individuals to Canada from around the world. Third, at the time of cancellation, costs of the programme were shown to be decreasing by hundreds of millions of dollars, making the aircraft more than competitive with others in its class. Fourth, the requirement for such an aircraft was not in doubt worldwide. Why, then, the cancellation and no American acquisitions?

From the Canadian perspective, several reasons have been identified, save for one, which has it that Prime Minister John Diefenbaker saw the programme as a Liberal government initiative and disliked the corporation. Some people say that his alleged personality conflict with Crawford Gordon,

the president of Avro, led him to cancel the programme and order everything destroyed. Perhaps,
but the records do not support any of this, unless
of course Diefenbaker was telling Defence Minister Pearkes what to say and do, orchestrating the
affair from behind the scenes.

In his book, Jon McLin concludes that the primary reason for cancellation was cost. However,
he notes that the Prime Minister maintained it
was the changing threat from missiles to manned
bombers. He notes, too, that when asked directly if
cost was the reason, Defence Minister Pearkes said
no, a view supported by his top-secret brief to Dulles in 1958. McLin next maintains that the Chiefs
of Staff had decided the issue was economics; however, the evidence presented earlier does not support this contention, since the Chiefs were all for
continuing the project to March 1959. Not one is
shown in Cabinet records as having complained
that they should receive the money from the
Arrow programme when the Minister of Finance,
Mr. Fleming, stated that it could be used elsewhere than defence. Also, it was only General
Foulkes who stated that Bomarcs would be a less
expensive way to go and was all for immediate termination, against the advice of the Chief of the
Air Staff, who maintained that interceptors would
be required.

As to why the United States would not purchase
the Arrow, especially in the face of decreasing cost,
McLin states that the Americans had doubts about
the aircraft's capabilities and that there were

doubts the fire control system would perform. Information presented earlier shows that the best
engineers in the United States had every confidence in Avro; it was American aircraft developments that were experiencing technical problems.
McLin next states that the range of the aircraft
was limited, but then admits there would be in
creased fuel capacity and therefore greater range
due to the installation of the Hughes and Falcon
system, which was smaller than the Astra plus
Sparrow system. Nor does he acknowledge that
flight testing was showing that range was in fact
much better than originally predicted. Finally,
McLin mentions that missiles were becoming the
new threat, and as proof he cites the U.S. cancellation of the F-106C and F-106D as well as the
long-range F-108, unaware perhaps of the U.S.
statements about the programmes for these aircraft being in technical difficulties. So why then
did the Americans not purchase the Arrow? Perhaps a better way to determine the answer is to
ask, "What, if anything, did the Americans stand
to gain by the cancellation?"[12]

The following modern-day analogy may help explain. In June 1987, Canada announced its plan to
obtain ten to twelve nuclear-powered submarines.
Of the two contenders, the British Trafalgar class
submarine had been designed using American
technology, whereas the French submarine had
not. Negative reaction from the United States was
swift as two central themes arose.

Writing in *Proceedings*, a U.S. Naval Institute

magazine, Norman Friedman commented on the
first theme, that of technology transfer:

> [T]he secret in naval nuclear reactors is likely to
> be the thousands of apparently minor manufac-
> turing tricks . . . and not the overall form of the
> plant. These tricks would not be evident from,
> say, a rough drawing of a reactor, but they would
> have to be transferred to a reactor builder. . . .
> Canadians do not have a reactor building or
> maintaining industrial base. . . . [W]ithout such
> an industrial base . . . they may find it difficult
> to build submarines even close to the advertised
> cost. They have already suggested that they will
> use competition to control reactor costs. That, in
> turn, will increase the transfer of information,
> because no potential builder can bid without a
> full design package.[13]

The implication in this comment is that American
manufacturing secrets or tricks would be spread to
too many sources should the Trafalgar be chosen.
The problem lay in the way that Canada does business. In the competitive process, Canada requests
several manufacturers to bid for the production.
However, to provide proper cost estimates, each
potential manufacturer has to be given the manufacturing secrets. As any intelligence expert will
admit, any increase in the number of individuals
who have the secrets increases the problem of
maintaining security and the likelihood of this information falling into unfriendly hands.

As discussed in previous chapters, the Arrow was not without its manufacturing secrets. Avro and its related companies had broken new ground in aerodynamics, metallurgy, electronics, engine technology, and more. Although considerable information had been made public, the secrets of manufacture and the test data had not. In addition, some of the data had come from the United States. Was this information sensitive? *Aviation Week* magazine of March 2, 1959, carried the following about the Canadian government's refusal to release information: "[I]t will not release that test data that has been collected thus far, because, although no Western power is interested, . . . it feels that the information possibly could aid a potential enemy."[14] The potential enemy, of course, was the Soviet Union. The data, along with the aircraft, drawings, and so forth, were all subsequently ordered destroyed.

While conducting research for his book *For Services Rendered*, about Soviet infiltration of the Royal Canadian Mounted Police (RCMP), journalist and author John Sawatsky discovered that a Soviet double agent, code-named Gideon, was

> being given responsibility for handling Green, a Canadian working as a KGB agent in Toronto with access to confidential information on the Canadian aircraft the Avro Arrow. . . . As a factory worker, Green's access was not classic but through planning and sleuthing he produced two sets of plans for the Arrow, one for the fuselage

and another for a portion of the engine. Green's spying posed a dilemma for [Terry] Guernsey [RCMP agent monitoring Green and Gideon under Operation Keystone] because the Green-Gideon connection was putting secret information into Soviet hands. The fundamental purpose of the Security Service was to stop espionage. Do you stop the leak or keep the case running? Was it worth sacrificing Operation Keystone and forego-ing possible future benefits to secure the confi-dentiality of the Arrow project? Some of the classified information belonged to the United States and an agreement of confidentiality re-quired that Canada keep it safe. Neither the United States nor the Avro company knew about the leak or about Operation Keystone. The offi-cial owner of the information was the Canadian government. Finally, Guernsey decided that since there was no war and the information would become obsolete in a few years, he would let it go. [15]

Similar statements about Soviet infiltration of A. V. Roe were made in the revealing book *Spycatcher* by Peter Wright. What is being stated in the above quote is that an RCMP officer was in-tentionally allowing Arrow secrets to fall into enemy hands for the sake of a case. Under what possible logic did he reason that the information on such an advanced aircraft would soon be obso-lete and that it would be all right?[16]

Mr. Guernsey believed that the United States

was unaware of the leak. Perhaps, but not likely. It has been proven that the Central Intelligence Agency (CIA) was operating in Canada in this time period. They were involved in the hallucinogenic experiments being carried out in Quebec in the late fifties and early sixties. They were also very much aware of the work at Avro since, in a parallel effort, the USAF was funding their own top-secret development project at Avro, Project Y. Project Y was a "flying saucer" allegedly capable of supersonic flight. Under American control, this project would have afforded an excellent opportunity for CIA agents to infiltrate Avro and keep abreast of what was going on in terms of espionage. CIA records show that the Agency was monitoring Project Y, but to what end?[17] That the RCAF was also fully aware of the espionage situation was confirmed to this author by the Air Member Technical Services, Air Vice Marshall Easton, on July 31, 1991. According to Air Vice Marshall Easton, at least one departmental employee was fired over this espionage.

Preventing the Soviets from obtaining the necessary manufacturing secrets would finally explain aspects of the destruction orders as mentioned in *Aviation Week*. Destruction of the aircraft themselves would prevent any likelihood of enemy agents ever obtaining any more information on the aircraft. For example, in the hands of the NAE, security around the aircraft could still be maintained. In a museum, though, it would be possible to break in and study the aircraft up close. It may sound like paranoia, but the country was in the midst of the cold war and the RCMP was knowingly allowing secrets to pass behind the Americans' back. Everything, then, would have to be destroyed. Retired Air Vice Marshall Easton confirmed to this author that security was the reason behind the blowtorching and destruction of all records. In the existing climate of the day, one simply could not risk having this information fall into the wrong hands.

While this was occurring, a media campaign on the obsolescence of the aircraft was begun. Was the media unknowingly taking part in a disinformation campaign? The media campaign and the destruction would send a clear signal to the enemy that, even if blueprints had been surreptitiously obtained, the aircraft would not be worth manufacturing. According to Air Vice Marshall Easton, everyone knew the Arrow was far in advance of anything in the world. Easton went so far as to say that had the programme continued, he had every confidence that the Arrow would have been purchased by the Americans. One is reminded of the British Harrier aircraft. For years, the Americans ignored it, but after it proved its worth during the Falklands crisis, the Harrier was placed in the American inventory, manufactured under licence in the United States. Ironically, as the Arrow was proving its worth, it had to be erased from existence, because it was too damn good!

The second important reason why the Arrow had

to be destroyed comes from the U.S. perspective. Although speculation, it, too, has its parallel in the submarine debate. The *Pacific Defence Reporter* stated in March 1988:

> [T]he U.S. is far from happy with the situation. The U.S. Navy is openly hostile to a fleet of Canadian submarines "trespassing" in the Arctic, which Washington regards as its own particular zone of operations. It visualizes complications arising from the necessity of having to cooperate with another country against Soviet submarines. . . . The likelihood of Canada demanding increased access to sensitive American information also irks the Reagan administration.[18]

Likewise, the *International Journal* stated: "When the Secretary of State for External Affairs declined to tell the House of Commons whether American submarines passed through Canadian waters, he did so to prevent 'Canada identifying travel patterns of submarines of friendly countries in our waters.' The submarine services of the world's navies are the most secretive of all military forces because their only real security lies in keeping their location imperfectly known."[19] In other words, the United States was worried that Canadian operations could compromise their own and those of other nations. In the 1950s, the American critical zone of operation was the skies.

In 1955, President Eisenhower had proposed an "open skies" policy which would have allowed planes to collect reconnaissance information over foreign countries, much like the policy proposed thirty-five years later in 1990. Eisenhower became discouraged when the Russians rejected his policy outright. Yet, the answer to the aerial reconnaissance problem had already been solved by the CIA in the form of the U-2 spy plane. Secretary of Defence Thomas S. Gates admitted in 1960 that U-2 overflights were "our best information" source. They flew under the cover of weather research, and their existence as spy planes had been continually denied.[20]

Conceived in the secret "skunk works" facilities of Lockheed Corporation, the U-2 was essentially a flying gas-tank glider. It could achieve altitudes of 70,000 feet and crisscross any country's airspace unmolested, much like the U.S. nuclear submarines under water. What may not be generally realized is that the U-2 was not a USAF programme. It was a CIA effort approved on December 1, 1954, by President Eisenhower. Allen Dulles was in charge. Together with his brother John Foster Dulles, the President, and others, Dulles discussed and individually approved each U-2 overflight.[21]

As Secretary of State, John Dulles was in the position of knowing both how the Arrow was progressing and, as pointed out in previous chapters, the programme's every vulnerability. According to *Kennedy and Diefenbaker* by Knowlton Nash, the Prime Minister distrusted Dulles, while Dulles saw Canada as a country to be humoured due to its strategic importance. The United States also believed that Canada was too close with Moscow. But how does this relate to the cancellation?[22]

In May 1960, Francis Gary Powers, piloting a U-2, was shot down by a surface-to-air missile. Before his ill-fated flight, Powers had been told: "There isn't any danger because no Russian plane or rocket can get to your altitude."[23] Eisenhower himself had been assured of the same when initially asked to authorize the flights in 1955. As in the submarine debate, the last thing the United States and Dulles, the hard-line anti-Communist, would want would be to have their U-2 overflights compromised; as late as 1990, these flights were still considered critical, as evidenced in the U.S. debates to cancel the super SR-71 spy plane overflights.[24]

Dulles, the CIA, and the President would have known that the Avro Arrow would have been the only aircraft capable of downing a U-2. The Arrow's role was precisely that — an interceptor — but one designed with a 60,000- to 70,000-foot altitude capability. In Soviet hands, even an unarmed Arrow could have been used to fly up to, photograph, and identify these high-altitude intruders, because at the time, while acknowledging the U-2's existence, the United States was telling the world that these were simply weather research aircraft. What better way was there to expose this operation than with an aircraft designed for the purpose? Any country flying the Arrow could do likewise, thereby seriously damaging U.S. intelligence-gathering operations. Moreover, it would give friendly and enemy countries alike the capability of overflying and attacking sensitive U.S. installations.

The Arrow could easily have evolved into the equivalent of the super SR-71 Blackbird, which was then on the drawing boards. Did it? By the late fifties, it was thought that the U-2 was becoming vulnerable due to the advances in surface-to-air missile technology and quite possibly from the Arrow. On September 1, 1959, less than seven months after the Arrow's demise, the CIA gave approval for the development of a high-altitude supersonic reconnaissance aircraft, the A-12, or Blackbird. This was a high-wing delta aircraft that maximized the use of titanium. It would have been in competition with the Arrow for this material, since in 1959 world supplies were low, with the bulk at Avro. The A-12 was capable of over a 70,000-foot altitude with a cruise at Mach 3. With aerial refuelling, it could overfly any country in the world. The A-12 eventually evolved into the YF-12 and finally the SR-71, which would be ordered by the USAF in December of 1962. What is interesting is that the specifications are very similar to those proposed to Jim Floyd by Dr. Courtland Perkins back in July 1957. Back then, Floyd had told Perkins the Arrow could achieve the required specifications except in range, where aerial refuelling would be required. It should come as no surprise, then, to learn that the SR-71 was in fact refuelled by American tanker aircraft during its missions.

Had the Arrow flown with the Iroquois engines and broken the altitude and speed records, it would have been virtually impossible to cancel. Therefore, it *had* to be terminated before any flights with the Iroquois. The United States and the CIA would be able to breathe a sigh of relief, and Canada would *never again* be involved in the high-altitude interceptor game.

It has to be more than coincidence that the USAF, which was encouraging Canada to continue the Arrow development, would begin changing its mind just as the project achieved first flight in March 1958 and began proving itself. Perhaps up to that point the United States and the CIA may not have believed that Canada, this banana republic to the north, could really do it! With CIA interests involved, it would not be stretching the imagination to think that after the USAF proposal to buy Arrows in January 1958, the USAF would have been told to back off. Having been so closely involved and being told all the project's vulnerabilities, the United States would have known that the simple refusal to purchase the aircraft, combined with the insistence to set up the Bomarcs, would be enough to kill it. In this way, the Bomarcs would be installed, the Arrow terminated, the manufacturing data (already in American hands) destroyed, the CIA U-2 programme protected, and the Canadians even willing to throw in their brilliant engineers and technicians for the avaricious prospect of obtaining lucrative deals in the United States. The Americans had everything to gain, and did.

Where was John Diefenbaker in all this? According to the Nash book and others, Diefenbaker saw President Eisenhower as his hero and went so far as to try to emulate him. As Nash explains:

> Diefenbaker's emotions about U.S. investment in Canada, U.S. trade restrictions, and the hawkishness of John Foster Dulles and the Pentagon were often calmed down by Ike. . . . Diefenbaker succumbed readily to the combination of Eisenhower charm, flattery, and considerations and to his own hero-worship of the American president. So much so that while bilateral issues continued to boil and differences sharpened between the two countries on specific issues, Diefenbaker spoke out in broad general support of Eisenhower and his policies.[25]

Was Eisenhower responsible for the change in attitudes about the Bomarcs and the Arrow, which began taking shape after the July 1958 summit with Diefenbaker? It seems it would have been a simple task for the President and his policy makers to convince Diefenbaker and his ministers of the need to stop this seemingly costly Arrow programme and opt for less expensive American missiles. Could Eisenhower have been one of those whom Diefenbaker claimed had persuaded him to cancel against his own wishes? This may never be known for certain. Still, the scenario fits the overall picture of trying to find an excuse for cancelling an otherwise brilliant programme.

And what of Minister Pearkes's attitude? If he had not been persuaded by July, he was most certainly a convert by August, after being told or perhaps threatened with nuclear devastation over Southern Ontario and Quebec. Was this a Dulles ploy?

When Gary Powers and his U-2 were shot down over Russia in 1960, Minister Pearkes admitted there had been U-2 overflights over Canada, as well, but insisted that these were weather planes only. Still, he conceded that the CF-100 could not police the skies against such intrusions; without interceptors, there could be no Canadian surveillance of Canadian airspace. Where was this argument before the Powers incident? It had been briefly discussed in an RCAF memorandum, but not by Cabinet. The intercept role would fall on the obsolete Voodoos, which did not have the range, altitude, speed, or manoeuvrability to affect U-2 or SR-71 operations.

After the Powers incident, the game was revealed and Diefenbaker must have realized he had been had by his hero. He had destroyed a viable industry for no good reason. To add insult to injury, it was the Bomarc development that would fall flat and become obsolete before it was installed. It is incredible that the government put so much faith in the unproven Bomarc and so little faith in the Arrow. If correct, it would also help explain Diefenbaker's hatred of a new president who was younger and to whom he owed nothing: President John F. Kennedy. The Canadian Prime

Minister would be able to vent all his anger on Kennedy, and he did exactly that. It is most ironic that back in July of 1958, when Diefenbaker introduced Eisenhower during his visit and spoke of the friendly relationship that had developed between the countries, he included these words in his address:

> We say what we have said on occasions in the past, that our countries are united in defence. I believe, sir, that the Soviet challenge demands that we can be no less in economic objectives. . . . And I go even further and suggest that, to meet the ever-enlarging expansion of Communist economic cold war, joint action is imperative. . . . We can on this occasion, in the simplicity of our faith, thank God that our nations know nothing of the ancestral hatreds or animosities. . . . Sir, as you came into our city you drove by and crossed over a small canal. Few know today when or why it was built. It was built more than 100 years ago to help protect this country from yours. Today it is a museum piece; it represents a past that is past.[26]

Or does it?

7 MYTHS AND MISCONCEPTIONS

For all its sleek technological excellence, the Arrow was a peace-lover's ideal weapon: it would self-destruct on use.
                    Toronto Star, February 20, 1986[1]

OVER THE YEARS, several myths and misconceptions have been fostered in a seeming effort to justify the cancellation and discredit the program, the company, and the personnel involved. These misconceptions have appeared in various historical texts, newspaper stories, and magazine articles and have essentially created a reverse Pygmalion psychology in Canadians — that is, when you continually tell somebody intelligent how foolish he is, eventually he believes it and reacts accordingly. How often has the phrase been heard, "Well, if it's Canadian, it can't be good," or the other, "Well, if it's Canadian, then it costs too much." It is high time this ridiculous psychology was stopped. The irony, of course, is that in the United States and other countries, Canadians and our products have always been recognized as world-class.

The comments on technical soundness by Air Vice Marshall Easton, RCAF pilot Jack Woodman, and Group Captain Ray Foottit, all individuals in key positions whose jobs were to assess the programme, point squarely to one of the largest attempts at brainwashing ever perpetrated on a nation in this reverse Pygmalion effect. These individuals and the supporting documentation prove that the Arrow was too good and that a disinformation campaign — either deliberately or not — has been in effect since 1959.

Following are some of those items of misinformation that have appeared in history texts and periodicals concerning the Arrow and A. V. Roe. Unfortunately, those in the history texts have done the most damage, for they are often quoted in other sources, giving young Canadians false and misguided impressions of their history and heritage. In a young country where heroes are few, to denigrate those who were legitimate is unconscionable. Only in Canada!

1. *The Arrow was obsolete.* False. The facts speak for themselves. With its fly-by-wire system, internal weapons carriage concept, and Iroquois engine, the Arrow was easily twenty-five years ahead of its time, if not more. Considered a long-range interceptor by the USAF, it met and exceeded its design specifications, a fact acknowledged by the government responsible for its cancellation.

2. *Arrow engineers were guilty of poor design in aerodynamics.* False. This comment, like the opening myth above, was predicated on the

basis of the internal weapons pack. The theory was that extending the weapons pack during supersonic flight would tear the aircraft apart. Yet the weapons pack was never designed to be lowered in flight. Desmond Morton, who propagated this information, has altered his text, *A Military History of Canada*, after an exchange of letters with this author and others. As for the engineers, they were eagerly sought by American and other foreign companies when the programme was cancelled and at least one government official thought they could be a useful bargaining tool in the defence-sharing negotiations.[2]

3. *The aircraft was not Canadian, having been designed by British engineers.* False. This is typical of Canadians unable to accept pride in their achievements. While some engineers did come from Great Britain, they also came from the United States, Poland, and just about every other country, as they do today, and became Canadian citizens. This raises the important question, what constitutes a Canadian? If a Canadian is only one who is born in this country, it is a tremendous slap in the face to the immigrant population. As for those who were born in Canada, this comment about British engineers ignores the contributions of individuals such as Jim Chamberlin, Mario Pesando, Carl Lindow, and the bulk of employees at Avro, Orenda, and the various subcontractors,

not to mention Fred Smye, a nonengineer with a dream. Do the propounders of this myth include Howe, the "minister of everything" who was an American by birth and who emigrated to Canada in his twenties?

4. *The company was mismanaged.* From the technical perspective, the answer is false. In a short period of time, Avro grew into one of the largest companies in Canada, producing aircraft more efficiently than comparable foreign companies, as explained in government documents. In 1957, a communications breakdown between the company and the RCAF did occur. Group Captain Ray Foottit at one point accused the company of mismanagement. In a letter to this author, Ray has explained that before the Arrow, the RCAF was having some difficulties with Avro. By 1957, because of the complexity of the Arrow programme and the numbers of individuals involved, misinformation was being obtained on performance reports. It was thought that perhaps this misinformation was the result of a throwback to the pre-Arrow days, so the RCAF decided to nip the situation in the bud and essentially put the company on notice. Avro responded by requesting central points for coordination of information. After this, Ray reports no further problems. Coupled into this equation, it must be remembered that until 1957, as incredible as it might seem for such an undertaking, there was no dedicated

government project office established for the Arrow. If there was any mismanagement, it certainly was not on the engineering side.

5. *The Arrow had too many technical flaws, including a poor undercarriage.* Two problems occurred with the undercarriage and both were corrected. In a complex development programme such as this, two problems of note represent an excellent track record. Doubters have only to look at the development problems of the F/A-18, B-1 bomber, JAS Grippen, YF-22 advanced tactical fighter, or any other supersonic aircraft development to appreciate the significance. As for other technical flaws, this comment may stem from the doubts put forward by the National Aeronautical Establishment, doubts that were disagreed with not only by the best aeronautical experts in the United States and the United Kingdom, but which were put to rest by the successful flight trials of the aircraft. Pilot Jack Woodman, the only RCAF pilot to fly the Arrow, commented at length on the aircraft's speed and manoeuvrability. In April 1956, the Canadian Armament Research and Development Establishment (CARDE) was given the task of performing an assessment of the Arrow and Astra system. The report was completed in April 1958 and concluded: "a) Targets up to 58,000 feet altitude can be intercepted in co-altitude attacks; b) Targets up to 70,000 feet altitude

can be intercepted in climbing or snap-up attacks."[3] The problem with this report is that it was *not released* until 1961, two years after cancellation. Even then, it was classified secret and is only now being revealed.

6. *The Arrow was too costly.* Arrow costs were decreasing, especially when it was decided to adopt the Hughes Falcon weapons system rather than the ill-fated Astra plus Sparrow combination. This was admitted by the government, as outlined in a lengthy letter from the Chief of the Air Staff to the Minister of National Defence. The cost was on a par with U.S. aircraft, and Canada would be gaining a world-class industry, as well. In fact, once the Arrow was introduced into service, it is likely to have been purchased by other countries, just as the CF-100 and the British Harrier were. This would have driven the cost down even further. A year after cancellation, when the government had to react to a NORAD request for supersonic fighters in Canada, the issue was not one of cost but of national security. In his top-secret brief of July 8, 1958, Minister Pearkes stated that the Arrow cost could be accommodated but not with the SAGE and Bomarc system, as well. Cost was never given as the official reason for the cancellation.

It has also been mentioned that the Navy and Army would have been left without funding for their programmes. While it is true that some concern was expressed, the Army and Navy supported continuation at least until March. It had been suggested that the RCAF was consuming a disproportionate share of the defence budget. This is true, but not because of the Arrow. RCAF expenses also included SAGE, Bomarc, gap-filler radar, coastal marine aircraft, updates to the CF-100, the Sparrow development, and so on.

7. *The aircraft was no good because the Iroquois was untried.* It is true that the Arrow plus Iroquois was an untried combination, but to criticize the programme because of this is most puzzling. Both airframe and engines were meeting design specifications in trials, and the next logical course in the development was to fly them as one unit. To criticize the development because this never was allowed to happen achieves new heights of hypocrisy.

8. *Diefenbaker cancelled the Arrow because of personality clashes with Crawford Gordon.* Based on the evidence, this contention remains difficult to believe, although it is acknowledged that Gordon had sent many strongly worded letters to Diefenbaker during the course of the project.

9. *The United States pressured Canada into cancellation.* Given that the fate of the programme was vested in U.S. hands from the

start, to say that Canada was pressured may be extreme. The United States knew the programme would be terminated if it refused to purchase the aircraft, so the need for overt pressure was undoubtedly small. The United States had everything to gain through the cancellation. It was privy to all the technical breakthroughs and developments and would gain the engineering talent, as well. The U.S. aircraft industry did not have to worry about competition from the north, and the much-valued CIA U-2 spy programme would remain safe and intact because the only aircraft capable of bringing down a U-2 at that time would have been the Arrow. As for the Gary Powers incident, no one could have guessed in 1958–59 that the U-2 would eventually be brought down by a missile in 1960.

10. *Diefenbaker had everything destroyed.* The evidence suggests that Diefenbaker may truly not have known of the order to mutilate the aircraft and all records and documentation, although he was ultimately responsible. The disposal itself was not ordinary, and the RCAF had the opportunity to save what they wanted. They were advised otherwise. A public announcement recorded in *Aviation Week* pointed to security reasons for this destruction, and this has been substantiated by Air Vice Marshall Easton.

11. *The United States would not buy the Arrow.* The USAF was interested, proposing as late as December 1957 that they wanted to purchase Arrows and station them in Canada. Attitudes changed in 1958 when the Arrow proved its worth. It is obvious that U.S. industry would be concerned about competition, but what about the CIA and their spy flights? It seems that from 1958, the USAF was shut out of further negotiations.

12. *All records are now open.* False. The personal records of John Diefenbaker remain closed. This author could find only those not related to defence matters. The personal records of George Pearkes are *nonexistent.* Those of some of the participants in the Cabinet Defence Committee remain closed. Those of Air Marshall Hugh Campbell are not to be found. Several from the Department of Defence Production, on production sharing, remain closed. Files on the Velvet Glove development remain closed. Some files from the National Research Council were destroyed in the eighties, before the rest were released to the public. Archival files on the Jetliner and Project Y were destroyed before they could be released to the public. The Eisenhower Library in Kansas contains the following information, which remains classified, but whose titles are unclassified:

- DDE [Dwight D. Eisenhower], Dulles, Merchant, Diefenbaker, Smith, and Robertson, re review of world situation; NORAD; proposal for joint Cabinet Defense Committee — 7/8/58.
- DDE and Diefenbaker, re U.S.–Canadian governments — 7/8/58.
- DDE, Dulles, Merchant, Diefenbaker, and Canadian cabinet members re U.S.–Canadian relations — 7/9/58.
- Dulles, Merchant, Sidney Smith, Donald Fleming, et al, re economic problems — 7/9/58.
- Dulles, Thompson, Greene, Smith, Pearkes, et al, re Canadian–U.S. Defense Problems — 7/10/58.
- Aide Memoire for Minister of National Defense for Discussions with the U.S. Secretary of State on Canada's Defense Problems — 7/10/58.

13. *One aircraft got away.* Highly unlikely, although many pieces keep turning up. No government records have yet been found acknowledging that the destruction of all aircraft was completed. RL25202 was not on the tarmac, as it was being repaired and fitted with the Hughes and Falcon system at the time of the scrapping. Was it spirited away? Rumour has it that late one evening the entire plant was cordoned off and several covered trucks were seen leaving the premises. If one did es-

cape, it would have to have been done with the knowledge of the Arrow Termination Co-ordination team. Even the pieces and engine on display at the Aviation Museum in Ottawa were released by this group. If it really is in hiding, logical places to look would be Canadian military bases rather than farmers' fields.

14. *The Arrow would not compare against aircraft of today.* Comparing aircraft is difficult at the best of times, since one must look at the operational scenario involved. For example, the F/A-18 engines produce in the order of 11,000 pounds thrust each and 16,000 pounds with afterburner. The Iroquois was rated at 19,500 pounds thrust and 25,600 with afterburner, with a potential for 30,000 pounds thrust each. F/A-18 top speed is on the order of Mach 1.8, and Arrows flew to Mach 1.98 with the less powerful J-75 engines and had power to spare. The F/A-18 is a fly-by-wire aircraft, as was the Arrow. An aircraft that comes closer to the Arrow on specifications alone is the Soviet MIG-31. Its engine thrust outputs and speed are similar. Still, the Arrow's feature of internal weapons carriage is gaining in favour since it reduces aerodynamic drag and radar cross-section, a significant feature in Stealth aircraft design. Would the Arrow compete today? Would new Arrows rolling off the assembly line today compare at all with those of 1959? Is Wayne Gretzky as good as Gordie Howe?

15. *Cancelling the Arrow was a good thing, other-wise we would have had Arrows involved in Vietnam and other world conflicts, and this would not be something to be proud of.* This is more an argument than a myth, but is included here to show the lengths Canadians will go to disparage themselves. This argument has not so much to do with the Arrow as it does with the righteousness of war. It applies equally well to patrol frigates, submarines, and so on. As well, by logical extension, it implies that strafing Iraqi patrol boats and other such acts in war are fine because the aircraft used were and are F/A-18s built in the United States. Unfortunately, this argument, like some of those above, has been proposed by university professors, who by their position and knowledge should be more responsible.

16. *No one wanted the Jetliner.* False. Like the Arrow, the Jetliner was unwanted only in Canada. Howard Hughes was negotiating contracts to get the Jetliner for his airline company, as was Mr. George T. Baker of National Airlines. The U.S. military was interested in purchases for use in training missions. The Jetliner was acknowledged as a milestone in aviation development, hailed as a marvel in the United States, and denigrated in Canada.

17. *The Avro saucer was another Avro failure.* The Avro saucer and the engineering team under

John Frost that built it were completely separate from the core group working on the Arrow.
Frost reported directly to Smye, not Jim Floyd,
because of the nature of the project. In denigrat-
ing Avro as a whole, the saucer is often mentioned as another example of the poor talent
and fanciful ideas of the overall engineering
team. But is even this criticism founded?

In 1953, the USAF contracted Avro to build a circular wing air-cushion vehicle for the demonstra-
tion of vertical takeoff principles. Known as the
Avrocar, it did just that, hovering a few feet off the
ground. To describe this concept, Avro produced
several brochures that spoke of Avrocars, trucks
and the like, each with the circular wing. In addition, Avro was contracted to build Project Y, a supersonic flying disc. A CIA memorandum from the
Applied Science Division, Office of Scientific Intelligence, CIA, and dated October 19, 1955, states:

The present study calls for a circular wing 30 ft
in diameter and about 1.1 ft thick. Its performance is to be as follows:

Speed M (Mach) — 3
Rate of climb — 120,000 ft min
Ceiling — 102,000 ft
Range — 700 n.m.

The present effort consists of wind-tunnel testing sponsored to the extent of $800,000 by the

U.S. Air Force. . . . Project "Y" is being directed by John Frost.[4]

In 1961, USAF funding ceased. Information from the United States suggests that the project may have gone underground, perhaps into the "skunk works" that built the U-2, SR-71, and Stealth aircraft. Files from the United States on the supersonic saucer remain classified. Was it really a failure or has work been ongoing?

18. *The Iroquois engine did not have enough thrust to power the aircraft.* False. This gem was put forth on a radio talk show early in 1991. Here again the facts speak for themselves — demonstrated static runs of over 20,000 pounds thrust from an engine rated at 19,500! It was said the B-47 aircraft used in the flight testing of the Iroquois suffered severe fuselage damage from the power of the engine trying to wrench itself free.

After cancellation, it was as if the spirit of the nation had been broken, just as had been predicted by some of the politicians. It was decided that Canada simply did not have the talent, the population base, the resources, and the will to embark on major programmes. The blow to national prestige was great. As a result, some of the best people, not just in the scientific fields but in the arts, as well, were lost to the United States and elsewhere. Kay Shaw's book, *There Never Was an Arrow*, is full of examples of people and ideas who have since abandoned this country in order to have their ideas developed elsewhere. As well, by cancelling the Arrow, Canada suffered a blow to her high-technology research and development base from which industry is still recovering. Unfortunately, the value of research does not appear to be appreciated in this country as it is in others — witness the cutbacks at the National Research Council and universities.

Contrary to the title of the Shaw book, though, there definitely was an Arrow. It is time for Canadians to recognize this fact and march ahead with confidence. It is time to wake up and rechallenge the world.

EPILOGUE

As the Space Task Group's burden was threatening to
overwhelm it, the Canadian government unintentionally
gave the American space programme its luckiest
break. . . . The Canadians never gained much public
recognition for their contribution to the manned space
program, but to the people within the program their
contribution was incalculable. . . . They had it all over
us, in many areas . . . just brilliant guys. . . . They
were more mature and they were bright as hell and
talented and professional, to a man.
                    Apollo: The Race to the Moon[1]

B Y 1958, CANADA HAD a thriving aviation industry,
acknowledged to be among the best in the
world. The Avro and Orenda teams at Malton included top engineering and manufacturing personnel from many countries in addition to the
predominantly Canadian staff. The "foreigners"
had emigrated to Canada specifically to join in the
state-of-the-art work going on at Malton and to become members of the talented team producing
world-class aircraft and engines.

After the cancellation, this influx of brain power
reversed; and the teams that had been dedicated to
putting Canada on the map as the best in the world
were scattered all over the globe in a massive brain

drain. Many of the engineers went into jobs at the leading edge of technology in other countries, but their unique capability as a tightly integrated team was lost forever. Avro was not just a faceless industry. It had become a multicultural family in the best of Canadian tradition wherein engineers, technicians, mathematicians, secretaries, and the like all worked together as a team for their belief in the project.

Jim Floyd, the vice president and director of engineering at Avro and the man ultimately responsible for all technical decisions (his hair turned from brown to snow-white during the Arrow project), received a number of lucrative job offers in the United States, but instead accepted a position as chief engineer of an Advanced Projects Group at Hawker-Siddeley Aviation in England. His group, which included a number of ex-Avro Canada engineers, carried out feasibility studies on the U.K. supersonic transport, which later evolved into the Concorde, and was also involved in in-depth studies on high-technology military projects and space technology, including orbital and horizontal take-off space vehicles.

After Floyd left Hawker-Siddeley Aviation to set up his own consulting practice, he carried out major studies for government and industry in the United Kingdom and was retained by the British Ministry of Technology as consultant on the Concorde during the eight years of early development of that project. He was awarded the Royal Aeronautical Society's George Taylor Gold Medal for his work on the subject of supersonic flight and its problems. On his retirement in 1980, after fifty years in the aviation industry, Floyd and his family came back home to Canada. The supersonic Concorde, which still flies after more than ten years of service, beat the American supersonic transport (SST) to the air. The SST would later be abandoned as a nonviable project.

Bob Lindley, the dynamic chief engineer at Avro, went to work for McDonnell Aircraft in St. Louis and was put in charge of engineering on the work that McDonnell was doing on the Gemini space programme for NASA. Lindley later joined NASA on the shuttle programme, becoming director of engineering and operations for manned space flight. In 1972, he was appointed director of project management at the Goddard Space Flight Center and later went to Europe as consultant on the European Space Agency development of "Spacelab."

Jim Chamberlin, the chief of design at Avro Canada and the man described by Jim Floyd as the genius behind the remarkable flying characteristics of the Arrow — the "best technical man I have ever worked with" — went to NASA with twenty-five of the ex-Avro engineers. Chamberlin was vital to much of NASA's space technology. In charge of engineering and contractual administration on the Mercury project, he headed a staff of 160 and played a major role in the design of the capsule used by John Glenn. As head of the U.S. Space Task Group's engineering division, he directed the $500 million project Gemini and became deeply involved in project Apollo, which put the first man on the moon.

Chamberlin received the NASA Gold Medal for his work on Gemini and was described by one of NASA's managers as "probably one of the most brilliant men ever to work with NASA." This extraordinarily talented man, although a native of Kamloops, British Columbia, never returned to work in Canada. At the time of his death in 1981, he was technical director for McDonnell at the Johnson Space Center in Houston.

Many of the other Avro engineers who went to NASA with Chamberlin also made their mark: John Hodges became flight director on the Gemini and Apollo programs; Fred Matthews became backup flight director to Chris Kraft; Tex Roberts was in charge of the trajectory group in the mission control centre; and all the others played major roles in the U.S. space programmes.

Mario Pesando, the chief of project research at Avro, went to RCA in Massachusetts to work on their space programmes and was subsequently placed in charge of a group working on the NASA Saturn V project to launch the astronauts to the moon. He eventually became the senior engineering scientist, involved in studies on the control of night flying and electronic jamming systems for military aircraft. In 1971, Pesando returned to Canada to work for DAF Indal as programme manager on a unique helicopter recovery system for small ships. He retired as director for new products in 1984.

The Boeing Aircraft Company in Seattle bene-
fitted greatly from the Arrow cancellation, with
many ex-Avro engineers finishing up in that company. Two of the senior engineers from the Arrow
programme went to Boeing and made widespread
contributions to both their civil and military
programmes.

Carl Lindow, the project manager on the Arrow,
was project engineer on the Boeing Saturn S-1 and
S-1B proposals and development programme manager on the Boeing studies for advanced space
launch systems, the aerospace plane, and nuclear
propulsion systems. In 1967, he was appointed
manager of intermediate-range aircraft design in the
commercial airplane division of Boeing, communi-
cating with their potential customers. Later he became systems integration manager for Boeing's
military and space programmes.

Frank Brame, who was chief of technical design
on the Arrow, was at Boeing for over twenty-seven
years. Among his many roles during that time
were supervisor of design studies on the 737; chief
project engineer on systems and avionics on the
Boeing SST proposals; project engineer on systems
and flight deck design on the 767 and other 7X7
series aircraft; and prior to his retirement in 1988
he was programme manager on the renewed Boeing SST studies.

John Morris, the chief of aerodynamics at
Avro, went to work with Floyd at the Hawker-
Siddeley Aviation Advanced Projects Group in the
United Kingdom. His work there on the cause and

implications of the sonic boom, outlined in a paper that he presented to the Royal Aeronautical Society, was acknowledged worldwide to be a milestone in supersonic research. He later went to McDonnell Douglas in charge of work on the DC-10 and is still there as director of advanced engineering.

And so the story of the ex-Avro engineers goes on . . . ad infinitum. Many of the key engineers from Avro were recognized as among the best in the business, readily snapped up by the United States, the United Kingdom, and other countries. For instance, Alan Buley, who was project designer on the Arrow Mark 2, went to Fokker Aviation in Holland, where he became vice president of sales and later managing director of Fokker International.

Rolf Marshall, transport research engineer at Avro, joined the New York Port Authority in their research and development operations as engineer in charge of equipment and systems research, working on novel transportation systems, including hydrofoil, catamaran, and air-cushion concepts. Among many other projects, his group was involved in in-depth studies on airport facilities, passenger control, and air-cargo operations, also satellite communication terminals and other facilities for a world trade centre.

Fred Mitchell, project designer on Arrow Mark 1, became president of Orenda Engines and was involved in the development of gas turbine engines for industrial use. He later joined the Matthews construction group as president and CEO. Prior to his retirement, he was vice chairman and chief executive officer.

Jack Ames, chief of product design, stayed with the greatly reduced Avro team, trying to bring together the pieces out of the ashes of the Arrow massacre. He became general manager of Avro and was the man who handed over the keys of the Malton plant to de Havilland Canada when they took over the facility in mid-1962. After a period as general manager of Canadian Steel Improvement and later general manager of Hawker-Siddeley in Nova Scotia, he finally became general manager of Ingersoll-Rand in Sherbrooke until his retirement in 1981.

Few Canadians are aware of the major contributions made in almost every field of aviation and space technology by the extraordinarily talented team of engineers at Malton, who found themselves rejected in their own country.

Back at Avro, the remaining 200 employees continued work on various projects, including Project Y, the circular-wing, vertical takeoff vehicle, or flying saucer, for the USAF. Then, in 1962, Avro closed its doors, leaving a legacy of concepts and ideas, including a vertical takeoff CF-100 (a forerunner to the British vertical takeoff Harrier?), a supersonic transatlantic transport (like the Concorde?), a space plane concept, a monorail, an anti-tank missile, satellites, and numerous others, testimony to the advanced thinking of one of the best engineering design teams ever assembled.[2]

Fanciful ideas? Ludicrous concepts? Hardly! For developments and breakthroughs to occur, ideas are required. The ability to think freely without constraint is essential. From there, the goals are established, followed by the necessary studies to determine the feasibility of achievement. Even if Avro determined that the costs of implementing their concepts would be too high, the possibilities of teaming up with European if not American industry would have been there. True, Canadian companies have started to make inroads and regain some of that lost prestige, but it has been a long and heavily travelled road.

Why was Avro so technically successful with the Arrow? The answer may be very simple. They were never told they were not supposed to be able to do it!

POSTSCRIPT

. . . in fact, any defence of Canadian territory is but a by-product or extra dividend to the main purpose, which is the defence of SAC bases and Northeastern United States.

Top-secret memorandum from Lieutenant-General
H. D. Graham to General Foulkes, August 21, 1958

SINCE THE ORIGINAL PUBLICATION of this book, I have continued my research in the hope of obtaining additional information concerning the demise of the Arrow. New material has indeed come to light on a number of the subjects I dealt with, including what is perhaps the "smoking gun" in the Arrow debacle.

For example, in searching through the National Archives, I found a previously undiscovered cache of files on the C-102 Jetliner. I am indebted to archivist Carl Vincent for placing them in some semblance of order for examination. The files, left by Jas T. Bain, cover the development of the Jetliner but unfortunately end in 1949, just prior to the first flight. Still, there is a noteworthy letter by Bain, then Director Engineering and Maintenance, Trans-Canada Airlines (TCA). He is writing to W. F.

English, Vice-President Operations, TCA Winnipeg. The letter is dated Montreal, May 2, 1949:

> ... Further to my memo this date in regard to the experimental operation of the C-102, I can bring you up-to-date on my last talk to the Avro Company during a recent visit ... It was interesting to see the evidence of *interest shown by most of the major airlines on this continent.* In particular, *Eastern Air Lines are serious* enough in their discussions that the second prototype will be built with the double slotted flap which will meet Eastern's low landing speed requirement. *A physical examination of the aircraft showed a quality of workmanship which I have never seen surpassed on a prototype aircraft nor indeed by many production aircraft.* Taken by and large, *the skinning and metal work is beautiful and far surpasses the quality achieved by Canadair in production North Stars.* They appear also to have left very few ends untied and even in the prototype *the general equipment installation design shows enough care and foresight to make the C-102 a really modern aircraft incorporating the best of present installation knowledge.*[1] (Italics added)

Within months of the writing of this letter, the Jetliner lived up to and surpassed all expectations with its prolonged maiden flight. It is hard to believe that after receiving such praise from the customer's own specialist and after that successful first flight,

The Arrow truly looked like it had flown in from the future. (DEPARTMENT OF NATIONAL DEFENCE)

Jan Zurakowski *(Second from Left)* is congratulated after the successful first flight. (DEPARTMENT OF NATIONAL DEFENCE)

Four Arrows await destruction with a fifth already in partial disassembly. Note second Arrow from top left with CF-100 in front. (AVIATION MUSEUM)

The second Arrow from the top has disappeared, along with its CF-100. Did it escape destruction? (HERB NOTT/*WEEKEND MAGAZINE*)

This photo of the destruction appeared several months after the cancellation.
(Aviation Museum)

Because of its increased thrust, the Iroquois engine bent and distorted the fuselage
of the test aircraft it was mounted on. (Orenda Engines Ltd.)

The Arrow prepares for its flight into history. (Jim Floyd)

What should have been. (Department of National Defence)

the Jetliner was not allowed to go into production by C. D. Howe. Instead, all work was ordered stopped, allegedly to concentrate efforts on the CF-100 production. Was this the real reason behind the Jetliner cancellation, or was there a more sinister influence involved? One can only hope that additional files like those of Bain will be forthcoming. There is one certainty, though: they will not come from the C. D. Howe collection. On more than one occasion I have been advised by archival staff that in the early sixties, many of the Howe files surrounding the Jetliner episode disappeared.

Not only was the Jetliner a success story of quality and workmanship, but so was Avro itself. In response to cries that it was an inept and poorly run company, I cited numerous documents showing otherwise. Here are two more to confirm the fact. On December 9, 1953, Frank Rackley, President of the Jessop Steel Company, wrote to Crawford Gordon:

> . . . I have been through quite a few similar operations and, while every industrial facility has its own assets and liabilities, I think when the score is totalled A. V. Roe is way out in front. I speak of such things as plant maintenance, production flow lines, general layout, employee morale and quality of workmanship . . . I did want to write . . . to extend my sincere compliments to you and your staff on your operation . . . it makes me feel real good to see our products going into an end product such as yours.[2]

The above letter was unsolicited, as was this one from General O. P. Weyland, United States Air Force. After touring the plant facilities, he wrote the following to Crawford Gordon on August 26, 1954:

> . . . These facilities are as modern and well organized as any I have ever seen, and additionally you appear to have more expansibility than many of our U.S. concerns. *Geographically we are all American* and share the same security problems, so *I am more than happy that your capability is additive to that of U.S. industry* . . .[3] (Italics added)

Avro was not only first-rate but was better than its giant U.S. counterparts. The reference to all being American and the relief expressed in the last statement, that it was a good thing Avro was on the good guys' side, may have been prophetic in terms of the eventual cancellation of the Arrow. After the Arrow proved itself in flight trials, perhaps Avro was seen as being too good, too big, and too powerful.

With regard to the Arrow itself, I received a copy of a report dated June 10, 1957. It is titled "Reconnaissance Arrow Drag and Power Summary." This report presents the design for a reconnaissance version of the Arrow. It shows a Mach 2.5 Arrow with canards and ramjet pods on its wingtips. The report concludes with the following: "The indications . . . are that a M=2.5, 90,000' altitude Reconnaissance Arrow is feasible within the present state of the art." From the profile shown and the specifications given, it could not be much closer to the SR-71

Blackbird design, whose prototypes went onto the drawing boards seven months after the Arrow's cancellation. As for the ramjets, *Jane's Defense Weekly* of May 29, 1996, reported that General Dynamics Convair had on its books a ramjet-assisted aircraft that had been proposed to the CIA in the late fifties or early sixties. The files on that proposal remain classified but it would be surprising if the Avro report never made its way to Convair. A second report I received shows proposals for long-range versions of the Arrow with Mach 3 performance.

Motive, opportunity, method. These are three essential elements which must be established during the course of police investigations into crimes. In many ways, the demise of the Arrow has been likened to a capital offence in which the perpetrators have never been truly identified. When *Storms of Controversy* first came out, I revealed the existence and contents of numerous documents which, in effect, pointed the finger at the United States as the prime suspect with then Defence Minister George R. Pearkes and Chairman Chiefs of Staff Charles Foulkes, along with a gaggle of others, as willing or coerced accomplices. Prime Minister John George Diefenbaker, the principal suspect for over thirty-five years, was, on the other hand, partly exonerated. I now wish to introduce new evidence that has been discovered, including the "smoking gun," with fingerprints.

As a brief recap, the Arrow development was begun in earnest in 1953, in response to a Royal

Canadian Air Force requirement for a new, supersonic interceptor. In fact, the existence of this
not-so-secret project was first announced by the
Globe and Mail, on January 3, 1952. Crawford
Gordon Junior, President of A. V. Roe, issued a
complete and immediate denial, noting that it was
up to the RCAF to make such announcements and
not the media, ". . . even if there was good basis for
the story."[4]

By 1954, Avro had become embroiled in heated
technical debates with the National Aeronautical
Establishment (NAE), an arm of the National
Research Council, which began acting as watchdog
over the project. The NAE fiercely questioned the
technical capabilities of Avro and of the Arrow
itself. According to the NAE, the Arrow would fall
far short of the specifications and perhaps even
break apart in flight. The RCAF was forced to
approach an independent arbiter, the National
Advisory Committee for Aeronautics (NACA), forerunner to NASA. It has been said by those present at
the time that the reason the NAE went after Avro
was simply that individuals within the NAE felt
industry was no place for the kind of research and
development required for the Arrow.

With Avro absent from the meeting, NACA
agreed that on the basis of the presentation from
the NAE, the Arrow had serious problems.
Undoubtedly upset by this finding, the RCAF gave
Avro a chance to respond. A second meeting with
NACA was held and Avro personnel provided their
reasoning and logic. All of the problems raised by

the NAE were addressed and in every case NACA agreed with Avro's responses. Needless to say, the NAE did not come out looking very astute.

The rivalry between Avro and the NAE was solidified, however, and may even have been a contributing factor to developments in February 1959, when the NAE was offered but turned down an Arrow for research. Had it been accepted, at least one Arrow would definitely have been saved. Still, that such an offer was even made to the NAE at the time of cancellation had never been made public before publication of *Storms*. The significance is that through its silence the NAE helped propagate the myth that all the aircraft were immediately ordered destroyed by the Prime Minister as an act of vengeance. In fact, although legitimate reasons may have been given for not accepting the aircraft, it was the NAE that sat idly by watching the Arrow die. Had the destruction order come from Diefenbaker, an Arrow would never have been offered to the NAE under any circumstances.

By November 1955, the RCAF was once again at the doorstep of the United States. This time, however, they were asking the USAF flat out whether, if the Americans were in the RCAF's shoes, they would continue or abandon the programme. The answer that came back from the USAF was that Canada should continue the programme. By now, it was clear who was actually in control. The Arrow would exist as long as the Americans wanted or needed it to. This last comment is in reference to the fact that during the development, Avro was repeatedly asked by the USAF if and how the performance of the aircraft could be enhanced. This leaves one to wonder whether Avro wasn't in fact naively solving technical problems being encountered by U.S. aircraft manufacturers. One thing is certain: the technical advances that Avro was making were benefitting all aircraft companies privy to the information, including those in Europe and Eastern bloc countries who were getting the information through covert means. While on a train trip, I was surprised by a retired German colonel I occasioned to meet. Not only did he know about the Arrow, but he told me that during its development it was the subject of monthly technical briefings in the German Air Force.

By 1958, after the Arrow's successful maiden flight, the USAF, which previously had expressed tremendous interest in the aircraft, began backing off. In fact, by July 1958, the U.S. and Canada signed the Defence Production Sharing Arrangements, wherein Canada agreed to accept the Bomarc missile as part of the continental defence strategy. At that July meeting, Canada tried to sell the Arrow to the Americans, noting that while we could afford to continue the development ourselves, we could not do so if we now also had to purchase the Bomarc. Actually, Canada did not have to purchase the Bomarc, as it was purely an American defence requirement solely for protection of the American Strategic Air Command bases and of the United States itself. Nevertheless, Canada succumbed and the Arrow's fate was effectively placed in American hands. Thus, by pressing for the Bomarc and refusing to buy into the Arrow programme, the U.S. had both opportunity and method.

What was the Americans' motive? There were several, including pressure from U.S. companies and a significant concern that the Arrow plans and manufacturing secrets were indeed falling into the wrong hands. I speculated that the CIA would have been particularly perturbed by that eventuality, as an Arrow in the wrong hands would destroy their secret U-2 spy operations and perhaps even turn the tables. John Foster Dulles, U.S. Secretary of State and one of those who advised Canada that the U.S. would not purchase the Arrow, was brother to Allen Dulles, head of the CIA.

One additional motive I did not discuss previously was linked directly to keeping Bomarc alive. By being able to advise Congress that another country was interested in Bomarc, the USAF would not only get more funding for that programme but would win an internal struggle with the U.S. Army for overall continental defence protection and, in particular, protection of the American Strategic Air Command.

That the United States was at the heart of the Arrow cancellation is evidenced in the now declassified "Top Secret minutes of the Canada-United States Ministerial Committee on Joint Defence," which met in Montebello on July 12 and 13, 1960. Discussion covered a range of topics, from nuclear weapons storage to the failing Defence Production

Sharing Arrangements to the acquisition and need for American F-101 Voodoos to fill the gap left by the Arrow cancellation. The following exchange sheds light on the Arrow termination:

Mr. Gates [Thomas S. Gates Jr., Secretary of Defense] then referred to the aircraft deal again, sixty-six F101s for one hundred and five million versus thirty-five transports for one hundred and fifty million; . . . He said that if you [Canada] want to modernize your forces and contribute to continental defence, *this is the decision to be made*; that they [United States] were under *considerable pressure from the aircraft industry* and they could buy air transports from Boeing much more cheaply . . . Mr. Green [Howard C. Green, Canadian Secretary of State for External Affairs] stated *they were told two years ago that the manned bomber was on its way out and that is why they cancelled the Arrow. Now they have to go back and say that both are still needed.* Mr. Fleming [Donald M. Fleming, Canadian Minister of Finance] referred to the fact that they *tried to interest the Americans in buying the Arrow at the Paris Conference but had been turned down flat by Mr. McElroy.* Mr Pearkes . . . said *we did not cancel the CF105 because there was no bomber threat but because there was a lesser threat and we got the Bomarc* in lieu of more airplanes to look after this. Now he said perhaps *the expectation of two years ago that the bomber threat was lessening has not been fulfilled.* At the same time he said *we expected Bomarcs to cover the whole country. These had been reduced*, and therefore some more protection to the western part must be made in those areas which were to be protected by Bomarc. *It wasn't fair, he said, for Canada to fill this western gap which had been created by the Americans all by themselves . . .*[5] (Italics added)

Imagine Secretary Gates telling the Canadians that if they wanted to modernize their forces and contribute to continental defence, they should purchase the obsolete Voodoo! Where was this requirement a year and a half earlier, when the Arrow could have not only modernized but revolutionized continental defence? Finally, but much too late, Pearkes and company realized the mistake in cancelling the Arrow. More importantly, it was realized that the Americans had in fact orchestrated the whole bomber/Bomarc scenario for their own purposes and were once again dictating the decision Canada should make regarding aircraft. Most pathetic is the lament from Pearkes that *it wasn't fair*. It never is! It should be noted that Minister of Finance Donald Fleming was at this meeting and neither he nor anyone else in the Canadian delegation made any mention that the cancellation of the Arrow had anything to do with cost.

How did Canada allow itself to get into this situation? Several factors have been detailed in *Storms*, not the least of which centred around the

influence of Charles Foulkes, Chairman Chiefs of
Staff. I have pointed out that it was General
Charles Foulkes who did not listen to his Chief of
the Air Staff, Air Marshall Hugh Campbell. While
Campbell was insisting on the need for the Arrow
or an aircraft just like it, Foulkes ignored him and
advised the Diefenbaker government that the
military had no requirement for the Arrow. Both
Foulkes and Pearkes had been sold on the virtues
of Bomarc and the potential benefits, which never
materialized, from the Defence Production
Sharing Arrangements. I pointed out how Pearkes
was threatened with the installation of nuclear-
tipped Bomarcs just south of the Great Lakes,
should the missiles not be purchased by Canada
and placed on Canadian soil. The threat of nuclear
devastation over southern Ontario might have
been enough to bring Pearkes on side, but what
about Foulkes?

In *The Generals*, Jack Granatstein provides
a significant clue. He notes that General Guy
Simonds, a contemporary of Foulkes, although
praised for his abilities to command, ". . . preferred
to keep Canada close to British standards and
methods . . . That was a fault in American eyes."[6]
The Americans regarded Foulkes, though, as

> . . . pleasant but unimpressive, restrained and
> thin-skinned. He is not a forceful leader nor is he
> endowed with any great brains. He appears to
> think highly of US military leaders and enjoys
> associating with them. In dealing with him a

little flattery and personal attention on a "first name" basis would be helpful!⁷

Granatstein adds that Foulkes went on ". . . and masterminded the scrapping of the Avro Arrow,"⁸ only to retire in 1960. This raises two interesting questions. First, if the Arrow was costing too much, why would anyone have to "mastermind" its cancellation? Second, if he did, why? In fact, if he was as obtuse as the Americans surmised, how could he mastermind anything without help? Charles Foulkes would have made the perfect American puppet in the Arrow story. Were his strings being pulled, Canadian defence requirements and the fate of the Arrow would be placed squarely in American hands. But is there any solid evidence of this?

Lending credence to the questionable actions of Foulkes and those of the Americans is the following declassified Top Secret memo addressed to Foulkes. Written by Lieutenant-General H.D. Graham, Chief of the General Staff, on August 21, 1958, it says:

Reference your "Report on the Development of the CF105 and Associated Weapon System 1952–1958" dated 19 Aug 58 . . . one is left with the impression that our air defence plan is designed for the defence of Canada. My understanding is that *our air defence plan is not for "the Defence of Canada"* . . . *I think it is wrong to leave the impression with the Minister and the Government* that our air defence plan is primarily for the

defence of Canadian territory when, in fact, *any
defence of Canadian territory is but a by-product
or extra dividend to the main purpose, which is
the defence of SAC bases and Northeastern
United States.*[9] (Italics added)

This is exactly what I had concluded. Now it
turns out that someone had actually put it in
writing in 1958.

Now for the smoking gun and fingerprints. In
the meeting of September 21, 1958, Cabinet had
approved the installation of Bomarc missiles. Its
members also agreed that the Arrow programme
should be reviewed in March 1959 and that the
Chiefs of Staff should investigate and report on any
requirements for further missile installations or for
aircraft "of the nature of the CF-105 or alternative
types." Interestingly, in November 1958, Air
Marshall Roy Slemon, stationed at NORAD headquarters in Colorado, had stated that interceptors
would be required for years to come. Diefenbaker
rebuked Slemon for this comment because it was
in effect pre-empting the Chiefs of Staff investigation on the matter and was therefore not yet
government policy. Also, both Foulkes and Pearkes
were recommending abandoning the programme
even though Chief of the Air Staff Campbell was
asserting that at least 100 aircraft comparable in
performance to the Arrow (if not Arrows) would be
required. Why was there a split, with Slemon and
Campbell both saying yes to aircraft and Pearkes
and Foulkes saying no?

In his own words, Foulkes provides the answer. Writing (appropriately enough) on December 24, 1958, Foulkes gave this gift, the "smoking gun," to the people of Canada, entitled "Progress Report on the Implementation of the Decisions in Regard to Air Defence Taken by Cabinet on 21 September, 1958":

With regard to the Cabinet Decision (e), that the Chiefs of Staff should investigate and report on requirements, if any, for additional air defence missile installations in Canada and for an interceptor aircraft of the nature of the CF105 or alternative types; the Chiefs of Staff have this matter under active study but *wish to defer making any recommendations until they have had an opportunity to study the plans of the Commander-in-Chief, North American Air Defence Command.* It is expected that the Commander-in-Chief, North American Air Defence Command, will be presenting his revised plans to the Canadian Chiefs of Staff in January. *After the Chiefs of Staff have an opportunity of carefully studying these plans, they will be prepared to make recommendations for any* additional air defence missile installations or for *interceptor aircraft of the nature of the CF105 or alternative types.*[10] (Italics added)

So it *was* the United States. It seems that Charles Foulkes was waiting for his orders. So it didn't matter a damn what the Chief of the Air Staff recommended and it didn't matter a damn what Roy Slemon, as second in command at NORAD, or anyone else in Canada for that matter, had to say. What mattered was only what the Commander-in-Chief of NORAD and the United States wanted, and so, the Arrow was cancelled. The chain was complete: Diefenbaker was being advised by Pearkes, who in turn was being advised by Foulkes, who in turn was following the agenda of the Americans. This explains why Hugh Campbell had been ignored and Slemon had been rebuked for having opposing views.

Is there any evidence that CINCNORAD did provide the anticipated information? Yes. First, two plans had indeed been submitted in December 1958, by CINCNORAD, to the Canadians. These were the North American Air Defense Objectives Plan 1959–1963 and the NORAD Air Defense Objectives 1959–1969, five- and ten-year plans respectively. Both plans remain classified, but some idea of what they contained, and of subsequent information provided in January 1959, may be gleaned from statements made shortly before and after the Arrow's cancellation.

At the Cabinet meeting of January 13, 1959, Pearkes advised his colleagues that the U.S. had 800 interceptors in service and enough funds to purchase another 650. As well, they had cancelled their F-106C and F-106D programmes in favour of the development of the long-range F-108 project. He noted that another 100 aircraft from Canada would make a minor contribution. In answer to questions, he stated that the Bomarc would provide a cheaper means of defence but that *Canada could rely on the United States for interceptor defence if required*.

At the meeting of February 4, Pearkes recommended that development of the Arrow be discontinued. He also advised that the Chiefs of Staff were studying the possibility of having American Bomarc squadrons moved to Western Canada. If the manned bomber threat was diminishing, it would be preferable to go with the missile system rather than interceptors; besides, terms of the NORAD agreement allowed for the temporary stationing of U.S. aircraft squadrons at Canadian airfields, should the need for interceptors arise. The following day, at a meeting of the Cabinet Defence Committee, it was learned that NORAD had advised that it might be possible to reposition two American Bomarc bases to Calgary and Swift Current. (The subsequent demise of this prospect is what may have prompted Pearkes to utter his lament in 1960 that the Americans had created a gap in protection of the West and were now expecting Canada to fill that gap by purchasing Voodoo aircraft.)

At the Cabinet meeting of February 10, it was pointed out that if the Arrow were cancelled, the U.S. would be defending Canada. The counterargument was that this was not true since Canadians would be manning the Bomarc bases and the related radar network.

At the meeting of February 23, the Cabinet was discussing damage control, i.e., how to counter any arguments that they should not have terminated the Arrow programme:

> . . . In defending the decision it could be said that it had been taken in the light of the best military advice available, and that the cost of the Bomarc, which was to perform the same role as the Arrow, was very much less than that of the Arrow . . .[11]

Presumably the best military advice was that from CINCNORAD. The wording of the discussion on the cost of the Bomarc is most interesting. It is true that the cost of the Bomarc was less, but why did they not elaborate on the alleged exorbitant cost of the Arrow? Why did they not say that continuing the Arrow would bankrupt the Army and the Navy and perhaps the country? The answer: because none of that was true, and they could easily have been challenged on that score.

Cabinet also tried addressing the question of new work to replace the Arrow programme. It seems there had been prospects about Canadair receiving a large U.S. contract:

> . . . but, unfortunately, this seemed to be less and less hopeful *in view of the pressure from the aircraft industry in the U.S.*[12] (Italics added)

So much for defence sharing.

Finally, the following gem is recorded:

. . . As regards the point that cancellation would mean that Canada would be still further under the wing of the U.S., it should be remembered that maintaining freedom from U.S. control was a continuous struggle. It might appear that the present decision was a retrograde step. But there would be other opportunities to assert Canadian sovereignty and independence . . . It would be unwise to blame the U.S. for the outcome of the Arrow contract.[13]

If maintaining freedom was such a struggle, why make it even harder by cancelling the Arrow? What other opportunities would there be to assert sovereignty? Crying on bended knee? The last statement is the final affront but bears some truth. While the U.S. provided the means, we willingly put our heads in the noose and kicked over the chair.

Astonishingly, less than a year after the cancellation, General Laurence Kuter, Commander-in-Chief of NORAD, was telling the RCAF that nine CF-100 squadrons should be replaced with six squadrons equipped with the Voodoo. At the Cabinet meeting of February 1960, Diefenbaker was beside himself on hearing this news, noting that he had been against cancelling the Arrow but had been persuaded otherwise.

Method, opportunity, motive, and accomplices; and so, the prosecution rests.

Did Diefenbaker want all memory of the Arrow destroyed? No. No such orders were ever given, for if they had been, the offer of an Arrow to the NAE/ NRC would never have been made. As well, the cockpit section of RL 206, which ended up at the Defence and Civil Institute of Environmental Medicine in Toronto, would never have been sent there. In fact, as the documents show, Pearkes would not have asked for a recommendation of what to do with the completed aircraft; he would have simply told the RCAF in no uncertain terms. Not only were orders not given to destroy photographs, but at least one memo on file shows that photographs of the aircraft would be allowed, after sensitive materials were removed. What was not allowed were photographs of the actual destruction.

Did one get away?

Unfortunately, no hard evidence has yet surfaced to suggest that one aircraft survived, but there are ongoing efforts to retrieve the eight-foot models in Lake Ontario. By the same token, there is little to suggest that all the aircraft were indeed destroyed. Proponents of the latter alternative point to the famous photographs taken of the destruction on the tarmac. These photos were taken in late June, 1959, by photographer Herb Nott and appeared in the August issue of *Weekend Magazine*.

Mr. Nott has informed me that, contrary to the published story, he did not rent a helicopter to overfly the restricted area of the tarmac at Malton. Rather, he rented a small aircraft from Toronto Island airport and made some five or six circuits before being told to get out by air traffic control.

The entire operation took on the order of fifteen or twenty minutes, during which time six photos were shot. It has since been taken for granted that the photos show all five aircraft being destroyed. But do they?

A photograph taken overhead and slightly in back of the Avro hangar and tarmac does show four aircraft awaiting destruction with a fifth already partially taken apart. A second photo shows four aircraft with debris to one side of the Arrow closest to the camera. This debris supposedly belongs to the fifth aircraft. However, if one looks at the overhead shot again, starting from the top of the picture is an Arrow, an oil drum, another Arrow, a CF-100 in front of this Arrow, and then the other three Arrows. In the second photo, starting from the furthest point from the camera, there is an Arrow, the same oil drum, an empty space where an Arrow should be, and then the other three, with the debris in the foreground. What happened to the Arrow that had the CF-100 in front of it?

Herb Nott does not recall seeing any aircraft being moved or any debris being disposed of. Given the size of the Arrow, there is no way it could be made to disappear in fifteen or twenty minutes. Such an act would rival those of magician David Copperfield. The suggestion is that the overhead photo was taken by someone other than Nott, at some point in time long before Nott made his flight. The removal of at least one aircraft would be consistent with the order to keep two of the best aircraft intact while it was determined if the NAE or

the British were interested in acquiring them. RL
202 would be a logical choice since it was or had
been fitted with the Hughes/Falcon missile system. The question, then, is not so much whether
one aircraft was moved but when it was moved and
to what location. Might it yet exist?

Group Captain Abe Lieff, the individual responsible for disposition, was contacted but does not
recall any specific effort to save one aircraft and
believes all were destroyed. Destruction was carried out by crews from Lax Brothers in Hamilton
and the resulting scrap sold through the Crown
Assets Disposal Corporation. In going through the
Crown Assets' records, one would expect to find
copies of invoices to verify the amount of scrap
sold and the money recouped. This would enable
a determination of how many aircraft or aircraft
parts were involved. Certainly, such records exist
and are available for other disposed-of equipment,
in the minutest of detail. Not so when one tries to
locate the records on the Arrow.

If anyone knows who took the photo showing
the five aircraft or if anyone has firsthand knowledge of what may have happened, the time to come
forward is now!

Several issues continue to be raised on the Arrow.
Following is a capsulized response to some of these
issues, as answered by the records themselves.
(Note: RG means Records Group and usually pre-
cedes files from the National Archives.)

(a) The Arrow costs were astronomical.

Arrow costs compare favourably with the somewhat less sophisticated aircraft in the USA . . .[14]

If this [Arrow] were the only requirement for
our air defence, we could perhaps make provision
for it in our succeeding defence budgets . . .[15]

The Minister of Finance said that in considering
matters of defence he naturally put the safety of
the country ahead of finance. When it had been
recommended a year ago that the CF-105 programme be continued, he supported the recommendation. Now, however, the military view
was that the programme should be cancelled. In
these circumstances, he did not see how the government could decide not to discontinue it.[16]

The Minister has forwarded to me a copy of
a letter he received from Mr. Fred T. Smye of
A. V. Roe Canada Limited, which makes a proposal for a fixed cost estimate for the production
of 100 CF105 aircraft, at an approximate cost of
3.5 million.[17]

The result of substituting MA-1/Falcon/MB-1 for
Astra/Sparrow together with a close analysis of
the programme has resulted in an overall saving
of . . . $452.5 million saving on the programme for
100 operational aircraft.[18]

(b) Did the Arrow even have a mission?

> With the object of economy and to avoid unnecessary duplication, every effort has been made to determine whether future U.K. or U.S. aircraft could meet our requirements . . . In the U.K. the only aircraft for consideration is the Javelin whose performance falls far short of the requirement. In the United States there is the Convair F-102 . . . does not meet the range requirement . . . The RCAF, therefore have had A. V. Roe Canada work out an engineering proposal for an aircraft to meet our specification.[19]

> [Major General G. E. Price] . . . did not foresee the day of the phasing out of the manned interceptors as he felt there would always be a need for judgement and mobility in a weapon system.[20]

> [The mission would be] . . . primarily in peacetime to expose violation of national airspace . . . In wartime, reconnaissance aircraft are targets the same as any other enemy aircraft . . . an alternative supersonic two-place all-weather interceptor that generally meets the operational requirement is defined in OCH 1/1-63. This aircraft would have to be equal to or superior to the Arrow Weapons System.[21]

(c) When the Arrow was terminated, was it really a disaster for Canada's aviation industry?

. . . It has been our experience in the past that the potentialities of the Canadian aircraft industry and its allied companies have not always been appreciated . . . Lack of an immediate and long-range programme will result in a deterioration of the industry's effective operating capacity . . . We believe the industry at the moment to be in serious jeopardy.[22] (The government response was to shut down what had become the largest player in the industry, A. V. Roe.)

. . . The arguments for continuing were that Canadian military requirements should be found in Canada, that cancelling the programme would throw upwards of 25,000 men out of work with serious effects on the economy, and that national prestige should be taken into account . . .[23] (A. V. Roe had developed into a talented team of people working on the cutting edge of high-technology. Disbandment of this group, like the removal of a supporting wall, dealt a severe blow to the Canadian aerospace industry, as predicted by the Air Industries and Transport Association.)

(d) Was Avro capable of delivering a first-class weapons system in the first place?

There is no doubt that the firm is capable with its present labour force and space of meeting the likely demands for the RCAF and in fact exceeding them considerably . . . Orenda Engines Ltd . . . is excellently equipped and there is no doubt

whatever of its ability to match the aircraft programme in mind by Avro Aircraft Ltd.[24] (The
report from which this quotation is taken, found
in the NRC library, took two years for declassifi-
cation from the U.K. It not only looks at technical
characteristics but examines work methods, production flow, morale, etc., and presents a strong
and convincing argument against the unfounded
notion that Avro was an inept and poorly run
corporation.)

(e) Questions remain about the Arrow's airframe
design, and its engine was still developmental.

This aircraft is now in the test flying stage and
flights to date indicate it will meet its design
requirements. The engine for the aircraft, which
is part of the Arrow programme, is also undergoing air tests. These tests indicate that it also will
meet its design requirements.[25]

Very few engineering problems are expected in
the production or flight testing of the Arrow 2
airframe . . .[26] (Both aircraft and engine test efforts
were proceeding better than comparable programmes then or since.)

(f) Even its proposed weapon system was still on
the drawing board.

The adoption of the MA-1/Falcon/MB-1 fire control and weapons to the CF 105 programme has

reduced the development time and will permit operational aircraft to be delivered for squadron use by September 1960 in place of the spring of 1961 . . .[27]

Regarding these issues, complaints have periodically surfaced that the so-called pro-Avro factions usually argue on the basis of emotion. These complaints are understandable, since the documentation revealed in this book has been unavailable to the general public for over thirty-five years. Now that it is out, it does corroborate the pro-Avro side of the story, perhaps to the dismay of the anti-Avro factions who also argue on emotion and consistently fail to cite the documented evidence.

With respect to evidence, the search continues. I am certain other files do exist, perhaps in the former Soviet Union and most assuredly in the United States. Even in Canada, files keep turning up, as they are not automatically declassified after so many years, partly because the archives do not have the staff. Access requests are required in both Canada and the United States, but in the case of the latter you must have U.S. citizenship or know someone who could apply on your behalf. If you want to look at the files of the Central Intelligence Agency, let me know what you find.

APPENDIX I

A Selection from the Secret Files

19 April, 1955

Mr. Crawford Gordon, Jr.,
President & General Manager,
A. V. Roe Canada Ltd.,
Box 430, Terminal A,
Toronto, Ontario.

Dear Mr. Gordon:

I am very pleased to learn from the copy of your letter of 11 April to Dr. Solandt of your complete support of the proposal that a member of the laboratory staff be attached to the project in your plant.

It is planned to have Mr. A.D. Wood, Associate Research Officer on the staff of this Division serve initially and to have him report at Malton on Monday, 25 April. It is also planned to have Mr. Wood sit in at the Coordination Meeting at Orenda Engines Limited on Friday, 22 April, and the initial Coordination Meeting with Avro Aircraft on the preceding Thursday.

I am confident that this arrangement will work out to the definite advantage of the C-105 project.

Yours sincerely,

Original signed
by Director

JHP/lkg

J. H. Parkin,
Director.

c.c. ↙Dr. O.M. Solandt,
Chairman, Defence Research Board.

Mr. H.H. Kelland
Mr. A.D. Wood

Government personnel worked hand in hand with A.V. Roe as evidenced in this letter from the director of the National Aeronautical Establishment.

(NATIONAL ARCHIVES, NATIONAL RESEARCH COUNCIL OF CANADA.)

DEPARTMENT OF THE AIR FORCE

Washington

Papers 9 nov.

Office of
The Secretary

Nov. 9, 1955

Dear Mr. Campney:

   At the request of Air Marshal Slemon and Dr. Solandt, representatives of the U.S. Air Force at Toronto on October 31 and November 1, evaluated the CF-105 all weather interceptor, including its PS-13 engine.

   The terms of reference of the evaluation were:

   "Should the RCAF proceed with development and production of the CF-105 in the face of a firm U.S. Air Force program for development and production of the F-102B medium range interceptor; the F-101B long range interceptor; and the LRIXI, which is being developed to replace the F-101B?"

   A summary of the evaluation is attached.

   It is the recommendation of the U.S. Air Force that development and production of the CF-105 proceed as now planned.

                         Sincerely yours,

                    (Sgd) Donald A. Quarles

1 Incl
   USAF Evaluation of the CF-105
   Acft and PS-13 Engine

The Honorable Ralph Campney
Minister of National Defense
Ottawa, Ontario
Canada

The Avro Arrow and Iroquois engine programmes get the green light from the United States. (NATIONAL ARCHIVES, DEFENCE RESEARCH BOARD)

OFFICE OF THE CHAIRMAN, CHIEFS OF STAFF
OTTAWA

8310

4 November, 1958.

Referred to *C. ...D7. PT.*

NOV 6 1958

File No. *...32 C.V. 17*

Chgd to ....

C.A.S.

1.   The Minister has forwarded to me a copy of a letter he received from Mr. Fred T. Smye of A.V. Roe Canada Limited, which makes a proposal for a fixed cost estimate for the production of 100 CF105 aircraft, at an approximate cost of $3.5 million.

2.   The Minister has directed that the Chiefs of Staff review this matter; and in making any such review it will be necessary to clarify the question of the future costs of this aircraft and to ascertain what will be required to complete development before any fixed price contract can be considered.

3.   I would suggest that your officers should discuss this matter with the Department of Defence Production and be able to come up with agreed figures for the cost of completing the development and a clear understanding of what is included in any fixed price contract as suggested in Mr. Smye's letter.

(Charles Foulkes)
General,
Chairman, Chiefs of Staff.

c.c. Mr. D.A. Golden,
Deputy Minister of Defence Production

Arrow production costs were being reduced as evidenced in this memo, but even as late as January 1959, with the production schedule advancing and success of the flight trials, the Chief of the Air Staff was unable to convince the Minister of National Defence to move forward to production. (NATIONAL ARCHIVES.)

OFFICE OF THE DEPUTY MINISTER

OTTAWA

C Lafore aircraft Branch ly.

207 - 6 - 3   8

March 4, 1959

Assistant Deputy Minister,
Department of Defence Production,
No. 2 Building,
Ottawa, Ontario.

Dear Sir:

Re: Screening of Surplus Inventories Resulting
from the Termination of the Arrow Programme

     The RCAF has formed a Termination Group and is ready to discuss any matters that you have in mind at your call.

     In the meantime, AMC is examining material which is still in use in the RCAF and for which there is a future requirement. This should lessen the work of the termination team if there is any delay in getting things started.

     The coordinating officer of the termination team is G/C A.H. Lieff, C/Mat/DMP, Local 2-0413.

     As there are a number of policy matters which must be settled before the termination team can actually undertake the work of screening, it would be appreciated if an early meeting could be arranged to discuss the termination procedures.

              Yours sincerely,

              L. M. Chesley,
              for Deputy Minister.

Formation of the Arrow termination team that saw the eventual disposition of Arrow-related matériel. (NATIONAL ARCHIVES)

1038CN-80 (CAS)

APR 2 1959

26 Mar 59

MEMORANDUM

The Minister (Through Deputy Minister)

Arrow Cancellation - Disposal of Materiel

1   In your approval to my recommendation of
13 March 1959 on courses of action to be taken in respect
to disposal of materiel arising out of the cancellation of
the Arrow, you desired to be informed before final action
was taken on the method of disposal being considered for
the disposition of the airframes and the Iroquois engines.

2   Two methods may be followed:

    (a) Declaring as surplus materiel to Crown Assets
        Disposal agency. This course is not recom-
        mended for the reason that this agency has
        the prerogative of selling this materiel in
        its original state. This course could lead
        to subsequent embarrassment, that is, air-
        frame and engine could conceivably be placed
        on public view or even, in fact, used as a
        roadside stand. This, I am sure, you will
        agree is most undesirable.

    (b) Relinquishing any DND interest in the air-
        frames and engines to DDP for ultimate
        disposal by that agency. In this case DDP
        can reduce it to scrap. This course is
        recommended.

3   I would appreciate being advised whether you
concur in the method recommended.

(Hugh Campbell)
Air Marshal
Chief of the Air Staff.

cc: Deputy Minister.

D.M. May I have your comments
please Smith/Leader

The infamous recommendation to reduce the Arrows to scrap originated with
Hugh Campbell, Chief of the Air Staff. It did not come from John Diefenbaker
as has been alleged for thirty-three years. He probably never saw it. (DIRECTORATE
OF HISTORY RECORDS, DEPARTMENT OF NATIONAL DEFENCE)

Aircraft Branch

April 7, 1959.

Mr. G.A. Hore,   J.L. Bush,
Toronto.   Ottawa.

A15

(C 13)

Arrow/Iroquois Termination, Direction A15 O-13

The RCAF has advised that there are no plans for further flights by the completed CF-105 aircraft. It is expected that they will be returned to the custody of DDP for mutilation prior to declaration to C.A.D.C. However, there is still a remote possibility that one or two aircraft may be required by D.N.D. , and therefore, the two best aircraft should be retained intact for the present.

With respect to plant clearance, you are authorized to:

(A) Declare all jigs and tooling, completed or in process, which has scrap value only to C.A.D.C. It is understood that you, in consultation with representatives of the Machine Tool Branch, will salvage any items of material or equipment which have a foreseeable use in a future aircraft programme.

(B) Declare all work in process to C.A.D.C. Recognizable components and aircraft are to be mutilated to the extent that they cannot be assembled in the form of an aircraft.

NOTE: It is unnecessary to prepare inventories for (A) and (B) which are to be declared surplus by estimated weight and value. Priced inventories are required for salvaged items.

(C) Instruct prime and sub-contractors to prepare inventories of all raw materials, equipment and bought out parts. Further instructions with respect to disposal will be issued after it is determined if the RCAF or other contracts have any requirement for these items.

(D) All J-75 engines, with the exception of those in the two aircraft mentioned above, and spare parts, are to be inhibited and stored in containers pending disposal instructions.

(E) All G.S.M. is to be packed in accordance with RCAF instructions and returned to the RCAF.

(F) Moveable work stands are to be retained pending further instructions.

(G) Three Iroquois engines, as selected by the RCAF, are to be retained pending possible requirements. The balance of the engines and parts are to be mutilated to the extent that they cannot be assembled in the form of an engine and declared to C.A.D.C.

(H) Retain one complete set of reproducible drawings, process sheets, technical reports, specifications test reports, tool order cards, work order cards, manuals, master glass cloth production lofts, tool drawing masters, master record of tool inspection, master I.B.M. run of components, master gauges.

(I) One complete cockpit in the configuration established by the RCAF is to be made available to the Institute of Aviation Medicine.

Disposition of Arrow matériel, including the nosepiece of Arrow 206, which now resides in the Aviation Museum in Ottawa. (NATIONAL ARCHIVES)

CANCELLED

MIN. FILE..................................

H. Q. FILE 1038-CN-80 TD9072

Ottawa, April 8th, 1959

CAS

ARROW Cancellation - Disposal of Materiel

With reference to your memorandum of March 26th on the above subject, my understanding of the proposal is as follows:

a) There is no intention of attempting to fly or maintain in service the completed aircraft.

b) Every effort will be made to salvage engines, instruments and parts that can be used or returned to the original supplier for credit.

c) The aircraft, as whole aircraft, will not be put up for disposal but will be reduced to scrap after all useful and creditable materiel has been removed.

On the above understanding I agree to your proposal.

[signature]

MINISTER

George Pearkes, Minister of National Defence, concurs with the recommendation to scrap the Arrow. (DIRECTORATE OF HISTORY RECORDS, DEPARTMENT OF NATIONAL DEFENCE)

1038CN-80

May 12, 1959.

Dear Mr. Miller:

Arrow Cancellation
Disposal of Airframes and Iroquois Engines
Your Letter 1038CN-80 dated April 27, 1959

I am in complete agreement with your understanding as expressed in the referenced letter and confirm that airframes and engines will not be disposed of in a useable condition. The five completed Mark I aircraft are being retained "as is" pending a decision by the United Kingdom, but, all others are being reduced to scrap. Equipment and parts with better than scrap value are being segregated and disposed of separately.

For your information, arrangements are being made to return the MA-1 Electronic Systems and J-75 Engines to the U.S.A.F.

Yours faithfully,

D. A. Golden,
Deputy Minister.

F. R. Miller, Esq.,
Deputy Minister,
Department of National Defence,
Ottawa, Ontario.

Deputy Ministers concur with the order to scrap but indicate interest in the Arrow from the U.K., an interest that was not actively pursued. (Directorate of History Records, Department of National Defence)

Aircraft Branch

207-6-3

Ottawa, Ontario,
July 7, 1959.

Mr. Louis Richard,
President and General Manager,
Crown Assets Disposal Corporation,
88 Metcalfe Street,
Ottawa, Ontario.

Dear Sir:

As you requested, I am submitting herewith
a copy of a letter dated April 27, 1959 from the Deputy
Minister of the Department of National Defence to the Deputy
Minister of the Department of Defence Production confirming
that all completed Arrow Aircraft are to be disposed of
as scrap.

Yours very truly,

J. L. Bush,
Chief,
No. 1 Division.

Encl.

JLB/ro

Memo to the Crown Assets Disposal Corporation. Lax Brothers in Hamilton
won the contract to reduce this multimillion-dollar development into a few
hundred thousand dollars' worth of scrap metal. (NATIONAL ARCHIVES)

Aircraft Branch

c/o Avro Aircraft Limited,
Box 4004, Terminal "A",
Toronto, Ontario.

January 21st., 1960

Mr. J. C. Wilson,
Arrow Termination Co-ordinator,
Avro Aircraft Limited,
Malton, Ontario.

Dear Mr. Wilson:

Termination Instruction No. 81"A"
Records, Drawings, etc.

Instruction No. 77"A" dated December 9th, 1959,
required you to retain certain records and publications.

As the R.C.A.F. have now advised that there
appears to be no purpose in retaining the engineering data
on the Arrow aircraft, you are instructed to dispose of it
in the same manner as you have disposed of other records,
drawings, etc.

Yours very truly,

(Original Signed By)
C. A. HORE
C. Allen More
Senior Representative.

CAH/hs
cc Mr. J. L. Bush

Final order to destroy the remaining data on the Arrow. Was this order carried out, or do original drawings still exist? (NATIONAL ARCHIVES)

JESSOP STEEL COMPANY

Washington, Pennsylvania

Office of the President   December 9, 1953.

Mr. Crawford Gordon, Jr.
A. V. Roe, Canada Ltd.
Box 430 - Terminal A,
Toronto, Ontario.

My Dear Mr. Gordon:

During a most recent visit to your fair city, your Mr. Wm. MacDonald extended to us the courtesy of a conducted tour through your jet engine plant. I thought you would like to know that, in my humble opinion, this is the finest facility of its type in the world today. I have been through quite a few similar operations and, while every industrial facility has its own assets and liabilities, I think when the score is totalled A. V. Roe is way out in front.

I speak of such things as plant maintenance, production flow lines, general lay-out, employee morale and quality of workmanship. Therefore, I did want to write, and would have done so at an earlier date had I been in my office, to extend my sincere compliments to you and your staff on your operation and a very positive thank you from myself and my associates for the courtesy extended. You know it is fun for me to sell but it makes me feel real good to see our products going into an end product such as yours.

With kindest regards for the forthcoming holiday season, I am,

Sincerely,

JESSOP STEEL COMPANY

"Frank B. Rackley"

Frank B. Rackley,
President.

FBR/a/j

This letter speaks to the professionalism of A. V. Roe. (NATIONAL ARCHIVES)

Headquarters

Tactical Air Command

Langley Air Force Base, Va.

Office of the Commanding General

26 August 1954

Mr. Crawford Gordon, Jr.
President, A. V. Roe Canada Limited,
Malton, Ontario.

My dear Mr. Gordon:

May I express my sincere thanks and
appreciation to you and, through you, to your key staff people
for the many courtesies extended to my group on 23 - 24 August.

I was most impressed with the possibilities
of the special project on which you have John Frost working. I
certainly hope the arrangements for assisting you on this project
can be firmed up soon. I also appreciated the tour through your
principal plant facilities. These facilities are as modern and
well organized as any I have ever seen, and additionally you
appear to have more expansibility than many of our U.S. concerns.
Geographically we are all Americans and share the same security
problems, so I am more than happy that your capability is additive
to that of U.S. industry.

Again, my thanks for your kindness and
hospitality. Please give my best to Fred Smye, McLachlan and
all the others, as well as to that fine son of yours.

Sincerely,

"O. P. Weyland"

General, United States Air Force

Commander

This letter also speaks to the professionalism of A. V. Roe, and alludes to the
Americans' security concerns. (NATIONAL ARCHIVES)

factories with work only for two. **Mr. O'Hurley** countered
by pointing out that of the 400 millions spent on the F104
by Canada, 150 million was being spent in the United States
for components. **Mr. Fleming** referred to the financial arrangements and it was confirmed by <u>Dave Golden</u> that the arrangements were to be spread over two U.S. fiscal years, which
meant over three Canadian fiscal years. <u>General Brown</u>
pointed out that the bill for spares would depend on the
rate of utilization; that the present bill for 47 million
was calculated on 25 hours a month per aircraft, and would
amount to 23 million dollars a year; the remainder was for
ground handling equipment and simulators and armament.

Mr. Gates said that you must decide the policy first. Do
you want the fighters, and then we can argue about price.

Mr. Green stated that they were told two years ago that
the manned bomber was on its way out and that is why they
cancelled the Arrow. Now they have to go back and say
that both are still needed. **Mr. Fleming** referred to the
fact they tried to interest the Americans in buying the
Arrow at the Paris Conference but had been turned down flat
by **Mr. McElroy.**

  Mr. Pearkes confirmed that the flying rate would
be about the same as the Americans and, therefore, there would
be no reductions in spares from that cause. He said we did
not cancel the F105 because there was no bomber threat but
because there was a lesser bomber threat and we got the
Bomarc in lieu of more airplanes to look after this. Now
he said perhaps the expectation of two years ago that the
bomber threat was lessening has not been fulfilled. At the
same time he said we expected Bomarcs to cover the whole
country. These had been reduced, and therefore some more
protection to the western part must be made in those areas
which were to be protected by Bomarc. It wasn't fair, he
said, for Canada to fill this western gap which had been

At the ministers' meeting in Quebec in July 1960, Pearkes felt betrayed by the
Americans. (Directorate of History, Department of National Defence)

created by the Americans all by themselves. **Mr. Gates**
referred once again that we must get this aircraft deal
settled if at all possible because they could not afford
to stand up to the political pressures at home too long.

Morning Session

The conference reconvened at 9 o'clock on
Wednesday, 13 July, and went over the previous day's
discussions to some degree.

Aircraft Deal

On aircraft, **Mr. Gates** offered to split the 47
million dollars for spares on a one-third, two-third ratio
which would mean that the U.S. would spend 150 plus 30
million dollars, and the Canadians would spend 122 million
dollars. **Mr. Fleming** appreciated the offer and said he
would report this fact to the Cabinet. **Mr. Gates** suggested
that the matter has already been discussed with the press
and therefore it would be wise if it could be settled as
soon as possible, especially at this meeting. **Mr. Fleming**
said that we now were aware of all the facts and would be
able to decide as soon as possible. **Mr. Pearkes** asked
when these aircraft would be available and it was confirmed
that they would come off production in the period August
through December and would be the last 66 on the production
line.

"SKY SHIELD"

Referring to "SKY SHIELD", **Mr. Green** said that he
would have to take back the proposed public relations policy
to the Prime Minister. As to the question that the first
announcement had been agreed to, the reply was yes. **Mr. Irwin**
pointed out that the proposed policy guidance was for NORAD
who would be required to answer questions arising from
the first announcement, and **Mr. Gates** stressed the fact
that the intent was to focus all releases through NORAD
and to give them this guidance. **Mr. Fleming** felt that the

.../13

May 27, 1960

MEMORANDUM FOR DEPUTY SECRETARY OF DEFENSE

SUBJECT: Combined Procurement with Canada of F-101B and CL-44 Aircraft

1. As we have recently discussed, we have under very serious consideration an arrangement on the above subject which should prove to be
of maximum benefit to both the United States and Canada. I believe
that our defense position can be greatly enhanced while, as part of the
same transaction, we will be able to make a substantial step toward our
MATS modernization goal.

2. The proposal is that the Canadians procure 66 F-101B aircraft,
now in U.S. inventory and procured with funds from previous fiscal
years, for approximately $105 million. As part of the transaction, the
USAF would procure 35 CL-44 aircraft for $155 million to be assigned to
MATS to meet requirements for immediate modernization prior to procurement of the SOR aircraft. On a strictly FY 1961 cash basis, the U.S.
would obtain 35 CL-44 aircraft for $50 million, which is $1.4 million
each. This compares with a figure of $4.4 million each, the actual
program cost including spares.

3. From our point of view, modern interceptor aircraft will be
deployed as far north as practicable with very significant gains to
North American defense as an immediate benefit. In addition, the interim modern aircraft needed so badly in MATS, can be obtained on a
much more economical basis than is otherwise possible.

4. There are also some significant related benefits to be realized.
As I have previously mentioned, a sensitive political situation has
arisen in Canada due to a series of events involving the CF-105 cancellation in favor of BOMARC and SAGE joint procurement with the U.S.,
followed by reductions in BOMARC and SAGE super combat centers. In
addition, the production sharing program initiated 18 months ago has not
produced the expected results from the Canadian viewpoint. The
exchange-procurement discussed above presents an ideal opportunity to
improve this situation while simultaneously attaining a significant
benefit to the United States. In this regard, it is important to note
that neither procurement would be likely to take place without the other
also being made.

5. This suggestion has been given to the Canadians informally and
their reaction is expected when their Prime Minister visits the
President next month. The proposal is also subject to Congressional
approval.

JOSEPH V. CHARYK
Acting Secretary of the Air Force

It is clear that the United States wanted interceptors in the north, obviously as
long as they were their own. Paragraph 4 notes the cancellation of the Arrow in
favour of Bomarc and the defence sharing program, which was not working.
(Eisenhower Library)

THE DEPUTY SECRETARY OF DEFENSE
WASHINGTON 25, D. C.

June 1, 1960

5

MEMORANDUM ON PRODUCTION SHARING PROGRAM --
UNITED STATES AND CANADA

The current program dates back at least to 1941 and the
Hyde Park Agreement. This agreement provided generally that
Canada and the U. S. should attempt to coordinate activities so
that each would produce in areas of greatest capability. In 1950
a Statement of Principles of Economic Cooperation was issued by
the Truman Administration. It advocated, among other things,
a coordinated program of requirements, production and procurement; the exchange of technical knowledge and productive skills;
the removal of barriers impeding the flow of essential defense
goods. In 1950 a DCD Directive on Defense Economic Cooperation
with Canada was issued. A Presidentially approved NSC paper,
5822/1, dated 30 December 58, reaffirmed the Statement of
Economic Principles and provided for equal consideration to be
accorded the business communities of both countries.

Prior to the NSC paper, and following a visit of the President
to Canada in July 1958, Canada took the following actions with the
understanding that her defense industry depended largely upon the
U. S. channeling defense business into Canada: Cancelled the
CF 105 and related systems contracts; decided to make maximum
use of U. S. developed weapons, integrated into NORAD; worked
with the U. S. toward a fully integrated continental air defense.

The U. S. in turn established a Production/Development
Sharing Program with Canada with the first quarterly meeting
in October 1958. Since then, policy obstacles impeding a free
flow of business have been modified in a number of areas such
as: Buy American Act; duty free entry of defense goods; security
requirements; etc. Also, working groups have been set up on
programs of mutual interest (for example, BOMARC); cost sharing
agreements have been worked out; and possible joint development
programs are being explored.

This memorandum implies that a deal was struck between Canada and the United
States concerning the fate of the Arrow. (Eɪsᴇɴʜᴏᴡᴇʀ Lɪʙʀᴀʀʏ)

The last quarterly meeting of the Production Sharing
Policy Group was held on 25 May. Despite all efforts, over the
period 1 January 59 through 31 March 60, Canadian defense
business in the United States almost doubled that placed in Canada.
Canada is not satisfied with these results, nor do they appear
acceptable from our view.

We must: re-emphasize the program of development
sharing activities; encourage American industry to subcontract
in Canada; and seek out other legitimate techniques to stimulate
the program. Canada should be encouraged to energize her
industry which has not displayed the necessary aggressiveness.

CHIEF OF THE GENERAL STAFF

21 Aug 58

Chairman
Chiefs of Staff

1   Reference your "Report on the Development
of the CF105 and Associated Weapon System 1952-58"
dated 19 Aug 58 and, in particular, paragraph 5
of the paper titled "Development of CF105 Weapon
System".

2   Upon reading paragraph 5, one is left with
the impression that our air defence plan is
designed for the defence of Canada. My understanding is that our air defence plan is not for
"the Defence of Canada", but is a part of a Canada-
US air defence plan for the defence of North America.
This Canada-US plan places first priority on the
defence of SAC bases, second priority on certain
other installations, and only third priority on
certain centres of population in North America,
of which four are in Canada, namely, Montreal,
Toronto, Hamilton and Vancouver.

3   I think it is wrong to leave the impression
with the Minister and the Government that our air
defence plan is primarily for the defence of
Canadian territory when, in fact, any defence of
Canadian territory is but a by-product or extra
dividend to the main purpose, which is the defence
of SAC bases and Northeastern United States.

(HD Graham)
Lieutenant-General
Chief of the General Staff

Lieutenant-General H.D. Graham indicates that Foulkes is misleading the
Canadian government and states flatly that defence of Canadian territory is but a
by-product of the defence of Strategic Air Command bases and the United States
(DIRECTORATE OF HISTORY, DEPARTMENT OF NATIONAL DEFENCE)

PROGRESS REPORT ON THE IMPLEMENTATION OF

THE DECISIONS IN REGARD TO AIR DEFENCE

TAKEN BY CABINET ON 21 SEPTEMBER, 1958

1.   Action to implement Decision (a) of the Cabinet, for the installation of two BOMARC bases in Northern Ontario and Quebec, the installation
of two additional heavy radars in Northern Ontario and Quebec, and the
associated gap filler radars, has already been taken, and cost-sharing
arrangements have been negotiated with the United States. Now that cost-
sharing arrangements have been completed, it will be possible to make
the necessary arrangements for construction and acquisition of this equipment.

2.   With regard to Recommendations (b), (c) and (d) referring to
the development programme of the Arrow aircraft and the Iroquois engine,
which required a careful and comprehensive review of requirements for
the Arrow aircraft to be made before 31 March. This matter is still
under study by the Chiefs of Staff. However the Chiefs of Staff wish to
report that there are no new military factors, either in regard to the
manned bomber threat or new developments to meet this threat, which
the Chiefs of Staff consider would have any bearing on this matter. The
RCAF and the Department of Defence Production, however, are studying
a proposal of the A.V. Roe Company for a fixed price contract for the
production of the Arrow aircraft and the Iroquois engine and Fire Control
System.

3.   Avro proposal has not yet been finally submitted, but as
we understand it, it will be as follows:

he "smoking gun": In paragraph 4, Foulkes clearly states that he is awaiting
irection from the Commander-in-Chief of NORAD, before finalizing recommenda-
ons concerning the need for aircraft like the Arrow. (DIRECTORATE OF HISTORY, DEPARTMENT
 NATIONAL DEFENCE)

(a) A fixed amount to complete the development, plus a
5% fee. The approximate amount being discussed is
$28,000,000. If Avro better this amount of money
in development they will collect their whole fee; if
they exceed the amount their fee will remain the
same;

(b) a fixed amount of $7,000,000 to complete the tooling;

(c) a fixed amount yet undetermined for tool maintenance,
and once this amount is established Avro will have to
get along with that or pay money out of their own
resources for the maintenance of tooling;

(d) to complete the remainder of the first 20 aeroplanes
on a cost plus fee basis, it is estimated that these
aircraft will average about $5,000,000 per copy;

(e) a fixed price for all aircraft after the twentieth
aircraft at a fly-away cost of $3.75 million; i.e.,
approximately $5,000,000 for each aircraft plus
one year's spares and support.

4.   With regard to the Cabinet Decision (e), that the Chiefs of
Staff should investigate and report on requirements, if any, for
additional air defence missile installations in Canada and for an
interceptor aircraft of the nature of the CF105 or alternative types;
the Chiefs of Staff have this matter under active study but wish to
defer making any recommendations until they have had an opportunity
to study the plans of the Commander-in-Chief, North American Air
Defence Command. It is expected that the Commander-in-Chief,

North American Air Defence Command, will be presenting his revised plans to the Canadian Chiefs of Staff in January. After the Chiefs of Staff have an opportunity of carefully studying these plans, they will be prepared to make recommendations for any additional air defence missile installations or for interceptor aircraft of the nature of the CF105 or alternative types.

5.   With regard to Recommendation (f) regarding the termination of the Astra fire control equipment and the Sparrow missile, the RCAF after investigating the alternative fire control systems and weapons available in the United States, have recommended the Hughes Aircraft Company fire control system and Falcon and Genie missiles.) They report as follows:

> Preliminary arrangements have been made with USAF, Hughes Aircraft Company and Avro for the prototype installation of MA-1 integrated fire control system and Falcon MB-1 missiles. *?? confusion here* Engineering evaluation has clearly indicated that the fitting of this system into the CF105 is feasible. Progress to date indicates that there will be no difficulties in adapting this fire control system and weapon to a new aircraft. Indications are that the new fire control system, weapons and aircraft are compatible and will produce a satisfactory all-weather interceptor.

6.   An extract of Cabinet Decisions of 21 September, 1958 is shown in Appendix "A" attached.

Chairman, Chiefs of Staff
24 December, 1958.

Cabinet Decisions – Air Defence Requirements

At its meeting on 21 September 1958 the Cabinet:

a)   approved in principle the installation of two BOMARC bases in
northern Ontario and Quebec and the installation of two additional
heavy radars in northern Ontario and Quebec and associated
gap-filler radars in the Pinetree system;

b)   decided that the development programme for the ARROW aircraft
and the Iroquois engine should be continued until March 31st,
1959, within the scope made possible by the amounts available
for it in the estimates for the current fiscal year;

c)   decided that production of the ARROW aircraft and Iroquois
engine should not be ordered at the present time;

d)   agreed that a careful and comprehensive review of the requirements for the ARROW aircraft and Iroquois engine should be
made before March 31st, 1959, in order to reach a decision
before that date as to whether development should be continued
or production ordered;

e)   agreed that the Chiefs of Staff should investigate and report
upon the requirements, if any, for additional air defence missile
installations in Canada and for interceptor aircraft of the nature
of the CF-105 or alternative types;

f)   agreed that further consideration should be given to the possibility of continuing the development of the Astra fire control
equipment and the Sparrow missile in Canada only; and

g)   agreed that no statement of these decisions should be made
until the following day or the next succeeding day pending
further consideration of the Astra and Sparrow programme.

Subsequently, the Cabinet agreed that the programme for the development of the Astra fire control equipment and the Sparrow II missile
should be terminated forthwith and that this decision should be
announced the following day, along with those decisions on the air
defence programme taken the preceding day. "

M E M O R A N D U M

28 Mar 58

AMTS

Arrow Cost Versus Cost of Comparable Aircraft

1   Previous attempts have been made to assemble, design and development costs for the USAF F106 in order that they might be compared with our
Arrow programme. While the costs directly attributable to the various
USAF orders for the F106 have been obtained it has been impossible to
assemble true costs of the F106 design and development phase. This
situation results from the manner in which the F106 has developed, i.e.
it is first of all a development of the F102 and a portion of the costs
of design and development of this aircraft should be borne by the F106.
In addition the MA-1 electronics system of the F106 is developed from the
$360.0M MG-10 and 14 programmes and an unknown portion of this cost should
be borne by the F106 in any true comparison. There are other major areas
of this nature which preclude the desired comparison, the most important
of which are the fact that USA contractors enjoy the use of certain Government facilities without cost and that the J75 has several applications
whereas the more advanced Iroquois is still in the development stage.

2   Notwithstanding the foregoing, costs attributed by the USAF to
their many orders for Century series aircraft have been assembled and are
summarized as Appendix "A". If these are viewed in the light of the
qualifications in para 1 it is apparent that Arrow costs compare favourably
with the somewhat less sophisticated aircraft in the USA. Production costs
included for 200 Arrow aircraft were obtained from DDP and are of course
only an estimate which is subject to change as more information becomes
available during the development phase.

3   It has been interesting to learn that RCAF fly-away costs for
the CF-10? from production were less than for the comparable F89 Scorpion.
Similarly, quantity production of the F86 and T33 was undertaken in Canada
at a lower per aircraft cost than from USA production.

4   It may, therefore, be concluded that quantity production of an
aircraft as complex as the Arrow can be undertaken in Canada at a cost
comparable to that for production of a like aircraft in the U.S.A.

(Signed) G. G. Truscott

(G.G. Truscott) A/C
CAE
6-6273

Attach.
JCSmith/MC
MP2/AWS
2-0282
Circ
MP2
CAS

This memo indicates that costs for the Arrow were comparable to those of less
capable American fighters. (NATIONAL ARCHIVES)

COST OF ALTERNATIVE AIR DEFENCE PROGRAMME
PROVIDING 100 CF105 AIRCRAFT
(80 from production; 20 from preproduction)

	Expenditures to 31 Mar 58	Forecast Total Future Capital Expenditures	FORECAST EXPENDITURES BY FISCAL YEARS					
			1958/59	1959/60	1960/61	1961/62	1962/63	1963/64 & future years
Arrow Preprod. (37)	221.0	568.2	203.2	237.9	112.0	12.1	3.0	—
Arrow Production (80)	—	589.6	4.0	114.0	201.0	176.0	90.0	4.6
Sparrow	15.1	170.3	26.2	21.1	24.2	33.8	50.0	15.0
Additional facilities CF105	—	34.4	—	5.2	7.2	7.0	9.0	6.0
Bomarc 2x60 – Estimated total cost	—	164.0⚡						
Additional Radars & Gap Fillers	—	35.2						
SAGE – Estimated total cost	—	108.0⚡						
Total Capital Costs	236.1	1,669.7						

⚡ – These figures are estimated total cost – no cost sharing has been taken into consideration.

NOTE: Should the existing Arrow/Sparrow programme be cancelled effective 1 Sept 1958

(a) Amount spent from 1 Apr 58 to date of cancellation is estimated at $67 M. (Arrow – $55.6 M, Sparrow – $11.4 M)

(b) ⚡ In addition the amount which may be spent for cancellation is estimated at $102 M. (Arrow – $89.4 M, Sparrow – $12.6 M)

⚡ DDP is of the opinion that in the final event the cancellation charges may be $80 M to $100 M.

The costs of the Arrow program, calculated in September 1958. A fly-away cost of $5 million was used instead of the actual $3.75 million. The costs of SAGE/Bomarc were factored into these numbers. Note the cancellation charges. (NATIONAL ARCHIVES)

COST OF ALTERNATIVE AIR DEFENCE PROGRAMME
CANCEL ARROW/SPARROW, ADD TWO ADDITIONAL BOMARC SITES

	Expenditures to 31 Mar 58	Forecast Total Capital Expenditures	FORECAST EXPENDITURES BY FISCAL YEARS					
			1958/59	1959/60	1960/61	1961/62	1962/63	1963/64 & Future Yrs.
Arrow Cancellation Charges (from 1 Apr 58)	221.0	145.0	120.0	25.0	-	-	-	-
Sparrow Cancellation Charges (from 1 Apr 58)	15.1	24.0	18.0	6.0				
Bomarc 2 x 60 - Estimated Total Cost	-	164.0 *						
Additional Bomarc West Coast 1 x 60 Tie into Existing SAGE	- / -	88.3 / 6.0						
East Coast 1 x 60 Tie into SAGE Sector	- / -	87.0 / 6.0						
Additional Radars & Gap Fillers	-	35.2						
SAGE Estimated Total Cost	-	108.0 *						
Total Capital Costs	236.1	663.5						

These figures are estimated total costs - no cost sharing has been taken into consideration.

The costs of the Bomarc. Note the cancellation charge estimates. (NATIONAL ARCHIVES)

COST OF ALTERNATIVE AIR DEFENCE PROGRAMME
CANCEL ARROW/SPARROW AND 100 F106C AIRCRAFT

	Expenditures to 31 Mar 58	Forecast Total Future Capital Expenditures	FORECAST EXPENDITURES BY FISCAL YRS					
			1958-59	1959-60	1960-61	1961-62	1962-63	1963-64 & Future Yrs
Arrow Cancellation Charges (From 1 Apr 58)	221.0	145.0	120.0	25.0				
Sparrow Cancellation Charges (From 1 Apr 58)	15.1	24.0	18.0	6.0				
100 - F106C Aircraft c/w Weapons System - #US Production	-	457.0	-	114.0	160.0	137.0	46.0	
Additional Facilities F106C A/C	-	34.4	-	5.2	7.2	7.0	9.0	6.0
Bomarc 2 x 60 Estimated Total Cost	-	164.0 Ø						
Additional Radars and Gap Fillers	-	35.2						
SAGE Estimated Total Cost	-	108.0 Ø						
Total Capital Costs	236.1	967.5						

Ø - These figures are estimated total costs - no cost sharing has been taken into consideration

NOTE: # Increased cost for Canadian Production $74.3 M

The costs of the F106/Bomarc alternative. Politically, the Canadian government couldn't justify acquiring American aircraft on cancellation of the Arrow. (NATIONAL ARCHIVES)

CF-105 ARROW PROGRAM

I PRE-TERMINATION ACTIVITY

1. GENERAL BACKGROUND

The CF-105 Arrow Program commenced as a research project in 1953. In 1955 contracts were placed with Avro and Orenda for full scale development including the production of airframes and engines for use in an evaluation program. Subsequently, work was commenced on allied programs known as Astra, which was to provide an integrated electronic system, and Sparrow, which was to provide the armament. The two latter programs were cancelled in September, 1958, and were replaced by the MA-1 electronic system and the Falcon Missile.

By February, 1959, the following quantities of airframes and engines had been ordered from Avro and Orenda.

Avro Aircraft Limited -

     5 Mk.1 Aircraft   (J-75 engines)
    32 Mk.2 Aircraft (Iroquois engines)

Orenda Engines Ltd. -

    20 prototype Iroquois engines
    87 preproduction engines

2. PRE-TERMINATION COSTS

The cost of work completed before termination and the estimated costs to complete 37 aircraft plus 83 aircraft are detailed below. Costs vary slightly from those previously reported as a result of audits.

COST OF 37 AIRCRAFT PROGRAM
(Millions of dollars)

	To 20 Feb/59	To Complete	Total
AIRFRAMES			
Development	67.7	24.9	92.6
Tooling	30.3	13.9	44.2
Production & Support	81.9	126.5	208.4
ENGINES			
Development	55.4	53.0	108.4
Tooling	13.6	3.6	17.2
Production & Support	58.4	10.0	68.4
MA-1	1.7	13.3	15.0
J-75 & MISCELLANEOUS	9.6	12.6	22.2
TOTAL 37 A/C	318.6	257.8	576.4

The true costs of the Arrow, totalled after the cancellation. Note that the costs to complete development of the fighter were far less than the predicted cancellation charges calculated in September 1958. (NATIONAL ARCHIVES)

ADDITIONAL 83 AIRCRAFT

	Total
Production at $3.75 each	311.2
Support (electronics, equipment and spares)	181.0
Combat stock of Falcon missiles	42.6
	1,111.2

NOTE: The additional 83 aircraft would have provided for the revised program of 20 development/evaluation aircraft plus 100 operational aircraft.

3. PHYSICAL PROGRESS & PLANNED DELIVERY

5 Mark 1 aircraft had been completed and flown at the termination date. The next three aircraft were in the final assembly line. Thirteen prototype Iroquois engines had been completed and 7 were in process. No Iroquois engines had been installed in aircraft.

Had the program continued on the basis of 120 aircraft, deliveries would have been:

1959	1960	1961	1962	1963	Total
12	12	30	57	9	120

II POST TERMINATION

1. ADMINISTRATION

An interdepartmental Ad Hoc Committee with representation from National Defence, Audit Services and Treasury Board staff, was established by DDP to co-ordinate all matters relating to termination of the program, to set policies and to monitor the settlement of problems arising from termination. Special contracts were placed with Avro and Orenda to consolidate all terminated contracts and to ensure the orderly channelling of contractual matters.

2. EFFECT ON INDUSTRY

The immediate effect of termination was felt most by employees of the two prime contractors. All employees were released the same day but rehiring began immediately and the re-engaged employees worked extra hours to inaugurate procedures to handle termination. Employment dropped at Avro from 8,800 to 2,000 and at Orenda from 5,000 to 1,100. Subcontractors in the Toronto Area were similarly affected but to a lesser degree. The prime contractors and some of the major sub-contractors were faced with heavy overhead costs which had to be absorbed by greatly reduced work loads.

The final $1.1 billion is less than the cost of the F106/Bomarc alternative calculated in September 1958 if the costs for the Arrow to that date are added into this alternative. (NATIONAL ARCHIVES)

CONFIRMATION

TOR 2181

TO   AVRO ATTN J L PLANT MALTON (TCO VIA CN TELEGRAM)

FROM   D L THOMPSON   D D P OTTAWA

TAKE NOTICE THAT YOUR CONTRACTS BEARING THE REFERENCE NUMBERS SET
OUT BELOW INCLUDING ALL AMENDMENTS THERETO ARE HEREBY TERMINATED AS
REGARDS ALL SUPPLIES AND SERVICES WHICH HAVE NOT BEEN COMPLETED AND
SHIPPED OR PERFORMED THEREUNDER PRIOR TO THE RECEIPT BY YOU OF THIS
NOTICE STOP YOU SHALL CEASE ALL WORK IMMEDIATELY, TERMINATE SUB-
CONTRACTS AND ORDERS, PLACE NO FURTHER SUBCONTRACTS OR ORDERS AND
INSTRUCT ALL YOUR SUBCONTRACTORS AND SUPPLIERS TO TAKE SIMILAR ACTION
STOP YOU ARE REQUESTED TO SUBMIT TO THE DEPARTMENT OF DEFENCE
PRODUCTION, OTTAWA, ONTARIO FOR CONSIDERATION, ANY CLAIM WHICH YOU MAY
HAVE AS A RESULT OF THIS TERMINATION STOP SUCH CLAIM AND THOSE OF YOUR
SUBCONTRACTORS AND SUPPLIERS, IF ANY, ARE TO BE SUBMITTED ON
THE PRESCRIBED DEPARTMENTAL TERMINATION CLAIM FORMS STOP ON RECEIPT
OF THIS NOTICE, YOU SHOULD MAKE APPLICATION IN WRITING TO THE CHIEF
SETTLEMENT OFFICER, DEPARTMENT OF DEFENCE PRODUCTION OTTAWA, FOR THE
REQUISITE SET OF FORMS STOP YOUR CLAIM AND ALL CORRESPONDENCE
CONCERNING IT SHOULD BE ADDRESSED TO MR. D. B. WALLACE, CHIEF
SETTLEMENT OFFICER, DEPARTMENT OF DEFENCE PRODUCTION STOP
REFERENCE NUMBERS OF TERMINATED CONTRACTS: BX69-12-44; SERIAL 2-B-5-309;
BX18-26-97; SERIALS 2-B-4-715; 2-B-4-593; 2-B-7-1455; 2-B-8-27;
BX18-772778 SERIAL 2-BX-8-14; BR18-872803 SERIAL 2-BR-8-149

FEB 20/59   12.30 PM   DC

CONFIRMATION

TOR 2183

TO AVRO ATTN J L PLANT MALTON (TCO VIA CN TELEGRAM)

FROM D L THOMPSON D D P OTTAWA

YOU ARE HEREBY AUTHORIZED TO CEASE IMMEDIATELY ALL PURCHASING
OR OTHER ACQUISITION AND INSTALLATION OF THE CAPITAL EQUIPMENT LISTED
IN SCHEDULES "A", " B" AND "C" TO THE CF-105 AIRCRAFT CAPITAL
EQUIPMENT AGREEMENT DATED SEPTEMBER 29, 1955, AS AMENDED, BEARING
REFERENCES B.18-38-4540 AND B.69-12-44 STOP TAKE NOTICE THAT THE COST
OF ANY CAPITAL EQUIPMENT PURCHASED SUBSEQUENT TO THE
RECEIPT BY YOU OF THIS NOTICE SHALL NOT BE SUBJECT TO REIMBURSEMENT
UNDER SECTION 4 OF THE SAID AGREEMENT

FEB 20/59   12.40 PM   BC

This government order makes it clear that *all* work and acquisitions were to cease immediately. (National Archives)

Improvements in air defence; replacement aircraft for CF-100's in Canada
(Previous reference Feb. 4)

1. **The Minister of National Defence**, using a map, informed the Cabinet on the location of interceptor and BOMARC squadrons in Canada and indicated the depth of the defences these weapons provided. The coverage of this form of defence was governed by the location of the Pinetree stations and the warning lines. If, several years ago, it had been physically and financially possible to have situated the Pinetree radars further north, this would probably have been done and the BOMARC and interceptor bases consequently would have been further north too. The expected range of the BOMARC "B" was between 400 and 500 miles, that of the "A", about 150 to 200 miles.

2. **Mr. Pearkes** also read a copy of a letter sent to the U.S. defence authorities, when the Pinetree stations were first being installed in August, 1951, recording the understanding of the Canadian Government that the conclusion of the agreement for a one-third: two-thirds cost-sharing arrangement in no way implied that Canada was to be regarded as a recipient of aid. Perhaps a cost-sharing arrangement for the F-101B's could be regarded in a similar light.

3. **The Prime Minister** said that a committee of the Ministers who were members of the Cabinet Defence Committee plus Messrs. Churchill, Harkness, Nowlan and MacLean should meet to consider the proposal and make recommendations. If the Committee reported that security demanded the acquisition of these aircraft, then that would have to be the decision. To purchase them, however, would cause great difficulties. It would place him and the Minister of National Defence in impossible positions. On the other hand, failure to re-equip would be bad for the morale of the R.C.A.F. He thought the public had been convinced of the wisdom of the government's decision to cancel the Arrow. To obtain other aircraft now in the face of statements that the threat of the manned bomber was diminishing and that the day of the interceptor would soon be over would be most embarrassing unless a reasonable explanation could be given. Additional BOMARC's in Canada might be an alternative. The Committee should first examine carefully what had been said publicly by himself and other Ministers about cancelling the Arrow and, in the light of that, consider what was possible. In any event, the safety of the nation should be the paramount consideration no matter what the consequences. He had been against cancelling the Arrow but had been persuaded otherwise.

4. **During the brief discussion** it was said that, even though a logical, reasoned case might be made for obtaining the F-101B's, such a decision could not be explained to the public. The repercussions of telling CINCNORAD that Canada was not prepared to re-equip the CF-100 squadrons would not be too great.

5. **The Cabinet** agreed that a Committee consisting of the members of the Cabinet Defence Committee, other than the Prime Minister, together with Messrs. Churchill, Harkness, Nowlan and MacLean, review and report on the proposals of the Minister of National Defence for authority to discuss with the United States various possible arrangements for re-equipping on a smaller scale, the air defence force of the R.C.A.F. in Canada.

In these Cabinet minutes, John Diefenbaker realizes his error in cancelling the Arrow. He would have committed political suicide if Canada had purchased American fighters. At no point in this memo is there discussion of the alleged exorbitant costs of the Arrow, only that the U.S. wanted Canada to purchase American aircraft. (NATIONAL ARCHIVES)

27 Chatham Street
Brantford, Ontario
May 8, 1959

Prime Minister J. Diefenbaker
House of Commons
Parliment Hill
Ottawa, Ontario

Dear Mr. Diefenbaker:

I would like to ask you and your government not to scrap
the Avro CF-1o5 Arrow RL 2O1 if such is your intention.

I believe that this Arrow should be kept for historical
purposes. It was the first Canadian aircraft to exceed one
thousand miles per hour and it is one of the finest achievements in Canadian aeronautical engineering to date.

To-day in Canada there are many people who are trying to
salvage the historical items in the aviation field. The
Ryerson Aeronautical Club of the Ryerson Institute of Technology are trying to find a Vickers Vedette to rebuild, so as
to fill in one of the gaps in the history of this country.
However, none of these efforts will be effective if we do not
preserve what we already have. Will we treat the Arrow the
same way we did the Bluenose and then when the damage is done
wish we had it back. Will the Arrow follow the same path as
the Jetliner, first jet transport in North America and now in
some scrap heap. Is not this country proud snough to want to
save any of its achienements?

If it is a matter of storage, I am sure that if you asked
there would be a company or individual who would take it to
preserve it. If not then if you give it the Ryerson Aeronautical Club of which I am President I am sure we could find a
place for it.

If security prevents you from giving it away then perhaps
Avro could keep it until such time as it would be safe for
the craft to be allowed out.

Whatever is done this craft must be saved to show future
generations of Canadians what their forefathers did.

Yours truly

Robert MacMillan

A valiant attempt to save the Arrow by Robert MacMillan, a concerned Canadian.
(NATIONAL ARCHIVES)

, June 9, 1959.

Dear Mr. MacMillan:

As you were advised on May 15th, 1959, your letter of May 8th concerning the retention of one Arrow Aircraft has been referred to my office.

Although I sympathise with your desire to preserve the Arrow as an item of historical interest, I cannot grant your request for economic reasons. At the present time the completed aircraft are being stripped of equipment and will be scrapped in the near future. We will be able to salvage several hundred thousands of dollars from the sale of equipment, particularly engines, and to this saving must be added the costs which would be incurred for transportation, etc. if the aircraft was turned over to your club.

Yours sincerely,

Minister.

Robert MacMillan, Esq.,
27 Chatham Street,
Brantford, Ontario.

DLT:c

The grim reality, according to George Pearkes, in response to MacMillan's letter in regard to keeping one Arrow for posterity. (NATIONAL ARCHIVES)

BRIEF FOR MINISTER OF NATIONAL DEFENCE

FOR DISCUSSIONS WITH THE

UNITED STATES SECRETARY OF STATE

CANADA'S DEFENCE PROBLEMS

Our major defence problems arise mainly from our geographical and political position vis-a-vis the United States. This is particularly true in regard to air defence, which is our major problem, and an activity on which we now spend almost half of our defence budget; and present indications are that we may be forced to spend a larger proportion of our budget on the air defence effort in future. It has sometimes been said that we would not be required to spend so much on defence, particularly on air defence, if Canada had been an island instead of the northern outpost of the United States; however we fully realize the Canadian position both geographically and politically in the current east-west struggle between the Soviet Union and the United States.

It will be recalled that at the time of Korea the Canadian Government found it necessary to accelerate our defence programme, including the setting up of a considerable defence industry to support our defence effort. We embarked on an extensive programme of building ships, developing and producing aircraft and other defence requirements. In these efforts we have had the closest co-operation from the United States development and production services in our effort to produce modern equipment for our services and for mutual aid for our NATO partners.

Many of our defence projects have had of necessity a considerable United States content, which at times has given us some concern about our balance of payments position. For example the production of the Argus maritime aircraft has a U.S. content of 35% and in spite of

In this brief from July 8, 1958, George Pearkes makes it clear that, while provision could have been made for the Arrow, addition of SAGE/Bomarc and radar improvements would increase the defence budget by 25 to 30 percent. There is no indication whatsoever that production of the Arrow in the absence of these other U.S.

the fact that we have had the closest co-operation with the U.S. Services
in determining the requirements for our various military equipments we
have never been able to persuade the United States to accept for their own
use a Canadian-produced aircraft; nor have we succeeded in jointly
developing or producing an aircraft or weapon system for common use by
the Canadian and United States forces. Therefore we have been forced to
follow a unilateral approach to these expensive projects or alternatively to
accept a fully developed U.S. project for manufacture in this country.
However the problem remains that with forces of only 120,000, our
requirements for equipment are quite small, and therefore including the
costs of development and setting up lines of production to meet our own
limited requirements makes the final cost of the equipment almost
prohibitive.

We are rapidly reaching a critical position, particularly in the
field of air defence development, because of these factors mentioned above.
The recent discussions with General Partridge regarding the future
requirements for continental defence confirm our concern. There are
two major problems facing us in the field of air defence:

    (1)   the development of defence against the ballistic missile; and

    (2)   the further requirement to round out the defence against

        the manned bomber.

In regard to the development of defence against the ballistic
missile, as you are aware, we are doing very little in this programme
except some research work at Prince Albert regarding the effects of the
aurora belt on radar signals and investigations into the upper atmosphere
which may be of use in the further development of defence against ballistic
missiles. We feel very strongly that this development of defence against
ballistic missiles in North America should be a joint effort and we are

requirements would bankrupt the defence budget or take funding away from the
Army and Navy. For clarification, SAGE was required for the Bomarc and the
American F106 but not for the Arrow. This fact was pointed out to the RCAF by
both Avro and USAF officials. (NATIONAL ARCHIVES)

concerned lest we spend too much on rounding out the defence against the manned bomber and not have the funds available to participate in the development and production of defence against the ballistic missile.

Our second problem, which is much closer to us, is the rounding out of the defence against the manned bomber. In this field we have been co-operating with the United States for many years and now, with the setting up of the Joint Air Defence Command in Colorado Springs, we should be able to develop a joint system of operational control which will be more effective in an emergency. However this arrangement is not likely to help us in the production and provision of the necessary improvements in the weapons systems to meet the continuing bomber threat.

As you are perhaps aware, we have had under development in Canada a supersonic aircraft known as the CF105, designed to deal with the manned bomber threat after the early 1960's. We have had the greatest possible co-operation with the United States Air Force in the development of a type of aircraft which was considered by both countries to be a requirement for the air defence of North America during the 1960's. This aircraft is to be equipped with the U.S. Navy weapon the "Sparrow" and a large part of the electronic equipment will have U.S. content. It is expected that the total United States content in the CF105 will be approximately 20% in the development and pre-production aircraft and 10 to 15% if this aircraft goes into production. The development of this aircraft to date has cost $250 million, and its development will be continued for the next two or three years, to cost about $530 million, making a total of $780 million. Our requirements for this aircraft will be relatively small, somewhere around 100, and therefore the individual cost of the aircraft will be about $5 million, plus the cost of development. If this were the only requirement for our air defence, we could perhaps make provision for it in our succeeding defence budgets; but in order that aircraft of this type and the type to be used by the United States can operate in Canadian airspace we will be required to introduce a semi-automatic ground environment into Canada. The introduction of SAGE in Canada will cost in the neighbourhood of $107 million. Further improvements are required in the radar and other associated communications which will also bring greater expense within the next few years. NORAD has also recommended the introduction of the Bomarc missile into the Ottawa - North Bay area to supplement the manned interceptor, to round out the U.S. Bomarc chain, and to push the defences 250 miles further north. This development will be a further commitment of some $164 million.

All these commitments coming at this particular time, between 1960 and 1963, will tend to increase our defence budget by as much as 25 to 30%. All these projects also contain a very large element of U.S. content, which may give rise to other fiscal problems. In approaching these joint problems in the past, we have been able to work out cost-sharing arrangements whereby each country contributed a portion of the capital costs and maintenance in Canada of these projects, which are designed for the defence of both countries but which because of geography had to be constructed in Canada. These projects included the Pinetree System, the DEW Line and the Mid Canada Line. We believe that perhaps a wider application of this principle of cost-sharing is now necessary to enable us to continue our joint defence measures without Canada having to shoulder heavy additional defence burdens because of our geographical position. Some approaches have already been made to a solution of these cost-sharing problems in informal discussions with the USAF. Some initial discussions on the cost-sharing of SAGE and Bomarc projects have been commenced. Suggestions have also been made in other quarters that perhaps the United States could assist in the production of the CF105 by equipping the U.S. squadrons at Harmon Field and Goose B with this aircraft. These are all very useful approaches which are worthy

...5

further consideration in the light of our joint defence efforts. However we consider that these financial problems are of such magnitude that perhaps discussion on a level higher than the Service level should be initiated as early as possible.

There are of course defence problems, which we realize will have to be discussed in detail with the defence authorities; but these are brought to your attention at this time to emphasize the need for current consultations on these urgent defence matters.

It appears apparent that we are reaching a stage in Canada when it will not be possible for us to develop and produce further complicated weapons purely for Canadian use. As the future weapons of war become more complicated, it appears that the defence of North America will have to depend upon the joint development and production of these weapons and weapons systems for our joint use. While perhaps Canada may not be able to produce all these complicated weapons in Canada, arrangements should be possible whereby we could produce certain components for joint weapons so that our defence industry would still have a stake in the provision of weapons for Canadian forces.

There is one remaining defence problem which should be mentioned, and that is the question of storage of nuclear warheads for United States and Canadian use on Canadian territory. In December last the U.S. authorities suggested that military talks should take place on the requirements for both U.S. and Canadian Services to have immediately available atomic warheads for the defence of North America. The military discussions were authorized but these discussions have not yet been finalized and therefore the matter has not yet been given final consideration by the government.

Chairman, Chiefs of Staff.
8 July, 1958.

APPENDIX II

The Forgotten Tapes and Costs Revealed

The assumption in 1958–59 had been that the threat of the manned bomber was changing. . . . This was one of the reasons which prompted the U.S. Air Force to urge the Canadian government to accept the Bomarc anti-aircraft missile and to consider phasing out its interceptor force.
Melvin Conant, "Canada's Role in Western Defence,"
Foreign Affairs: An American Quarterly Review, April 1962

Many believe that Prime Minister John Diefenbaker made the decision to scrap the Arrow on his own, out of vengeance for all things Liberal and a profound hatred of Avro president Crawford Gordon. Others have stated the real reason was the exorbitant costs of the program. It has been said the Arrow was going to cost more than 12 times that of comparable American aircraft. In this book, using archival records, I have shown both of these contentions to be false. The documents point the finger at Minister of National Defence George Pearkes, Chairman, Chiefs of Staff Charles Foulkes, and Chief of the Air Staff Hugh Campbell, whom the records clearly show proposed the subsequent destruction of all completed aircraft, engines, tooling, and technical information. Many of these documents are reproduced in Appendix I.

I have also detailed the role of the United States in the cancellation, showing first how the program was supported by certain members of the USAF but was later not accepted by Secretary of the Air Force James Douglas and Secretary of State

John Foster Dulles. I provide possible reasons for this change in attitude, which included a fear of manufacturing secrets falling into Soviet hands and pressure from U.S. industry.

New material added to the second paperback edition, released in 1997, in particular the memo by Charles Foulkes dated December 24, 1958, makes it clear that the U.S., through NORAD, was pushing its own agenda for continental defence regardless of the political and economic consequences to Canada. The U.S. wanted Canada to buy and use its hardware: the Bomarc missile and its Semi-Automatic Ground Environment (SAGE) control network. Both Pearkes and Foulkes bought into the argument and recommended cancellation of the Arrow as early as August 1958.

On the question of cost, I now have details that show that while the program was expensive, as I had noted earlier in the book, the costs were not going to bankrupt the government. In fact, I had previously shown that the problem was not the cost of the Arrow alone, but the combined cost of the Arrow *and* the SAGE/Bomarc, which was too much for Canada. New information added to this edition not only bears this out but also shows that the cancellation charges being anticipated by the government at the time would have paid for completion of the development of the airframe and engines. Completion of the Arrow alone, without SAGE/Bomarc, was never an option, even though SAGE/Bomarc entered the equation long after the Arrow program had begun.

In November 1997, after the publication of that edition, the staff of the University of Victoria provided me with tapes made in 1967 of Dr. Reginald Roy interviewing George Pearkes. In the tapes, portions of which I have transcribed and included below, Pearkes admits to U.S. persuasion as a major factor in his recommendation to cancel. He makes a surprising admission about his defence plans that the Canadian public would never accept today. It was top secret even then. Whether there was malicious intent on the part of some U.S. officials, as I had speculated, remains unresolved.

Other observers, including U.S. writer Melvin Conant, continue to focus on the role played by the U.S. In his paper in *Foreign Affairs* (1962), Conant makes no reference to the fact that the alleged exorbitant cost of the Arrow led to its undoing. Rather, he says the cancellation was prompted by the U.S. Air Force's assertion that the bomber threat was diminishing and the nuclear ICBM threat in 1959 was growing. He then notes that no sooner had the Arrow been cancelled than the USAF changed its mind again about the nature of the bomber threat and requested that Canada purchase American aircraft. "Needless to say, there ensued charges of either bad faith or purblind judgment," writes Conant. He notes that, as a result, the Canadian public lost confidence in both the American and Canadian governments.

New documents I cite in this edition support Conant's analysis, but they also substantiate Prime Minister John Diefenbaker's own pronouncements on the subject, that the perceived changing threat and the requirement to purchase SAGE/Bomarc, on top of the cost of the Arrow, led to its cancellation. Diefenbaker writes in his memoirs that "the Canadian government was asked to approve the expenditure, exclusive of new interceptor costs, of between $120 million to $190 million . . . to modernize control and data handling [referring to SAGE]. . . . The CF-105 program, taken together with the other air defence items . . . provided for expenditures of almost a billion dollars in the 1958–60 period to improve our defence against a threat that could disappear shortly after these improvements were operational." It is clear something had to be dropped and it was not going to be the additional air defence military commitments that the U.S. required.

George Pearkes, on the other hand, flip-flopped on the reasons for the Arrow cancellation, as noted by Jon B. McLin in his 1967 book *Canada's Changing Defence Policy, 1957–1963*. In 1960, according to the Halpenny Committee proceedings cited by

McLin, Pearkes says the cancellation was due to cost. At other times he emphasizes that it was scrapped based on the perceived reduction in the bomber threat. McLin quotes Pearkes as stating on January 23, 1958, that the future of the Arrow depended "entirely on the nature of the threat, not on its cost." The manned bomber threat was diminishing, so the government was turning its attention towards missile defences, in no small measure due to insistence from the U.S., as noted by Conant.

Pearkes's top secret briefing notes of July 1958 support Conant's argument and further substantiate Diefenbaker's memoirs. In the notes, Pearkes explains that the government could make provision for the Arrow itself, but not for the Arrow *and* the NORAD requirements. Pearkes states, "Further improvements are required in the radar and other associated communications, which will also bring greater expense within the next few years. NORAD has also recommended the introduction of the Bomarc missile into the Ottawa–North Bay area to supplement the manned interceptor, to round out the U.S. Bomarc chain, and to push the defences 250 miles further north. This development will be a further commitment of $164 million. All these commitments coming at this particular time, between 1959 and 1963, will tend to increase our defence budget by as much as 25 to 30%."

The commitments Pearkes spoke of all dealt with satisfying the American NORAD defence requirement for SAGE/Bomarc. Without American help, he argued in his briefing note, the costs of all these programs would be too much for Canada alone to shoulder. This same sentiment had been echoed in 1957 at a meeting of the 273rd Air Council, where the Air Member Personnel argued that the cost of purchasing both the Bomarc and the Arrow would be prohibitive. Canada could afford only one. The dilemma for Pearkes in 1959 was that if the Arrow was cancelled, the Bomarcs would still be several years away from being operational. In the interim, Canada would be defenceless.

Should any doubts remain about whether the Americans' role influenced Canada's decision to cancel the Arrow, consider the aforementioned interview between Dr. Roy and George Pearkes. From the interview tape, it is clear that Dr. Roy believed that the decision to introduce the Bomarc into Canada occurred separately from the decision to cancel the Arrow. Pearkes enlightens Dr. Roy about the sequence of events. This is crucial in understanding the nature of the two decisions made in 1959: to cancel the Arrow and to buy the SAGE/Bomarc. Initially, on the interview tape, Pearkes talks about the extremely high cost of the Arrow and emphasizes that the Arrow program, if it had survived, would have siphoned off money intended for the Army and Navy. This, of course, is one of the flip-flops from his earlier assertions that money was not a factor. On the tape, Pearkes then makes these startling statements:

Pearkes: I took chances. We were defenceless against the high-power bomber where we had the old CF-100. It couldn't compete with the modern Russian bombers. We had no supersonic fighter but the Americans emphasized the fact that they had lots of them. Now . . . one thing I had to face was, if you scrap the Arrow you've got nothing. What will you do? Will you buy American aircraft to fill in this gap?. . . Or, say here, you can rely on American aircraft, not having bought them, but putting your pride in your pocket and saying here, we will give facilities [to] American fighter squadrons to come and be stationed in Canada, so that they can get the advantage there or, if not actually stationed in there, when the situation deteriorates they can move forward and operate from Canadian airfields.

Unbelievably, Pearkes was ready to look the other way and let the Americans defend Canada. He reasoned that Canada could sacrifice a little pride and let the Americans, who were rich in fighter planes, defend our skies. All we had to do was allow them to station themselves in Canada or at least provide them with facilities to practise military exercises here so that they would be in a position to defend us.

But the reason Canada could not scrap the Arrow in favour of purchasing any American airplanes outright was purely political. This was amply demonstrated when the government delayed its acquisition of the American Voodoo aircraft for several years after the Arrow cancellation. In Cabinet, Diefenbaker himself said that to turn around and purchase American aircraft after having convinced the Canadian public of the wisdom of cancelling the Arrow would be a tremendous embarrassment. So, according to Pearkes, rather than purchase American aircraft, the plan was to let the Americans defend us at the cost of a little pride.

The agreement to let the Americans practise and station aircraft in Canada is common knowledge, but that this was done to defend Canada is not widely known. This is borne out in the interview.

> *Pearkes*: I said . . . let us make full arrangements for these American fighter squadrons to come in, to practise from our airfields. Let them store equipment and aircraft if they want to, at places such as Cold Lake and various other points all across Canada, and they came there and then carried out training exercises, moving a squadron up at short notice to one of these airfields. Now, that was how I filled in this defenceless gap during those times. He [name of another author whose name is not clear] doesn't bring that out and I don't know how he would have known . . . [that the Americans were not just carrying out exercises but that it was part of the agreement to allow the Americans to defend us].

> *Dr. Roy*: No, he probably wouldn't. It certainly wouldn't be something that would be advertised.

Pearkes: It was not anything which was advertised at all, but people like Hugh Campbell, who was Chief of the Air Staff, he knows about it . . . . I had the assurance that the Americans at this time had lots of fighters. That was when I was talking to [the] Undersecretary of Defense. I flew out from Washington to Colorado Springs the first time I went to see NORAD. On that aircraft he told me, "We have got lots of fighters" [Pearkes pounds the table with each word]. We were sitting together like this and talking. He said to me, and we can't quote this [his voice goes soft here], "If I was you I wouldn't put all that money into that aircraft. If you don't want to buy aircraft from us you may rest assured that we have got lots of them [emphasis here] which we can use to help in the defence of the North American continent if a crisis comes." That's what convinced me more than anything else.

So, not only did the Americans strongly urge Canada to abandon the Arrow, they also sweetened the suggestion by offering to defend Canada. Was the U.S. Undersecretary of Defense really just trying to help Pearkes out, or was there more behind his generous offer? We will likely never know, but Pearkes bought into it. That he asks Dr. Roy not to quote the statement suggests that there indeed was more to it. What would happen today if the Canadian government accepted such a charitable offer from the U.S. and then scrapped its own fighter squadrons? Indeed, what would have happened if Canadians other than just Hugh Campbell knew about this offer?

Pearkes, knowing that Canada couldn't afford both the Arrow and the Bomarc, needed a safety valve — the American offer of protection if Canada opted for the Bomarc. If the Arrow program was indeed going to bankrupt the military, it would have been far better simply to admit this and to look for defence alternatives that would not cost Canadians their pride. But Pearkes and his colleagues knew the Arrow program was not going to bankrupt the military or the country. They were also aware that the introduction of the Bomarc into the Canadian arsenal was essentially a fait accompli.

Other than Pearkes's briefing note of July 1958, what other evidence is there that the introduction of the Bomarc was a done deal? In earlier chapters I write about a document from the Canadian Department of Defence Production that suggests the NORAD agreement was completed as early as April 1958, months before the official announcement.

Also, at the cabinet meeting of August 28, 1958, Pearkes not only asked for abandonment of the Arrow in favour of the Bomarc, but he also noted the government's commitment to the SAGE control network, essential for the Bomarc and American interceptors but not required for the Arrow. At this meeting, Pearkes described "SAGE and the steps that had to be taken to introduce it, whether or not the government decided to proceed with the CF-105 [the Arrow]." This unnecessary SAGE commitment was going to cost Canadians about $108 million over and above the costs of the Arrow, by the government's own estimates.

What did Pearkes say to Dr. Roy about the need for the SAGE/Bomarc? When Dr. Roy asked if anyone had suggested the Bomarc option to him, he responded:

Pearkes: Had anybody suggested [it]? Oh, yes. At this time, when we scrapped the Arrow? Oh, yes, well, the Bomarcs were in the plan! [Strong emphasis here by Pearkes as he refers to the American NORAD plan for continental defence.]

Dr. Roy: In the American plan?

Pearkes: Well, in the American plan . . . it was the Bomarc. This was all part of NORAD. As soon as NORAD was approved [May 1958], then the Americans came forward with a plan for the defence of the North American continent, which included all these different agencies, the fighters, the warning systems, the Bomarcs, and I haven't got the map but there was a map which showed where all these stations were going to be. . . . Of course, there was a map and it was changed all the time but this was all the overall plan which when we joined NORAD was explained to us.

Dr. Roy: In brief, then, the two problems, although we deal with them in separate chapters, these were in time coming together, going along at the same time as the problem of NORAD, the problem of whether or not to continue on the CF-105 and so on?

Pearkes: Yes. Well, the NORAD plan came first. . . . In the original plans for the Bomarc distribution [Ontario and Quebec] were included.

Pearkes is clear about the requirement to acquire SAGE/Bomarc and that Canada was committed to this as soon as the NORAD agreement had been signed. The Americans had explained this requirement to the Canadian government — it was all part of their plan for continental defence. The NORAD agreement and the need to purchase Bomarcs occurred before the decision was made to cancel the Arrow. Because the Bomarc was in the American plan, the Canadian government had to allocate defence dollars for it and SAGE. Canada was committed to SAGE/Bomarc because of the NORAD agreement, so they absolutely had to allocate money for the American missiles. This commitment left less money in the budget for the Arrow. The Bomarc was not going to disappear from the equation, so the Arrow had to be sacrificed. Eventually, the Americans paid a substantial part of the SAGE/Bomarc cost, but this cost sharing was not agreed to until only days before the cancellation. Pearkes was considering the full costs of both the SAGE/Bomarc and the

Arrow programs when he recommended in August 1958 that the Arrow be abandoned in favour of the Bomarc.

What were the costs of the Arrow and SAGE/Bomarc? Three defence options and their costs were discussed at the 121st meeting of the Cabinet Defence Committee. The first option was to complete both the Arrow, with its Astra/Sparrow missile and fire control system, as well as to install the SAGE/Bomarc system, at a total combined cost of $1.67 billion. (This figure used a fly-away cost of $5 million per aircraft when in fact the fly-away cost was reduced to $3.75 million later in 1958, as I have explained in earlier chapters.) The second alternative was to cancel the Arrow and to increase the number of Bomarc bases to four, at a total cost of $663.5 million. The third choice was to cancel the Arrow and to purchase the American F106 fighter plane, with its Hughes/ Falcon missile and fire control system, and SAGE/Bomarc, at a total cost of $967.5 million. This total, which included Arrow cancellation charges, did not include the $236.1 million already spent on the Arrow up to March 31, 1958. Adding this cost would raise the total to $1.2036 billion for this package. Another alternative, simply dumping the SAGE/Bomarc and completing the Arrow, was never discussed.

The Arrow cost figures in these scenarios included the Astra/Sparrow missile and fire control system, which Avro argued should never have been part of the development. Indeed, Astra/ Sparrow development was scrapped in September 1958. By including the cost of the Hughes/Falcon missile and fire control system as with the F106 rather than the Astra/Sparrow, the costs of the Arrow decreased considerably. (All these costs are now included in Appendix I.) Even the Diefenbaker government had recognized that in order to compare the F106 with the Arrow, the less expensive Hughes/Falcon system had to be factored in the equation.

So what was the true cost of completing the Arrow? The answer is provided in a detailed memo from the Department of Defence Production (DDP) written just after the cancellation (the memo is partially reproduced in Appendix I). According to this

APPENDIX II

memo, at the time of cancellation on February 20, 1959, Avro was on contract to produce 37 aircraft and 107 engines. The figures in the memo show the amount spent as of this date and the amount required to complete the rest of the program, which included an additional 83 aircraft with weapons and spares support.

A closer look at the figures reveals that, at a total of $1.1 billion, the cost of completing the Arrow was going to be cheaper than the $1.2 billion ($967.5 million plus the $236.1 million cost of the Arrow up to March 1958) for the F106/SAGE/Bomarc alternative. With the real costs already spent on the Arrow up to February 20, 1959 — $318.6 million — removed from the equation, it would cost only $792.6 million more to complete the entire Arrow production, at a fly-away cost of $3.75 million per aircraft. Again, this figure is less than the $967.5 million total for the F106/SAGE/Bomarc alternative.

Speculation that it was going to cost several hundred million dollars to complete the Arrow development alone is incorrect. Completion was going to cost only $77.9 million. (This included $24.9 million for the airframe and $53 million for the engines, for a total of $77.9 million. The government was also expecting to pay over $100 million in cancellation charges alone — though the truer figure would be closer to $33 million in the end). It would cost $257.8 million to complete 37 aircraft and set up the rest of the production line to produce the other 83 aircraft, a fact not often mentioned by other writers on the Arrow.

Avro set out to establish the production line and production tooling simultaneously with the development program in order to save time and money in the long run. A significant amount of this money went into tooling, production, and support, whereas only $201 million in total ($92.6 million for airframes plus $108.4 million for engines) went directly into development of the aircraft and engines.

There is no question that the SAGE/Bomarc package without the F106 was less expensive than the Arrow. But buying the Arrow was not going to bankrupt the military, as some have alleged. Rather, the combination of the Arrow and the SAGE/Bomarc at $1.67 billion was too much for the Canadian government to handle, as Pearkes himself stated in his top secret briefing notes. Considering that the manned interceptor threat was diminishing (according to the USAF) and that at the cost of a little Canadian pride the Americans would provide us with air power in the interim, the SAGE/Bomarc package seemed like a good deal, since it allegedly afforded the same protection as the Arrow against this lesser threat. It was an argument of cost effectiveness. Today we know better.

Interestingly, at the Cabinet meeting of September 7, 1958, even Donald Fleming, the Minister of Finance, indicated that buying the Arrow alone would not bankrupt the military or the government. Also, the Army and Navy Chiefs, the ones who were supposed to lose their shares of the defence pie if production of the Arrow continued, are on record as supporting the Arrow program, at least until March 31, 1959, when it would be reviewed not economically, but in light of changing world military conditions. Fleming stated that he put the safety and security of the country ahead of finance, meaning he would provide the necessary funds for the Arrow. However, he noted that the military did not want the Arrow anymore. He was, of course, referring to the fact that Pearkes and Foulkes were both touting the Bomarc, while at the same time recommending the cancellation of the Arrow.

In the end, not only was the Arrow going to cost less than the combined F106/SAGE/Bomarc cost, but the Bomarc missile had yet to be proven. The first U.S. Bomarc base did not become operational until September 1959, and it was equipped with the Bomarc A missile, not the Bomarc B that Canada was to purchase. The Bomarc A used fuels so corrosive that they could not be stored in the missile for long periods of time. This meant that each missile had to be fuelled before it could be launched, giving the attacking aircraft the advantage. Another problem was that since these fuels ignited when mixed, there was always a danger of fire. In June 1960, a nuclear-tipped Bomarc incinerated on the launch pad at McGuire Air Force Base in New Jersey, leaving a heap of smouldering radioactive material on the launch pad.

The Bomarc B was test launched in May 1959 in the United States. Problems with the propulsion system adversely affected the first seven test flights, leaving Canadians wondering what they had gotten themselves into. The Bomarcs finally became operational in Canada in 1962, but by the fall of 1964 the Americans had already started to deactivate and dismantle their own Bomarc squadrons. Canada was left searching for new fighter aircraft since the bomber threat had not diminished.

In 1961, because of the admission by the USAF that the bomber threat was not diminishing, the Canadian government ended up having to purchase 66 aging and less capable American Voodoo aircraft. According to the Department of Defence Production records, had the Arrow program continued, 54 of the advanced Arrows could have been in the inventory at that time, and the rest delivered by 1963.

In addition, the Arrow performed far better on test flights than the Bomarc, and it was gaining recognition around the world, but this did not seem to matter in Canada. *Aviation Week* (October 21, 1957), which featured the Arrow on the cover, noted the "Avro CF-105 Arrow has given Canada a serious contender for the top military aircraft of the next several years. The large, decidedly advanced delta-wing fighter . . . was designed specifically as a long-range interceptor which would set new standards for combat ceiling and maneuverability at altitude." *Flight* magazine (October 25, 1957) carried the headline, "Arrow a World-Leading Interceptor by Avro Aircraft" and went on to explain the advanced nature of the aircraft. Today, even the prestigious *American Smithsonian Air and Space* magazine (May 1998) acknowledges the technological advances of the Arrow, while in Canada, questions are still being raised as to whether the aircraft was really that good.

On another note, some have argued that A.V. Roe should never have fired all of its employees in a single afternoon. But the government's order that the company cease and desist from any further work was clear. All contracts were cancelled, effective immediately, so if 14,000 people showed up for work the following day, there wouldn't have been anything for them to do. And, there was no more money to pay salaries, since they were funded by Avro's contracts with the government. (I lived through a project cancellation, and I can attest to the fact that once a project is cancelled, the funding dries up.) I believe the government did not fully appreciate the consequences of their stop-work termination order.

Finally, one question remains: what was the impact of the cancellation on the Canadian aerospace industry? Some suggest that the impact was minimal. In 1997 the Aerospace Industries Association (AIA) reported that the present Canadian aircraft industry is strong. It currently employs over 59,000 people and has made Canada the sixth largest supplier of aerospace products in the world. The AIA predicted that Canada will become the fourth largest producer of aerospace products in the world by the year 2000.

However, compare that bill of health with the December 2, 1957, brief from the Air Industries and Transport Association (AITA) to John Diefenbaker, at a time when Canada's population was far less than it is today. The AITA concluded that "Canada is today among the five leading producers of aircraft in the world." It further stated that the industry provided direct employment to "47,000 Canadians in the aircraft industry, some 59,000 including directly associated electrical and electronic companies and indirectly to a total of over 100,000."

It has taken only forty years for us to crawl back to where we were in 1957. Well done, Canada.

NOTES

Chapter 1: DREAMS

1. House of Commons, *Debates*, 20 February 1959, 1221–24; J. B. McLin, *Canada's Changing Defence Policy, 1957–1963* (Baltimore: The Johns Hopkins Press, 1967).
2. W. Manchester, *The Glory and the Dream* (Toronto: Bantam Books, 1990).
3. H. Weinstein, *Father, Son and CIA* (Halifax: Formac Publishing Co., 1990); J. Sawatsky, *For Services Rendered* (Markham, Ontario: Penguin Books Canada Ltd., 1986); J. C. Floyd, *The Avro Canada C102 Jetliner* (Erin, Ontario: The Boston Mills Press, 1986).
4. Scott Young, "The Way Up," *Jet Age Magazine*, A. V. Roe Canada Ltd., 1955.
5. Ibid.
6. J. C. Floyd, "The Avro Story," *Canadian Aviation Magazine*, 50th Anniversary Issue, June 1978.
7. Ibid.
8. Ibid.
9. R. Rummel, *Howard Hughes and TWA* (Washington, D.C.: Smithsonian History of Aviation Series, 1991).
10. Ibid.
11. Record Group (RG) 24/83/84/167, Box 6426, File 1038CN-180, National Archives, Ottawa; D. J. Goodspeed, *A History of the Defence Research Board of Canada* (Ottawa: Queen's Printer, 1958).
12. Ibid.
13. Ibid.
14. Ibid.
15. Ibid, F. Smye, *Canadian Aviation and the Avro Arrow* (Oakville, Ontario: Randy Smye, 1989).
16. RG 24/83/84/167, Box 6426, File 1038CN-180.
17. Ibid.
18. RG 77/85-86/180, Box 3.
19. RG 24/83/84/167, Box 6426, File 1038CN-180.

20. J. C. Floyd, *The Avro Canada C102 Jetliner* (Erin, Ontario: The Boston Mills Press, 1986); Report No. P/F.F.M./47 *C-105 Summary of Free Flight Model Tests and Results*, Directorate of Scientific Information Services, Department of National Defence, Ottawa, July 1957.
21. Report No. P/F.F.M./47; *Avro News*, 3, 4 October 1957.
22. Report No. P/F.F.M./47.
23. *Avro News*, 4 October 1957.
24. RG 24/83/84/167, Box 6426, File 1038CN-180.

Chapter 2: U.K. AND U.S. INTEREST

1. RG 24/83/84/167, Box 6430, File S1038CN-180A, Vol. 11, National Archives, Ottawa.
2. Ibid, Vol. 14.
3. Ibid, Vol. 11.
4. Ibid.
5. Ibid, Box 6426, Vol. 8.
6. Ibid.
7. Ibid.
8. Ibid.
9. Ibid.
10. Ibid.
11. Ibid, F. Smye, *Canadian Aviation and the Avro Arrow* (Oakville, Ontario: Randy Smye, 1989).
12. RG 24/83/84/167, Box 6426, File S-1038CN-180, Vol. 8.
13. Ibid, Box 6430, Vol. 11.
14. Ibid, Box 7319, File 0315-02, Vol. 3.
15. Ibid.
16. Ibid.
17. RG 24/83/84/167, File S-1038CN-180A, Vol. 14.
18. Ibid, Box 6433, File 1038CN-181, Vol. 1.
19. Ibid, Box 7319, File 0315-02, Vol. 2.
20. Ibid.
21. J. C. Floyd, personal records.
22. RG 24, Box 7319.
23. Ibid.
24. RG 24, Box 6433, File 1038CN-181, Vol. 1.
25. RG 24, Box 7319.
26. RG 24, Box 6433.
27. Ibid.
28. Ibid.
29. *Evaluation of the Canadian CF-105 as an All-Weather Fighter for the* RAF *Report by the Joint Air Ministry/Ministry of Supply Evaluation Team*, Aeronautical Library, National Research Council, Ottawa, ca. 1956.

30. Ibid.
31. Ibid.
32. Ibid.
33. RG 24/83/84/167, File S-1038CN-180A, Vol. 14.
34. Ibid, Vol. 20.
35. Ibid.
36. Ibid.
37. Ibid, Vol. 23.
38. "Arrow Memorial: The Story Continues," *Engineering Dimensions*, January/February 1989.

Chapter 3: THE ARROW

1. *Avro News*, Vol. 3, 4 October 1957.
2. Ibid.
3. "CF-105 Displays Advanced Engineering In Rollout," *Aviation Week*, 21 October 1957.
4. "Arrow: A World-Leading Interceptor by Avro Aircraft," *Flight*, 25 October 1957.
5. J. C. Floyd, "The Canadian Approach to All-Weather Interceptor Development," *The Journal of the Royal Aeronautical Society*, 62, December 1958.
6. Ibid.
7. Ibid.
8. P. Campagna, "An Aviation Chapter in Canadian History," *Engineering Dimensions*, September/October 1988.
9. Ibid.
10. D. J. Goodspeed, *A History of the Defence Research Board of Canada* (Ottawa: Queen's Printer, 1958).
11. RG 24/83/84/167, Box 7319, File 0315-02, Vol. 3, National Archives, Ottawa.
12. Ibid.
13. J. C. Floyd, personal records.
14. *Arrow 2 Armament System*, Report 72/System 26/8, Directorate of Scientific Information Services, Department of National Defence, Ottawa, June 1957; The Arrowheads, *Arrow* (Erin, Ontario: The Boston Mills Press, 1981).
15. "Low-drag Weapon Carriage," *Interavia Aerospace Review*, 45, January 1990.
16. *Flight*, 25 October 1957.
17. P. Brannan, "Arrow System Leads the Way," *Canadian Aviation*, March 1958.
18. *Flight*, 25 October 1957.
19. *Evaluation of the Canadian CF-105 as an All-Weather Fighter for the* RAF: *Report by the Joint Air Ministry/Ministry of Supply Evalua-*

tion Team, Aeronautical Library, National Research Council, Ottawa, ca. 1956.

20. The Arrowheads, *Arrow.*
21. *Preliminary Pilot's Operating Instructions Arrow 1*, A. V. Roe, April 1958 (author's collection).
22. Ibid.
23. The Arrowheads, *Arrow*; J. H. Baldwin, "Automatic Flight Control in the Arrow," *Aircraft*, June 1958.
24. *Avro News*, 4 October 1957.
25. P. Campagna, "An Aviation Chapter."
26. RG 24/83/84/167, Box 6426, File S-1038CN-180, Vol. 5.
27. Ibid.
28. *Iroquois Represents Major Advance in Gas Turbine Field*, from the J. H. Parkin files, National Research Council, Ottawa.
29. RG 24, Box 6433.
30. The Arrowheads, *Arrow.*
31. RG 24, Box 6430, Vol. 10 and 19.

Chapter 4: UP, UP, OR AWAY?

1. 73/1223 Series 1, File 12, Directorate of History, Department of National Defence, Ottawa.
2. F. Smye, *Canadian Aviation and the Avro Arrow* (Oakville, Ontario: Randy Smye, 1989).
3. J. Zurakowski, "The Flight of the Arrow," *Wingspan*, March/April 1987.
4. Smye, *Canadian Aviation and the Avro Arrow.*
5. Zurakowski, "The Flight of the Arrow."
6. *Arrow Flight Development*, Report No. 70/Eng Pub/7, Directorate of Scientific Information Services, Department of National Defence, Ottawa, 1 May 1958.
7. Zurakowski, "The Flight of the Arrow."
8. J. C. Floyd, personal records.
9. Zurakowski, "The Flight of the Arrow."
10. Ibid.
11. P. Campagna, "An Aviation Chapter in Canadian History," *Engineering Dimensions*, September/October 1988.
12. J. Woodman, "Flying the Arrow," paper presented at the Canadian Aeronautics and Space Institute Symposium, Winnipeg, Manitoba, 13 May 1978 (J. C. Floyd, personal records).
13. J. C. Floyd, personal records.
14. Ibid.
15. RG 24/83/84/167, Vol. 7319, File 0315-02, Vol. 3. National Archives, Ottawa.
16. J. C. Floyd, personal records.

17. RG 24/83/84/167, Box 6430, File S-1038CN-180A, Vol. 1–10 and 19.
18. *The Scientific and Industrial Resources of the Canadian Aircraft Industry*, from the J. H. Parkin files, National Research Council, Ottawa, 2 December 1957.
19. RG 24, Box 6430.
20. *The Scientific and Industrial Resources of the Canadian Aircraft Industry*,
21. J. B. McLin, *Canada's Changing Defence Policy, 1957–1963* (Baltimore: The Johns Hopkins Press, 1967).
22. RG 49, Interim 135, Vol. 67, File 151-9-1, part 3.
23. Ibid.
24. Subject Series, Canada, Trip of President, 1958, Dwight D. Eisenhower Library.
25. RG 49, Interim 135, Vol. 67, File 151-9-1, part 3.
26. RG 49, Vol. 427, File 159-44-B, part 1.
27. RG 2, Cabinet Conclusions, August 1958.
28. Ibid.
29. Ibid.
30. Ibid.
31. P. Grier, "What Do Weapons Really Cost?" *Military Forum*, November/December 1989.
32. McLin, *Canada's Changing Defence Policy.*
33. RG 2, August 1958.
34. Ibid, September 1958.
35. RG 2, August 1958.
36. RG 2, September 1958.
37. Ibid.
38. Ibid.
39. Ibid.
40. RG 49, Vol. 427, File 159-44-B, part 1.
41. Ibid.
42. Ibid.
43. J. Dow, *The Arrow* (Toronto: James Lorimer and Co., 1979); J. G. Diefenbaker, *One Canada: The Tumultuous Years* (Toronto: Macmillan, 1977).
44. RG 2, September 1958.
45. Ibid.
46. McLin, *Canada's Changing Defence Policy.*
47. E. K. Shaw, *There Never Was an Arrow* (Ottawa: Steel Rail Educational Publishing, 1981).
48. RG 2, December 1958.
49. D. M. Fleming, *So Very Near: The Political Memoirs of the Honourable Donald M. Fleming: Volume Two: The Summit Years* (Toronto: McClelland and Stewart, 1985).
50. RG 24/83/84/167, Box 6430; RG 49, Vol. 434, File 159-RO-5, Vol. 2.
51. RG 24, Box 6430.

52. RG 49, Vol. 5, File 159-RA-1, Vol. 2.
53. J. C. Floyd, personal records.
54. RG 24, Box 6430.
55. RG 49, Interim 84, File 159-RO-5, Vol. 10.
56. Ibid.
57. Ibid.
58. J. C. Floyd, personal records.
59. RG 24, Box 6433.
60. 73/1223 Series 1, File 12, Directorate of History, Department of National Defence, Ottawa.
61. RG 24, Box 6433.
62. Ibid.

Chapter 5: MUTILATION

1. J. Dow, *The Arrow* (Toronto: James Lorimer and Co., 1979).
2. RG 2, January 1959, National Archives, Ottawa.
3. Ibid.
4. National Security Council, *Certain Aspects of U.S. Relations with Canada*, NSC 5822/1, 30 December 1958, Dwight D. Eisenhower Library.
5. Folder Canada (3) (June-July 1960), Dwight D. Eisenhower Library.
6. RG 2, January 1959.
7. Ibid.
8. Ibid, February 1959.
9. Ibid.
10. Ibid.
11. Ibid.
12. Ibid.
13. Ibid.
14. Ibid.
15. Ibid.
16. J. B. McLin, *Canada's Changing Defence Policy, 1957–1963* (Baltimore: The Johns Hopkins Press, 1967).
17. Dow, *The Arrow.*
18. RG 24/83/84/167, Box 7319, File 0315-02, Vol. 3.
19. RG 24, Box 6428, part 26.
20. Ibid.
21. RG 49, Vol. 781, File 207-6-3.
22. 79/333, Directorate of History, Department of National Defence, Ottawa.
23. Ibid.
24. RG 49, Vol. 781, File 207-6-3.
25. Ibid.

26. 73/1223 Series 1, File 12, Directorate of History, Department of National Defence, Ottawa.
27. RG 49, Vol. 781, File 207-6-3.
28. Ibid.
29. Ibid.
30. Ibid.
31. Ibid.
32. Ibid.
33. Ibid.
34. RG 24/83/84/167, Box 7319, File 0315-02, Vol. 3; D. Noland, *Superflops, Air Progress World's Greatest Aircraft* (Los Angeles: Petersen Publishing Co., 1972).
35. RG 49, Vol 781, File 207-603.

Chapter 6: WHY?

1. RG 2, Cabinet Conclusions, July 1960, National Archives, Ottawa.
2. 30-E163, Vol. 17, Robertson Files, National Archives, Ottawa.
3. Ibid.
4. Ibid.
5. RG 49, Interim 135, Vol. 67, File 151-9-1 part 3.
6. RG 49, Vol. 781, File 207-6-3.
7. "Intelligence Schism," *Aviation Week*, 2 March 1959.
8. RG 2, February 1960.
9. Ibid.
10. RG 2, May 1960.
11. *A Limited Technical Evaluation of the Avro Arrow Interceptor System*, Aeronautical Library, National Research Council, Ottawa, completed in April 1958, not released until 1961.
12. J. B. McLin, *Canada's Changing Defence Policy, 1957–1963* (Baltimore: The Johns Hopkins Press, 1967).
13. N. Friedman, "U.S. Technology Transfers Debated," *Proceedings*, U.S. Naval Institute, Annapolis, Maryland, June 1988.
14. "Canada Seeks U.S. Defence Contracts," *Aviation Week*, 2 March 1959.
15. J. Sawatsky, *For Services Rendered* (Markham, Ontario: Penguin Books Canada Ltd., 1986).
16. P. Wright, *Spycatcher* (New York: Stoddart Publishing Co. Ltd., 1987).
17. Timothy Good, *Above Top Secret* (Toronto: Macmillan, 1988).
18. J. Dudman, "Nuclear Submarines Will Revitalize Defences," *Pacific Defence Reporter*, 16 March 1988.
19. N. Tracy, "Why Does Canada Want Nuclear Submarines?" *International Journal*, 43, Summer 1988.

20. S. Gramont, *The Secret War Since World War II* (New York: G. P. Putnam's Sons, 1962).
21. J. Ranelagh, *The Agency: The Rise and Decline of the CIA* (Cambridge Publishing Ltd., 1986).
22. K. Nash, *Kennedy and Diefenbaker: Fear and Loathing across the Border* (Toronto: McClelland & Stewart, 1990).
23. Gramont, *The Secret War.*
24. "U.S. Reconnaissance Weakened by SR-71 Program Termination," *Aviation Week,* 22 January 1990.
25. Nash, *Kennedy and Diefenbaker.*
26. R. F. Swanson, *Canadian-American Summit Diplomacy, 1923–1973* (Toronto: McClelland and Stewart, 1975).

Chapter 7: MYTHS AND MISCONCEPTIONS

1. "A Revisionist Perspective on the Avro Arrow," *The Toronto Star,* 20 February 1986.
2. P. Campagna, *An Aviation Chapter in Canadian History.*
3. *A Limited Technical Evaluation of the Avro Arrow Interceptor System,* Aeronautical Library, National Research Council, Ottawa, completed in April 1958, not released until 1961.
4. Timothy Good, *Above Top Secret* (Toronto: Macmillan, 1988).

EPILOGUE

1. Charles Murray and Catherine Bly-Cox, *Apollo: The Race to the Moon* (New York: Simon and Schuster, 1969).
2. J. C. Floyd, personal records.

POSTSCRIPT

1. RG 70, Vol. 401, File 1400-8.
2. RG 24, Vol. 4243.
3. Ibid.
4. Ibid.
5. File 79/469, Folder 19, Directorate of History, Department of National Defence.
6. J. L. Granatstein, *The Generals: The Canadian Army's Senior Commanders in the Second World War* (Toronto: Stoddart Publishing, 1993).
7. Ibid.
8. Ibid.

9. File 79/469, Folder 11, Directorate of History, Department of National Defence.
10. 73/1223, File 1348, Directorate of History, Department of National Defence. The original of this "smoking gun" was in the Cabinet Conclusions documents at the National Archives. I found this copy amongst unrelated material.
11. RG 2, Cabinet Conclusions, February 23, 1959.
12. Ibid.
13. Ibid.
14. RCAF memo, March 28, 1958, from RG 24, Box 6430.
15. Pearkes to Dulles, in explaining how adding SAGE/Bomarc would stress the defence budget. TOP SECRET brief, July 8, 1958, from RG 49, Vol. 427, File 159-44-B, part 1.
16. RG 2, Cabinet Conclusions, September 1958.
17. Charles Foulkes, Chairman Chiefs of Staff, to Chief of the Air Staff, November 4, 1958, from RG 24, Box 24.
18. Chief of the Air Staff to Pearkes, January 12, 1959, from 73/1223, Series 1, File 12, Directorate of History, Department of National Defence.
19. The Honourable Brooke Claxton to Cabinet, November 30, 1953, from RG 24/83/84/167, Box 6426.
20. General Price to the RCAF, after a two-day review of the entire project on October 31 and November 1, 1955, in which the USAF team concluded that the Arrow was superior to their F-101, that Falcon should be the weapon of choice, and that Iroquois would improve the performance of their own aircraft, from RG 24/83/84/167, Box 6426.
21. RCAF review of the project, late 1958, from RG 24, Box 6430.
22. Air Industries and Transport Association to the Prime Minister, December 1957, from "The Scientific and Industrial Resources of the Canadian Aircraft Industry," J.H. Parkin files, National Research Council, Ottawa.
23. RG 2, Cabinet Conclusions, September 1958.
24. "Evaluation of the Canadian CF-105 as an All-Weather Fighter for the RAF," report by the Joint Air Ministry/Ministry of Supply Evaluation Team, 1956.
25. RG 2, Cabinet Conclusions, August 1958.
26. RG 24, Box 6433, Assistant for Arrow Weapon System Office, January 1, 1959.
27. Chief of the Air Staff to Pearkes, January 12, 1959, from 73/1223, Series 1, File 12, Directorate of History, Department of National Defence.

INDEX